James Russell Lowell's
The Biglow Papers [First Series]

James Russell Lowell's

Northern Illinois University Press

The *Biglow Papers*

[First Series]

A Critical Edition

by Thomas Wortham

DeKalb 1977

The title page illustration is from James Joseph Jacques Tissot's cartoon entitled "Hosea Biglow," published in *Vanity Fair*, 21 August 1880.

CENTER FOR EDITIONS OF
AMERICAN AUTHORS

AN APPROVED TEXT

MODERN LANGUAGE
ASSOCIATION OF AMERICA

®

Library of Congress Cataloging in Publication Data

Lowell, James Russell, 1819–1891.
James Russell Lowell's The Biglow papers, first series.

Includes index.
1. United States—War with Mexico, 1845–1848—Poetry.
2. Slavery in the United States—Poetry. I. Wortham, Thomas,
1943– II. Title. III. Title: The Biglow papers.
PS2306.A1 1976 811'.3 74–12827
ISBN 0–87580–053–X

Copyright © 1977 by Northern Illinois University Press
Published by the Northern Illinois University Press,
DeKalb, Illinois 60115
Manufactured in the United States of America

Contents

THE BIGLOW PAPERS

Acknowledgments

I wish to express my appreciation to the Research Committee of the University of California, Los Angeles, for its generous support of my work.

For the use of their collections and permission to quote from unpublished materials, I thank the Boston Public Library; the Butler Library of Columbia University; the Houghton Library, Harvard University; the Massachusetts Historical Society; the Library of Middlebury College; the Pierpont Morgan Library; the New York Public Library; the Beinecke Library, Yale University; and, not least, the Research Library and the Clark Library, University of California, Los Angeles.

The Kemble illustrations are printed by permission of the Department of Special Collections, University of California, Los Angeles, and were a gift of Mr. Vincent Price.

My research assistants, who patiently checked my collations and assisted in reading proof, I name in gratitude: Leonard Feldman, Kathy Eileen Greenbaun, Barry Hoffman, Katherine Kline, and Ellen Samsell. My greatest debt in editorial assistance is to Julie Bates.

I thank my colleagues and friends—George Guffey, Charles Gullans, James H. Justus, J. A. Leo Lemay, David J. Nordloh, Hershel Parker, G. B. Tennyson, and Wallace Williams—for listening and correcting.

To Edwin and Norma Cady I dedicate my editorial work.

And to each of my parents, as always,

> *voi mi date a parlar tutta baldezza;*
> *voi mi levate sì, ch'i' son più ch'io.*

Introduction

Middle life and the tragedy of the Civil War sobered James Russell Lowell. In his 1865 essay on Thoreau he looked back with self-deprecating humor on the America of his youth, the America of the late 1830s and the 1840s:

> Every possible form of intellectual and physical dyspepsia brought forth its gospel. Bran had its prophets, and the presartorial simplicity of Adam its martyrs. . . . Plainness of speech was carried to a pitch that would have taken away the breath of George Fox; and even swearing had its evangelists. . . . Everybody had a mission (with a capital M) to attend to everybody-else's business. No brain but had its private maggot, which must have found pitiably short commons sometimes. Not a few impecunious zealots abjured the use of money (unless earned by other people), professing to live on the internal revenues of the spirit. Some had an assurance of instant millennium so soon as hooks and eyes should be substituted for buttons. Communities were established where everything was to be common but common-sense. . . . Conventions were held for every hitherto inconceivable purpose.[1]

Just so Emerson had reported early on to Thomas Carlyle: "We are all a little wild here with numberless projects of social reform. Not a reading man but has a draft of a new Community in his waistcoat pocket. . . . One man renounces the use of animal food; & another of coin; & another of domestic hired service; & another of the state."[2]

One can easily add to Emerson's list of "Apostles of the Newness": besides vegetarians and anarchists, there were polygamists,

1. *The Writings of James Russell Lowell in Ten Volumes* (Boston and New York: Houghton, Mifflin and Co., 1890), 1:362.
2. 30 October 1840: *The Correspondence of Emerson and Carlyle*, ed. Joseph Slater (New York and London: Columbia University Press, 1964), pp. 283–84.

feminists, socialists, suffragists, perfectionists, millennialists, and temperance men. But from this same general enthusiasm originated not only Brook Farm but also Thoreau's experiment at Walden Pond, a new code for the sometimes worthy tradition of civil disobedience, and, most importantly, an increasing acceptance by Americans of the ideas, if not the life-styles, of the abolitionists. One must, if only in fairness to those involved, distinguish between the necessary and beneficial reforms urged on society by responsible, serious men and women, and the cockeyed schemes of silly, disenchanted, and dangerous fanatics. It will not do to confound Henry David Thoreau and Joseph Smith. But neither will it do to suppose that the good and the foolish, the beneficial and the destructive worked in opposition to or in isolation from one another. Only by considering them as sharers of a common impulse can we begin to understand those in-between figures, those we should call mad had they not so often made such good sense—the Bronson Alcotts, the Margaret Fullers—and the age of which they are perhaps the most telling spirits.

The simple fact is that at mid-century many imaginations in the Western world were seized by a spirit of liberalism and reform, the not so simple effect both of an ever-increasing dissemination and acceptance of various forms of late eighteenth-century romanticism and of the emergence of a modern, industrial, and urban society. What had been suggested in the French Revolution, promised in the aborted Continental revolutions of 1830, and nearly made fact in the revolutions of 1848, would at length emerge in the shape of a modern, though not twentieth-century, Europe. Because America was already fundamentally democratic, there was less need for revolution, and reform manifested itself in ways sometimes more curious but not less serious. American reformers recognized a happy commonwealth of purpose with their European allies, as when Bronson Alcott spoke orphically in the January 1841 issue of *The Dial*:

> The trump of reform is sounding throughout the world for a revolution of all human affairs. The issue we cannot doubt; yet the cries are not without alarm. Already is the axe laid at

the root of that spreading tree, whose trunk is idolatry, whose branches are covetousness, war, and slavery, whose blossom is concupiscence, whose fruit is hate. Planted by Beelzebub, it shall be rooted up. Abaddon is pouring his vial on the earth.[3]

James Russell Lowell came of age during the first year of this decade: he shared in many of its follies and mistakes, he benefited from its strengths, and undoubtedly the years profited by his presence.

I

Being born a Lowell was a fact of some importance in New England. His father, Charles Lowell, was pastor of the West Church in Boston; his uncle was Francis Cabot Lowell, the great industrial entrepreneur and mechanical genius who led in revolutionizing New England economic life. In the generations of Lowells farther back one finds other ministers, judges, and civic leaders. Young Lowell was thus heir to two distinctive traditions in New England life: "the Brahmin caste of ministers and scholars" and the urban aristocracy, who became Proper Bostonians during the nineteenth century. Lowell accepted his social and intellectual prominence with the immature grace and impudence of a young, strikingly handsome, intelligent aristocrat. His popularity in the club rooms of Harvard, the ballrooms of Boston, and the parlors of Cambridge was no surprise: this was his birthright.

But the uncomfortable fact in New England life is that behind every true Yankee stands a Puritan ancestry: "men who sacrificed everything and came hither," as Lowell himself observed, "not to better their fortunes, but to plant their idea in virgin soil."[4] As the injustice of the social order and the wickedness of slavery became increasingly apparent to Lowell, the gentle manners of Cambridge and Boston and the natural congeniality of his temperament were insufficient to suppress that Puritan spirit. Though he had playfully

3. "Orphic Sayings," *Dial* 1 (January 1841): 351.
4. *Writings,* 3:246.

attacked transcendentalists and abolitionists in his Harvard *Class Poem* (Cambridge, 1838), it was the egotism of "fanatics" he had primarily objected to, and he soon repented his condemnation of these movements and their vital ideas. Native prejudices and habits of thought are not easily overcome, especially when the prospect of life is as seemingly comfortable as was young Lowell's. His conversion to the cause of abolition and, to a lesser extent, other reform movements was made at considerable cost: psychologically, socially, and professionally. In becoming a reformer and an abolitionist in the early 1840s, Lowell, in a very real sense, declassed himself. He was not alone; this too is a familiar tradition in New England life, embarrassing at the time but celebrated by posterity. A movement that could boast among its supporters Henry I. Bowditch, Francis Jackson, Charles Sumner, Wendell Phillips, Ellis Gray Loring, Samuel E. Sewall, and John Murray Forbes could hardly be said to lack intellectual and social distinction. Nevertheless, Edmund Quincy, Lowell's friend and the son of the Harvard president, found himself, after joining ranks with the abolitionists, "called the Prince of Bigots, His Anti-Slavery Highness, an aristocrat, a hyena, and a squash."[5]

Like many abolitionists, Lowell's reforming zeal was not solely directed against black slavery in the South. He wrote in his first antislavery editorial for *The Pennsylvania Freeman* (16 January 1845): "The aim of the true abolitionist is not only to put an end to negro slavery in America; he is equally the sworn foe of tyranny throughout the world."[6] There was the tyranny of the French monarchy, and Lowell celebrated in his poem "Ode to France" the February 1848 Revolution which overthrew the government of Louis

5. M. A. DeWolfe Howe, "Biographer's Bait: A Reminder of Edmund Quincy," *Proceedings of the Massachusetts Historical Society* 68 (October 1944–May 1947): 378.

6. *The Anti-Slavery Papers of James Russell Lowell*, ed. William Belmont Parker, 2 vols. (Boston and New York: Houghton, Mifflin and Co., 1902) 1:6. Lewis Perry's *Radical Abolitionism: Anarchy and the Government of God in Antislavery Thought* (Ithaca, N.Y.: Cornell University Press, 1973) is extremely helpful in pointing out the connections between the beliefs of the abolitionists and the general radicalism of the period.

Philippe. He expressed "Sympathy with Ireland" (1848) in its desire for self-government, even though he could not approve of the violent means John Mitchel and his followers had chosen to achieve freedom from England. He attacked the tyranny of the established and orthodox churches over the life of the mind and soul in "Bibliolatres" (1849), and he argued "true radicalism" in "Prometheus" (1843). Lowell participated in temperance meetings against a vice that was increasing with the growth of cities and factory towns, a vice he believed was caused by the new tyranny of the company and the machine over the workers. He wrote in 1845: "The system of labor and of its reward at the North we sincerely believe to be but little better than that at the South."[7] Poems titled "Hunger and Cold" and "The Landlord" indicate an imagination not innocent of the world and ideas then concerning Lamartine in France and Karl Marx in Belgium.

Yet, while "tyranny is of one complexion all the world over,"[8] Lowell recognized that for reform to be effective the objects of attack must be limited, and he chose to attack black slavery. In August 1845, he wrote to his friend Charles F. Briggs, the New York author and journalist, defending his position of reformer as abolitionist:

> I admit that when all these sore boils with which God hath smitten our social system spring from one disease, it would be idle to apply external remedies to *one* of them, meanwhile leaving all the rest to grow up to a more poisonous and incurable head. Nor is this the system of therapeutics which obtains among abolitionists. We believe that the only remedy for this terrible disease is the application of Christianity to life. We cry out most loudly against slavery because that seems to be the foulest blotch, and it is easier to awaken the attention of the worldly and indifferent to that than to any other. . . . Absolute freedom is what I want—for the body first, and then for the mind. For the body first, because it is easier to make men conscious of the wrong of that grosser and more outward op-

7. *The Anti-Slavery Papers*, 1:10.
8. *The Anti-Slavery Papers*, 1:106.

pression, and after seeing that, they will perceive more readily the less palpable chains and gags of tyranny.[9]

And in his position of reformer as poet, Lowell understood, at least for the moment, his vocation clearly. In the midst of seeing *The Biglow Papers* through the press he took time to write Mrs. Horace Mann:

> Surely the office of the poet was a happier one when the sole demand upon him was from within his own nature, & his calling was simply that of a shower of the Beautiful. But, while I would by no means acknowledge that the Beautiful is not also (to a clear vision) the Practical, yet I conceive that our age summons the poet to tasks peculiarly its own. He must content himself to be, in a certain sense, only a Schoolmaster. He must be a John the Baptist, a voice crying in the Wilderness, preparing for the simply Beautiful, for Art in its highest sense, a wider & more universal reception in a future age. The pulpit & the lecturer's desk must serve him for a Pegasus. He must submit to be nothing more than the plank over which happier spirits shall mount the vessel sailing to find a new world—himself to be left behind to rot upon the shore. I say this not in sadness, but only in selfvindication. After I have served my apprenticeship as a baker of bricks without straw (not without hope that of such bricks temples of the gods may chance be built) I hope also to be led to the promised land of Song, & to have my Sinais & my waters from the rock by the way. This much by way of apology (since you have expressed an interest in me) for my apparent deviation to preaching instead of singing, & for my seeming to prefer the husks of Hosea Biglow to more ambrosial diet. But I assure you that Mr Biglow has a thousand readers for my one, & that he has raised the laugh at War & Slavery & Doughfaces to some purpose.[10]

9. *Letters of James Russell Lowell*, ed. Charles Eliot Norton, 3 vols. (Boston and New York: Houghton, Mifflin and Co., 1904), 1:134–35.

10. 10 September 1848: A.L.s., Massachusetts Historical Society, Boston. Quoted by permission.

INTRODUCTION

In Hosea Biglow, Lowell had discovered how best to perform his task. In the satiric verses of this rustic Yankee he was able to denounce wrong and encourage right. Through the mask of humor the preaching sounded less like preaching and the morality less like morality. Hosea's voice was humane as well as righteous. But Lowell's discovery of Hosea Biglow was only the beginning of *The Biglow Papers*.

II

While visiting friends in a Boston law office in early June 1846, Lowell was interrupted in his conversation by the sound of drum and fife outside in Court Square. Recruiters had come to rally a company of Massachusetts volunteers for the Mexican War. Lowell's indignation rose immediately, but, as Judge Robert Burbank later told Francis Underwood, "his good sense and native humor soon got the better of his wrath. His friends in the office . . . long remembered the keen light in his eyes, and his caustic comments upon the humiliating scene."[11] Several days later the satiric reflections on the recruiting sergeant written by a Yankee farmer-poet who had been in town that same day and whose response to the incident was not unlike Lowell's were printed in the *Boston Courier* —the successful literary debut of Hosea Biglow. It is unlikely that Lowell's friends in Court Square had doubts about the authorship of the verses.

Many northerners agreed with Lowell and Hosea in "thinking the Mexican war . . . a national crime committed in behoof of Slavery, our common sin,"[12] but the background of the conflict and the issues and stresses involved in fighting this war were complicated. Wise men initially hesitated to condemn the government's action, while the less wise conveniently substituted for hard thought false notions of patriotism and loyalty.

11. Francis H. Underwood, *The Poet and the Man: Recollections and Appreciations of James Russell Lowell* (Boston: Lee and Shepard, 1893), pp. 31–32.
12. *Writings,* 8:155.

Ever since the migration of some 30,000 Americans to the Mexican state of Coahuila y Texas, in the 1820s, the "Texas question" had been an inflammatory issue in American politics. Many of these settlers were southern slave owners who had been prevented by the Missouri Compromise from pioneering land in the American territories to the north. But they retained their American allegiances, and relations between the American-Texans and the Mexican government quickly deteriorated. Finally, in 1836, the territory declared itself independent and fought a clumsy revolutionary war to substantiate the fact. Thus was created the Matter of Texas: James Bowie and his long knife, Davy Crockett and his rifle "Betsy," Sam Houston, the massacre of the Goliad prisoners, and "Remember the Alamo!" But for some Americans it was not Romance.

Resolutions calling for recognition of the new republic by the United States were passed by Congress in July 1836, but President Jackson delayed in this matter until March of the following year. Nor did he support the petition of Texas for annexation in August 1837. Not until 1844 was Texas again made an important public issue. In the presidential campaign of that year James K. Polk included annexation in his platform, and his success in the election encouraged President Tyler to push through Congress a joint resolution inviting Texas into the Union. Mexico broke diplomatic relations with the United States in March. When, on 4 July 1845, annexation became official, both sides maneuvered troops on opposite sides of the disputed territory, which lay between the Nueces River and the Rio Grande, land which Texas claimed but to which Mexico had not given up her prior rights. An attempt at a diplomatic settlement, wherein the United States offered to pay $30 million for New Mexico and California, failed early the next year; and in February 1846 Gen. Zachary Taylor was ordered to advance to the Rio Grande. The Mexican government considered Taylor's crossing of the Nueces River an act of hostility, and retaliated. When it was learned in Washington that eleven American soldiers had been killed and others wounded in a clash with Mexican cavalry, Polk asked Congress to declare war, an action the president and his cabinet had decided upon even before the news of the conflict had reached the capital.

INTRODUCTION

Abraham Lincoln believed in 1846 "that all those who, because of knowing too *little*, or because of knowing too *much*, could not conscientiously approve the conduct of the President . . . should, nevertheless, as good citizens and patriots, remain silent on that point, at least till the war should be ended"; but two years later the young congressman from Illinois declared in the United States House of Representatives "that the war with Mexico was unnecessarily and unconstitutionally commenced by the President."[13] By the time of Lincoln's speech, however, the war was over: the Treaty of Guadalupe Hidalgo would be signed on 2 February 1848 and ratified by both nations the following May. More than 1,500 Americans had been killed or wounded in battle; perhaps as many as 11,000 had died from disease. Mexican casualties were considerably higher. It was America's first successful offensive war, and she benefited from it immensely. Over one million square miles were added to the national domain, including California, where in January 1848 James Marshall discovered gold. But the price was high, much higher than the $15 million payment to Mexico, which some called "blood money": sectional hatred increased in the United States, and the Compromise of 1850, the political turmoil of the decade that followed, and, eventually, the Civil War were made inevitable. Daniel Webster said at the time: "I pretend to see but little of the future, and that little affords no gratification. All I can scan is contention, strife, and agitation."[14]

Historians still argue with one another about the causes of the war, and their opinions are tallied into schools. The mercantile interests of New England, the land hunger of the West, and a "conspiracy of the slaveocracy" eager for new slave territory and increased political power have each been used to explain the ag-

13. "Speech in United States House of Representatives: The War with Mexico" (12 January 1848), *The Collected Works of Abraham Lincoln*, ed. Roy P. Basler, 8 vols. (New Brunswick, New Jersey: Rutgers University Press, 1953–55), 1:432.

14. Quoted in James Ford Rhodes, *History of the United States from the Compromise of 1850*, 7 vols. (New York: Macmillan Co., 1893–1906), 1:92.

gression.[15] President Polk has been personally blamed; the Mexican government has been blamed. The facts are incontrovertible: there was a war; the president and his administration acted in an underhanded manner; slavery, whether by a conspiracy or by a "defensive aggression" of the South, did become an issue; and commercial and financial interests benefited. But facts are not always answers, and if one stands confused before the facts of public life he may be merely an honest man. Moral facts, on the other hand, can allow no confusion in the mind that recognizes them as such, however wrong or exaggerated the reasons formulated to justify and encourage the moral vision may be. Lowell recognized the ultimate irrationality of any moral position when he confessed: "I cannot reason on the subject [of slavery]. A man who is in the right can never reason. He can only affirm."[16] Lowell and his fellow abolitionists were not in doubt about the immorality of the war, and therefore felt no doubt about the opposition they need take. Lowell had written to Briggs several years before: "The question of Annexation is surely the most momentous of this century to the interests of Humanity & Civilization."[17] Believing—and time proved him right— that with annexation domestic slavery would be extended westward, Lowell used vigorously and persistently his literary talents and labors against that annexation. If he was wrong in making the ex-

15. The last view, popular among the abolitionists, including Lowell, was argued most carefully by Rhodes. Justin H. Smith's *The War with Mexico*, 2 vols. (New York: Macmillan Co., 1919), remains, in spite of its racist and imperialistic biases, the standard history of the military campaign, but it now can be supplemented by David M. Pletcher's excellent study of *The Diplomacy of Annexation: Texas, Oregon, and the Mexican War* (Columbia: University of Missouri Press, 1973). Ramón E. Ruiz has compiled a useful reader, *The Mexican War: Was It Manifest Destiny?* (New York: Holt, Rinehart and Winston, 1963), with an annotated bibliography.

16. *Letters,* 1:93.

17. 6 March 1844: A.L.s., Houghton Library, Harvard University. This and the other letters in the Houghton Library quoted in this edition are used by permission.

tension of slavery the paramount cause of the American aggression against Mexico, he was in error together with John Quincy Adams and Abraham Lincoln. What has become the most convenient and common explanation of the belligerent expansionism of the 1840s is Manifest Destiny. Lowell's temperament and education prepared him to accept in theory the idea as defined by editorial writers like John L. O'Sullivan: "the right of our manifest destiny to overspread and to possess the whole of the continent which Providence has given us for the development of the great experiment of liberty and federated self-government entrusted to us. . . ."[18] But Lowell's moral sense and his Yankee practicality enabled him generally to distinguish between good reasons and real reasons; and he could see that for no few Americans Manifest Destiny was merely a rationalization. There was a real difference between the congressman who envisioned the future states of Texas, Oregon, Nova Scotia, Canada, Cuba, Mexico, and Patagonia,[19] and Albert Gallatin who reminded Americans at the time:

Your mission was to be a model for all other governments and for all other less-favored nations, to adhere to the most elevated principles of political morality, to apply all your faculties to the gradual improvement of your own institutions and social state, and by your example to exert a moral influence most beneficial to mankind at large. Instead of this, an appeal has been made to your worst passions; to cupidity; to the thirst of unjust aggrandizement by brutal force; to the love of military fame and of false glory; and it has even been tried to pervert the noblest feelings of your nature. The attempt is

18. *New York Morning News*, 27 December 1845. Julius W. Pratt's researches conclude that O'Sullivan, the editor of the monthly *Democratic Review* and of the *Morning News*, was the first to use this term. See Pratt's "The Origin of 'Manifest Destiny,' " *American Historical Review* 32 (July 1927): 795–98.

19. John Wentworth of Illinois, *Congressional Globe* 14 (28 January 1845): 200.

made to make you abandon the lofty position which your fathers occupied, to substitute for it the political morality and heathen patriotism of the heroes and statesmen of antiquity.[20]

Or, as Hosea said more simply but none the less effectively:

> We 'd ha' scared 'em by growin' in peace,
> A plaguy sight more then by bobberies like these.

For Lowell and others of like mind, the nation's failure was not to be found so much in mistakes it had made as in opportunities it had ignored: not that it had been so wrong but that it should have been greatly right. If Frederick Merk argues correctly that public opinion opposed the doctrine of Manifest Destiny—"that Manifest Destiny and imperialism were traps into which the nation was led in 1846 and 1899, and from which it extricated itself as well as it could afterward"[21]—then it seems necessary to conclude that either public opinion is an invention of politicians, journalists, and historians; or that public opinion, even in a democracy, is generally of little power, that public opinion might as well be no opinion. Lowell wrote early (30 January 1845) during the annexation crisis:

> After all, the saddest part of the matter is that the moral sense of the mass of the people should be so dead, their intelligence in political affairs so limited, that they can be willing not only to submit to this iniquity, but to sustain it.[22]

III

Charles Sumner, Longfellow's houseguest about the time of the publication of *The Biglow Papers*, was left by his host on a sofa with Lowell's new volume one rainy afternoon when it was necessary for Longfellow to go out. Longfellow, on returning, asked the Massa-

20. *Peace with Mexico* (1847), in *The Writings of Albert Gallatin*, ed. Henry Adams, 3 vols. (Philadelphia: J. B. Lippincott, 1879), 3:583–84.
21. *Manifest Destiny and Mission in American History: A Reinterpretation* (New York: Alfred A. Knopf, 1963), p. 261.
22. *The Anti-Slavery Papers*, 1:13.

chusetts politician if he had enjoyed the poems. Sumner replied: "They are admirable, very good indeed; but why does he spell his words so badly?" Longfellow could not explain to the brilliantly humorless man Lowell's purpose in using New England dialect.[23]

Lowell's enjoyment at hearing this story, and he surely heard it, can be easily imagined. His emotional distance from the book usually considered his best is one of the more telling facts in the life of this complicated and generally misunderstood man. When, in 1859, two English publishers were rushing to issue editions of *The Biglow Papers* before the other, Lowell admitted to Charles Eliot Norton: "I confess I am a little jealous of people who like my humorous poems best. I guess they are right, 'up to date'—but I feel also as if it were a little unfair to tother half of me which has not fairly worked itself free so as to combine . . . the results of life with those of study."[24] In the introduction to the Second Series of *The Biglow Papers* (1867) he tells of his surprise at the popularity of the earlier Biglow verses:

> The success of my experiment soon began not only to astonish me, but to make me feel the responsibility of knowing that I held in my hand a weapon instead of the mere fencing-stick I had supposed. Very far from being a popular author under my own name, so far, indeed, as to be almost unread, I found the verses of my pseudonym copied everywhere; I saw them pinned up in workshops; I heard them quoted and their authorship debated; I once even, when rumor had at length caught up my name in one of its eddies, had the satisfaction of overhearing it demonstrated, in the pauses of a concert, that *I* was utterly incompetent to have written anything of the kind.

He then goes on to defend his use of humor and satire:

> If I put on the cap and bells and made myself one of the court-fools of King Demos, it was less to make his majesty

23. The story is told by Henry Cabot Lodge, *Early Memories* (New York: Charles Scribner's Sons, 1913), p. 280.

24. 20 September 1859: A.L.s., Houghton Library, Harvard University.

laugh than to win a passage to his royal ears for certain serious things which I had deeply at heart. I say this because there
is no imputation that could be more galling to any man's self-
respect than that of being a mere jester.[25]

But in 1848 his dread and frustration at being thought just a funny-
man (another Seba Smith, T. C. Haliburton, or Charles Augustus
Davis) were manifested in the Latin quotation Lowell composed for
the title page of the First Series, an insult probably never felt by
those readers who preferred Hosea's dialect verse to Lowell's lyrical
performances: "*Margaritas, munde porcine, calcâsti: en, siliquas
accipe.*"[26] This fear, in that it encouraged Lowell towards higher
creative levels, accounts considerably for the form the volume
finally took: something more than an anthology of dialect verses
written for various occasions; something more difficult perhaps, but
something better worth the time.

The nine poems by Hosea Biglow first appeared in newspapers,
either the *Boston Courier*, then a liberal, Whig-oriented daily edited
by Joseph T. Buckingham, or the *National Anti-Slavery Standard*,
the weekly journal of the American Anti-Slavery Society, edited in
New York City by Lowell's friend Sydney Howard Gay. It was probably not until the early fall of 1847 that Lowell thought of making
a book out of his Biglow material. Twenty years later he wrote of
the genesis of the papers:

> ... I imagined to myself such an upcountry man as I had often
> seen at antislavery gatherings, capable of district-school En-
> glish, but always instinctively falling back into the natural
> stronghold of his homely dialect when heated to the point of
> self-forgetfulness. When I began to carry out my conception
> and to write in my assumed character, I found myself in a strait
> between two perils. On the one hand, I was in danger of being
> carried beyond the limit of my own opinions, or at least of that
> temper with which every man should speak his mind in print,
> and on the other I feared the risk of seeming to vulgarize a

25. *Writings*, 8:157.
26. "Oh, swinish world, you have trampled pearls; so, take the husks."

deep and sacred conviction. I needed on occasion to rise above the level of mere *patois*, and for this purpose conceived the Rev. Mr. Wilbur, who should express the more cautious element of the New England character and its pedantry, as Mr. Biglow should serve for its homely common-sense vivified and heated by conscience. The parson was to be the complement rather than the antithesis of his parishioner, and I felt or fancied a certain humorous element in the real identity of the two under a seeming incongruity. Mr. Wilbur's fondness for scraps of Latin, though drawn from the life, I adopted deliberately to heighten the contrast. Finding soon after that I needed some one as a mouthpiece of the mere drollery, for I conceive that true humor is never divorced from moral conviction, I invented Mr. Sawin for the clown of my little puppet-show. I meant to embody in him that half-conscious *un*morality which I had noticed as the recoil in gross natures from a puritanism that still strove to keep in its creed the intense savor which had long gone out of its faith and life. In the three I thought I should find room enough to express, as it was my plan to do, the popular feeling and opinion of the time.[27]

This account was accurate enough in retrospect, but the actual growth from the newspaper verses to the volume was much more hazardous, more accidental, less obvious in the beginning than Lowell would have us believe, or, indeed, afterwards remembered.

The verses of the second paper were printed in August 1847, and those of the third on 2 November 1847. On the thirteenth of that month Lowell wrote to Briggs that Hosea "intends publishing a volume of his own before long," and that "Parson Wilbur is about to propose a subscription for fitting [Hosea] for college, and has already commenced his education."[28] Notes in one of Lowell's writing books from this period (see Textual Commentary, pp. 246–47) suggest that it was his early intention to build the volume around Hosea's adventures at college. The fictional possibilities of New England life intrigued him; the preceding year he had written to

27. *Writings*, 8:155–56.
28. *Letters*, 1:166–67.

Briggs, "I have always had it in my mind to write a New England novel which will astonish my friends if it ever gets delivered."[29] But the book did not develop along this line, and it is difficult to imagine it doing so effectively. "Remarks of Increase D. O'Phace" was printed in the *Courier* in December, and "The Debate in the Sennit," the last of the verses to appear first in the *Courier*, on 3 May 1848.

During the previous March, Lowell had become a "Corresponding Editor" of the *National Anti-Slavery Standard*. In return for an annual salary of $500, he was to contribute a weekly paper either in prose or verse. His first contribution under this arrangement was "Ode to France," 6 April 1848. He sent "The Pious Editor's Creed," accompanied by a letter from Parson Wilbur (see Appendix to this volume), for the 4 May issue. The verses of the remaining three papers appeared there during June, July, and September. By midsummer Lowell was thinking and working hard on *The Biglow Papers*, and on 22 August he wrote Briggs, "I am to begin printing Hosea forthwith. . . ."[30] It had been a difficult summer. Besides the *Standard*'s weekly paper or poem, *A Fable for Critics* (published in October) and *The Vision of Sir Launfal* (published in December) lay on his desk demanding attention, and his health had not been good: "I have suffered all this summer with a severe pain in the head which has entirely crippled me for a great part of the time. It is what people call a *fulness* in the head, but its effect is to produce an entire emptiness."[31] His biographers have not erred in naming it an *annus mirabilis*.

The emphasis on Birdofredum Sawin in the last papers and the disappearance of Hosea—though it is still he who is turning into verse Sawin's letters—probably resulted from Lowell's desire to give greater fictional and structural unity to the volume. Having abandoned the plan of sending Hosea to college, there was little Lowell could do with the country fellow that would provide something resembling a plot line. Hosea belongs to, just as he helped create, the tradition of New England rustic or Down East humor; but in Low-

29. *Letters*, 1:150.

30. A.L.s., Houghton Library, Harvard University.

31. 28 July 1848: *New Letters of James Russell Lowell*, ed. M. A. DeWolfe Howe (New York and London: Harper & Brothers, 1932), p. 29.

ell this Yankee type is primarily a voice, a point of view, a center of consciousness: a fine commentator but a poor actor. Birdofredum, on the other hand, provided rich possibilities both for humor and irony. He is a true picaro; his responses to and reflections on his adventures in Mexico and the South and his unfortunate career in politics portray his character more fully than Lowell managed to achieve with either Wilbur or Hosea. He is a supporting actor who nearly steals the show. For all this, he is nonetheless a type, what Howells would later call the Puritan rebel. But he is a human type; Birdofredum never becomes a monster, either of drollery or of wickedness. The men he admires—Cushing, Taylor, the petty politicians surrounding them—seem monstrous, however, largely because we have seen sympathetically, and with no slight regret, the flaws in a pathetic fellow who believes he can emulate their glory. A man who believes the lies by which he and his society live is too common to be despised. Increase D. O'Phace is a hypocrite, Birdofredum merely a fool.

Wilbur was mentioned in Ezekiel Biglow's letter to Buckingham which was printed with Hosea's first verses in the *Courier;* but the parson made no public appearance until his letter, refuting the attribution of Hosea's verses "to the pen of Mr. James Russell Lowell," was printed in the *Courier,* 6 November 1847. A fine letter (reprinted in paper No. III), it shows that Lowell grasped the character of Wilbur firmly in his imagination at the time when he was just beginning to consider the possibilities of Hosea's volume. It is probable that his own father, the Rev. Mr. Charles Lowell, or the Rev. Mr. Barzaillai Frost, Lowell's tutor in Concord while rusticated from Harvard in 1838, were in Lowell's mind when he drew Wilbur. And it is possible that the fictional parsons of Fielding and Goldsmith, to mention only two, were conscious antecedents. But the ministerial type was common enough to New England life and literature to make specific sources unnecessary. Great in learning—as Cotton Mather said of John Cotton: "his library was vast, and vast was his acquaintance with it"[32]—and great in pride of priestly status, Wilbur is yet a man humble in person and gentle in attitude. Forty

32. *Magnalia Christi Americana,* 2 vols. (Hartford: S. Andrus and Son, 1853), 1:274.

years earlier he would have been a worthy contributor to the *Monthly Anthology;* two centuries earlier he would have been an exemplary Puritan divine. Indeed his Jeremiah language, his moral earnestness, his belief that secular law is subservient to moral law, and his imagination, more sensitive to the spiritual and the prophetic than to the material and mundane, all suggest an earlier, and, for Lowell, finer period of New England history. His weaknesses—too much pride (how transparent is his lie that he has "never read a single line" of the *Liberator*) and pedantry—are shortcomings of a man born out of his right time. The weaknesses are a condemnation, however, of the modern age and its deficiencies, not Parson Wilbur. He must protect the dignity of his office because it is regarded too cheaply by his contemporaries: "So it has come to pass that the preacher, instead of being a living force, has faded into an emblematic figure at christenings, weddings, and funerals." His pedantry—a misuse of intellectual labor—is undeniable, but its extent and its damaging effect on the volume have been exaggerated by most critics. Wilbur's learning is often funny —though for the reader who fails to catch the joke it is annoying— and more often, even in its humor, of serious purport. Wilbur's part of the volume constitutes some of Lowell's best writing, by far the best prose he wrote before the Civil War. Not all admirers of *The Biglow Papers* have preferred Hosea to his spiritual father.

But it is not in characterization, though it has been generally praised, that the greatest strength of *The Biglow Papers* lies. Fine characterization is rarely remarkable in humorous satire; the chance for a hit, for humor, understandably diverts the author from anything so literary as consistency of character. What holds *The Biglow Papers* together, what makes it a book, are irony and its form, unique both in conception and execution. From its beginning in deft parodies of contemporary literary notices to its outrageous "Index," *The Biglow Papers* is a masterpiece of sustained irony, the irony of an earnest young man who sees the good sense of truth and justice, but realizes the blindness of those about him. It is irony that permits much humor, because the ironist believes that conflicts between the fact and the ideal may be resolved. It is irony not yet directed against the self, though there are times—for instance, Wil-

INTRODUCTION

bur's last paragraph in the last paper—when this final irony is strongly suggested: where the fun is turned on one's self, where the limits of society are glimpsed as limits—perhaps unchangeable —of that self.

Lowell's conception of the book went beyond the contents. It included the design. When he first imagined the Biglow volume, he had definite ideas about the book's appearance: "The book will purport to be published at Jaalam (Mr. B.'s native place), and will be printed on brownish paper with those little head and tail-pieces which used to adorn our earliest publications—such as hives, scrolls, urns, and the like."[33] Except in the prose and character of Wilbur, however, this desired effect of old-fashionedness was not achieved until sufficient time had passed so as to make all books printed in 1848 appear "old." But there is a quaint charm and simplicity about the first-book edition that was suppressed in later editions, though never entirely obscured. The table talks and essays of English writers of the eighteenth century taught Wilbur how to write, and editions of the classics suggested ways of putting books together. Sterne in *Tristram Shandy* and, more immediately, Robert Southey in *The Doctor* had done more with the book as a physical object; yet Lowell's solution was in its way original (just as Melville's would be in *Moby-Dick*); something new, not imitative.

Lowell had hopes the book would be published by the first of October, but the preparation of copy, the reading of proof, and the stereotyping went slower than he had anticipated, and publication was not until 10 November 1848, the day he wrote to Gay:

I shall send you a copy of Hosea in next week's "Liberator" bundle. It will be out, I suppose, to-day. So we are going to have Taylor after all. Tell Briggs that I had not so much faith in the brutality of the people as he had. I suppose we shall have another cursed Missouri Compromise.[34]

Three days earlier the Whig slaveowner and war hero, Gen. Zachary Taylor, had been elected president by the people of the United

33. Lowell to Briggs, 31 December 1847: *Letters*, 1:168–69.
34. *Letters*, 1:195.

States. *The Biglow Papers* came too late to turn voters from Taylor to Martin Van Buren, the Free-Soil candidate. If it therefore made the times no better, it is not likely that it could have. Joseph R. Chandler wrote in *Graham's Magazine* for December 1848:

> Men talk of an exciting *contest* for the presidential chair; but analyze that contest, and it is found to be only a newspaper discussion of the merits of certain existing or proposed acts of Congress, having nothing to do with the organic laws of the land, or with the form of government; the contest or discussion was closed on the 7th day of November last, and men scarcely remember the earnestness of the newspaper paragraphs, or the stump speeches.[35]

IV

Printed reviews and notices during the months following the publication of *The Biglow Papers* were few, and, as Lowell wrote Gay, generally unfavorable.[36] Almost all reflect, as one would expect, the political orientation and prejudices of the writer and journal. Though the abolitionist was no longer the pariah he had been a decade before, editors of popular periodicals in the North rarely allowed the discussion of slavery and its abolition. It was not good business. Poe's reaction to Lowell's satire was extreme, but it was shared to some degree by many readers.

> Mr. Lowell is one of the most rabid of the Abolition fanatics; and no Southerner who does not wish to be insulted, and at the same time revolted by a bigotry the most obstinately blind and deaf, should ever touch a volume by this author.[37]

35. "Reflections on Some of the Events of the Year 1848," *Graham's Magazine* 33 (December 1848): 324.
36. 20 December 1848: *Letters*, 1:198.
37. *Southern Literary Messenger* 15 (March 1849): 190.

As a result, it is in the lesser magazines that one finds mention of Lowell's book.[38] To quote from these reviews would be merely to add further illustrations to Wilbur's "Notices of an Independent Press." Only one really got beyond Lowell's "message" to the art of *The Biglow Papers*, and that was written by a friend, Charles Briggs. It begins:

> This is a new, an entirely new, and a very neat volume, which has manifestly been made up by the author without having an eye to any other work which has ever been published. There is nothing fashionable about it, nor yet is it unfashionable. It is simply fresh, and, which is not by any means a matter of course, refreshing. A book that is a book should be a book by itself, from the title-page to the finis; and such is the volume entitled "The Biglow Papers."[39]

More typical was the apology by Daniel March in the *New Englander*:

> It may surprise, and possibly offend, some very good people, that we take *any* notice of a book, which one class of critics will regard only as a foolish attempt to make people laugh, and another class will be sure to denounce, as full of the most wicked and diabolical mockery.[40]

When radicals are not forgotten, though most of them are, they often become heroes and saints. Lowell's apotheosis was to schoolroom poet, and among our national scriptures *The Vision of Sir Launfal* has had its hallowed place. But *The Biglow Papers* was too

38. Reviews or notices of the book appeared in the *Christian Examiner* 46 (January 1849); *Harbinger* 8 (23 December 1848); *Holden's Dollar Magazine* 3 (January 1849); *Literary World* 3 (2 December 1848); *New Englander* 7 (February 1849); *North American Review* 68 (January 1849); *Peterson's Magazine* 15 (February 1849); and *Spirit of the Times* 3 (2 December 1848).
39. *Holden's Dollar Magazine* 3 (January 1849): 50.
40. *New Englander* 7 (February 1849): 64.

honest for Sunday school, in spite of Wilbur's imprimatur, and its admirers have largely been of the dissenting sects.

But admirers there have been. Either way one interprets his statement, Barrett Wendell was wrong when he told Harvard students, "No one knows enough to read *The Biglow Papers.*" Linguists have studied the language and have been greatly impressed with Lowell's achievement in recording the New England dialect. H. L. Mencken praised Lowell both for his attempting "to depict with some care the peculiar temperament and point of view of the rustic New Englander," and for his "extremely successful effort to report Yankee speech. . . . He did a great service to the common tongue of the country, and must be numbered among its true friends."[41] Bret Harte and Edward M. Chapman favorably considered *The Biglow Papers* in terms of the New England culture it celebrates, and Arthur Voss studied the book in relation to its political and historical backgrounds. Walter Blair and Jennette Tandy in their studies of American humor both praise *The Biglow Papers*, the latter writing: Lowell "cuts deeper than any other into the gnarled fibers of the cross-grained Yankee. Hosea, Birdofredum, John P. Robinson, The Pious Editor, the Candidate, are a Hogarthian company. Lowell's range and penetration in satirical portraiture are unsurpassed in America."[42]

But these are as yet minority voices. Most academic critics have merely repeated Barrett Wendell's remarks made at the turn of the century:

41. *The American Language, Supplement 1* (New York: Alfred A. Knopf, 1945), pp. 129–31. The most thorough study of the dialect is James Walker Downer's dissertation, "Features of New England Rustic Pronunciation in James Russell Lowell's *Biglow Papers*" (University of Michigan, 1958).

42. Tandy, *Crackerbox Philosophers in American Humor and Satire* (New York: Columbia University Press, 1925), p. 63; Blair, *Horse Sense in American Humor* (Chicago: University of Chicago Press, 1942) and *Native American Humor* (San Francisco: Chandler Publishing Co., 1960); Harte, "A Few Words about Mr. Lowell," *New Review* 5 (September 1891): 193–201; Chapman, "The Biglow Papers Fifty Years After," *Yale Review*, n.s. 6 (October 1916): 120–34: Voss, see below, page 171.

The humour of Parson Wilbur's interminable introductions, to
be sure, seems mostly of the ponderous old English type; but
the verses themselves, amid all their extravagance of dialect
and puns, now and again state grave truths in solemnly plain
terms, and sometimes rise into noble poetry. . . . [Both, however, finally] fall into the same category. Both prove so delib-
erate, both so much matters of detail, that in the end your
impression may well be, that, taken all in all, each paper is
tediously ingenious. No one number of the 'Biglow Papers' is
so long as the 'Fable for Critics;' but none is much easier to
read through.[43]

The only adequate extended critical commentary on *The Biglow
Papers* is that of Leon Howard in his study of Lowell's early literary
career.[44] Howard's conclusions are no more favorable than Wendell's, but at least he reached them through an investigation into the
circumstances of the book and an honest consideration of the text.
Whether his southern point of view, however, caused him to over-
look certain Yankee virtues in the book is another matter.

William Rose Benét's prophecy, made three decades ago, remains
prophecy: "To us, Lowell accomplished no inconsiderable feat in
'The Biglow Papers.' Some day they will be 'rediscovered.' "[45]

V

*Peace, plenty, and contentment reign throughout our bor-
ders, and our beloved country presents a sublime moral
spectacle to the world.*
— James K. Polk, 5 December 1848[46]

43. *A Literary History of America* (New York: Charles Scribner's
Sons, 1900), pp. 508, 401.
44. *Victorian Knight-Errant* (Berkeley and Los Angeles: University of
California Press, 1952), pp. 232–60.
45. "Lowell, and Liberty," *Saturday Review of Literature* 25 (12 December 1942): 20.
46. Fourth Annual Message to Congress: James D. Richardson, ed.,

In December 1848, several days before the new year, Lowell, on the evening of his sister-in-law's wedding,

> . . . walked to Watertown over the snow with the new moon before me and a sky exactly like that in Page's evening landscape. Orion was rising behind me, and, as I stood on the hill just before you enter the village, the stillness of the fields around me was delicious, broken only by the tinkle of a little brook which runs too swiftly for Frost to catch it. . . . I was so happy as I stood there, and felt so sure of doing something that would justify my friends. But why do I not say that I *have* done something? I believe that I have done better than the world knows yet, but the past seems so little compared with the future. . . . I am the first poet who has endeavored to express the American Idea, and I shall be popular by and by.[47]

When the new year came, it found Lowell ready to leave his youth behind. The radicalism, the optimistic faith, the extraordinary energy which characterized his early life and work were being gradually replaced by a more considered, more cautious, and perhaps wiser approach to the problems of life and art. The man who had proclaimed in 1845, "Every success of wrong is a step toward its annihilation,"[48] now more hesitatingly wrote: "The longer I live the more am I convinced that the world must be healed by degrees."[49] There was a change in styles both of life and thought which has puzzled and disappointed his biographers; that change wherein a man looks to find himself after he has passed thirty. Lowell had achieved much for a young man; but it was, after all, a young man's achievement. In January 1850, he wrote Briggs:

A Compilation of the Messages and Papers of the Presidents 1789–1897, 11 vols. (Washington, D.C.: Government Printing Office, 1897–1914), 4:629.

47. Lowell to Briggs [29 December 1848]: *Letters*, 1:200–201; date determined from evidence in letter (Houghton Library, Harvard University) deleted by Norton.

48. *The Anti-Slavery Papers*, 1:14.

49. Lowell to Gay, 21 May 1849: *Letters*, 1:213.

INTRODUCTION

I begin to feel that I must enter on a new year of my apprenticeship. . . . I have preached sermons enow, and now I am going to come down out of the pulpit and *go about among my parish*. . . . I shall not grind for any Philistines, whether Reformers or Conservatives. I find that Reform cannot take up the whole of me, and I am quite sure that eyes were given us to look about us with sometimes, and not to be always looking forward. If some of my good red-hot friends were to see this they would call me a backslider, but there are other directions in which one may get away from people beside the rearward one.[50]

Lowell did try in the fifties "to write a Hosea Biglow," but the result, he told Edmund Quincy, was four lines.[51] Only after the Civil War had become a common-day reality was Lowell able to rediscover in his imagination the voices of his friends at Jaalam. But they were older voices, reflecting a quaint pathos and lyricism not in the First Series, and indicating an imagination no stranger to sorrow and death, but neither one defeated by life.

Were writers and the history of literature subject to laws and cycles, not unlike those that scientists sometimes claim to find in nature, Lowell, rather than continuing his apprenticeship in the 1850s, should have been ready with a masterpiece. His exact contemporaries, Melville and Whitman, wrote *Moby-Dick* (1851) and *Leaves of Grass* (1855); Thoreau, two years older, published *Walden* in 1854. But Lowell's masterpiece did not come, much to the frustration of later literary historians. There did follow a series of intriguing fragments of masterpieces: the brilliant essays, the contemplative poems, the public odes, the sometimes profound and

50. *Letters,* 1:232–33.

51. 19 April 1854: *New Letters,* p. 50. On 6 July 1859 Lowell wrote Charles Eliot Norton: "I have a new 'Biglow' running in my head these three weeks, & shall write it as soon as my brain clears off. . . . I *think* my new 'Biglow' will be funny. If not, you will never see it. It will be on the re-opening of the slave-trade, & some rather humorous combinations have come into my mind. We shall see." A.L.s., Houghton Library, Harvard University.

usually insightful criticism, and, not least, the later correspondence, all which need serious consideration before the literary and intellectual life in America during the second half of the nineteenth century can be fully understood. But there did not appear during the fifties that one book of which it could be said, "This is it!" It would seem Lowell's genius (to use the term of his day) was inadequate to produce such, unless it had already been achieved. So thought John Jay Chapman:

. . . at a crisis of pressure, Lowell assumed his real self under the guise of a pseudonym; and with his own hand he rescued a language, a type, a whole era of civilization from oblivion. Here gleams the dagger and here is Lowell revealed. His limitations as a poet, his too much wit, his too much morality, his mixture of shrewdness and religion, are seen to be the very elements of power. The novelty of the Biglow Papers is as wonderful as their world-old naturalness. They take rank with greatness, and they were the strongest political tracts of their time. They imitate nothing; they are real.[52]

52. *Emerson and Other Essays* (New York: Charles Scribner's Sons, 1898), pp. 104–5.

The Biglow Papers
[First Series]

Notices of an Independent Press.

[I have observed, reader, (bene- or male-volent, as it may
happen,) that it is customary to append to the second editions
of books, and to the second works of authors, short sentences
commendatory of the first, under the title of *Notices of the
Press*. These, I have been given to understand, are procurable
at certain established rates, payment being made either in
money or advertising patronage by the publisher, or by an
adequate outlay of servility on the part of the author.
Considering these things with myself, and also that such
notices are neither intended, nor generally believed, to convey
any real opinions, being a purely ceremonial accompaniment
of literature, and resembling certificates to the virtues of
various morbiferal panaceas, I conceived that it would be not
only more economical to prepare a sufficient number of such
myself, but also more immediately subservient to the end in
view to prefix them to this our primary edition rather than to
await the contingency of a second, when they would seem to
be of small utility. To delay attaching the *bobs* until the second
attempt at flying the kite would indicate but a slender
experience in that useful art. Neither has it escaped my notice,
nor failed to afford me matter of reflection, that, when a circus
or a caravan is about to visit Jaalam, the initial step is to send
forward large and highly ornamented bills of performance to
be hung in the bar-room and the post-office. These having been
sufficiently gazed at, and beginning to lose their attractiveness
except for the flies, and, truly, the boys also, (in whom I find it
impossible to repress, even during school-hours, certain oral
and telegraphic communications concerning the expected
show,) upon some fine morning the band enters in a gaily-
painted wagon, or triumphal chariot, and with noisy advertisement, by means of brass, wood, and sheepskin, makes the
circuit of our startled village-streets. Then, as the exciting
sounds draw nearer and nearer, do I desiderate those eyes of

Aristarchus, "whose looks were as a breeching to a boy." Then do I perceive, with vain regret of wasted opportunities, the advantage of a pancratic or pantechnic education, since he is most reverenced by my little subjects who can throw the cleanest summerset or walk most securely upon the revolving cask. The story of the Pied Piper becomes for the first time credible to me, (albeit confirmed by the Hameliners dating their legal instruments from the period of his exit,) as I behold how those strains, without pretence of magical potency, bewitch the pupillary legs, nor leave to the pedagogic an entire self-control. For these reasons, lest my kingly prerogative should suffer diminution, I prorogue my restless commons, whom I follow into the street, chiefly lest some mischief may chance befall them. After the manner of such a band, I send forward the following notices of domestic manufacture, to make brazen proclamation, not unconscious of the advantage which will accrue, if our little craft, *cymbula sutilis*, shall seem to leave port with a clipping breeze, and to carry, in nautical phrase, a bone in her mouth. Nevertheless, I have chosen, as being more equitable, to prepare some also sufficiently objurgatory, that readers of every taste may find a dish to their palate. I have modelled them upon actually existing specimens, preserved in my own cabinet of natural curiosities. One, in particular, I had copied with tolerable exactness from a notice of one of my own discourses, which, from its superior tone and appearance of vast experience, I concluded to have been written by a man at least three hundred years of age, though I recollected no existing instance of such antediluvian longevity. Nevertheless, I afterwards discovered the author to be a young gentleman preparing for the ministry under the direction of one of my brethren in a neighbouring town, and whom I had once instinctively corrected in a Latin quantity. But this I have been forced to omit, from its too great length.—H.W.]

From the Universal Littery Universe.

Full of passages which rivet the attention of the reader. . . . Under a rustic garb, sentiments are conveyed which should be committed to the memory and engraven on the heart of every moral and social being. . . . We consider this a *unique* performance. . . . We hope to see it soon introduced into our common schools. . . . Mr. Wilbur has performed his duties as editor with excellent taste and judgment. . . . This is a vein which we hope to see successfully prosecuted. . . . We hail the appearance of this work as a long stride toward the formation of a purely aboriginal, indigenous, native, and American literature. We rejoice to meet with an author national enough to break away from the slavish deference, too common among us, to English grammar and orthography. . . . Where all is so good, we are at a loss how to make extracts. . . . On the whole, we may call it a volume which no library, pretending to entire completeness, should fail to place upon its shelves.

From the Higginbottomopolis Snapping-turtle.

A collection of the merest balderdash and doggerel that it was ever our bad fortune to lay eyes on. The author is a vulgar buffoon, and the editor a talkative, tedious old fool. We use strong language, but should any of our readers peruse the book, (from which calamity Heaven preserve them!) they will find reasons for it thick as the leaves of Vallumbrozer, or, to use a still more expressive comparison, as the combined heads of author and editor. The work is wretchedly got up. . . . We should like to know how much *British gold* was pocketed by this libeller of our country and her purest patriots.

From the Oldfogrumville Mentor.

We have not had time to do more than glance through this handsomely printed volume, but the name of its respectable editor, the Rev. Mr. Wilbur, of Jaalam, will afford a sufficient guaranty for the worth of its contents. . . . The paper is white, the type clear, and the volume of a convenient and attractive size. . . . In reading this elegantly executed work, it has seemed to us that a passage or two might have been retrenched with advantage, and that the general style of diction was susceptible of a higher polish. . . . On the whole, we may safely leave the ungrateful task of criticism to the reader. We will barely suggest, that in volumes intended, as this is, for the illustration of a provincial dialect and turns of expression, a dash of humor or satire might be thrown in with advantage. . . . The work is admirably got up. . . . This work will form an appropriate ornament to the centre-table. It is beautifully printed, on paper of an excellent quality.

From the Dekay Bulwark.

We should be wanting in our duty as the conductor of that tremendous engine, a public press, as an American, and as a man, did we allow such an opportunity as is presented to us by " The Biglow Papers " to pass by without entering our earnest protest against such attempts (now, alas ! too common) at demoralizing the public sentiment. Under a wretched mask of stupid drollery, slavery, war, the social glass, and, in short, all the valuable and time-honored institutions justly dear to our common humanity and especially to republicans, are made the butt of coarse and senseless ribaldry by this low-minded scribbler. It is time that the respectable and religious portion of our community should be aroused to the alarming inroads of foreign Jacobinism, sansculottism, and infidelity. It is a fearful proof of the wide-spread nature of this contagion, that these secret stabs at religion and virtue are given from under the cloak (*credite, posteri!*) of a clergyman. It is a mournful spectacle indeed to the patriot and Christian to see liberality and new ideas (falsely so called,—they are as old as Eden) invading the sacred precincts of the pulpit. . . . On the whole, we consider this volume as one of the first shocking results which we predicted would spring out of the late French " Revolution " (!).

From the Bungtown Copper and Comprehensive Tocsin
(a tryweakly family journal).

Altogether an admirable work. . . . Full of humor, boisterous, but delicate,—of wit withering and scorching, yet combined with a pathos cool as morning dew,—of satire ponderous as the mace of Richard, yet keen as the scymitar of Saladin. . . . A work full of " mountain-mirth," mischievous as Puck and lightsome as Ariel. . . . We know not whether to admire most the genial, fresh, and discursive concinnity of the author, or his playful fancy, weird imagina-

7

Winslow Homer (1836–1910) portrays Zekle in the dress of a stage Yankee in this silhouette which appeared in a gift-book edition of The Courtin' *(Boston: James R. Osgood and Co., 1874). This was the only book entirely illustrated by Homer.*

tion, and compass of style, at once both objective and subjective.
. . . We might indulge in some criticisms, but, were the author other
than he is, he would be a different being. As it is, he has a wonderful
pose, which flits from flower to flower, and bears the reader irre-
sistibly along on its eagle pinions (like Ganymede) to the " highest
heaven of invention.". . . We love a book so purely objective. . . .
Many of his pictures of natural scenery have an extraordinary subjective clearness and fidelity. . . . In fine, we consider this as one of
the most extraordinary volumes of this or any age. We know of no
English author who could have written it. It is a work to which the
proud genius of our country, standing with one foot on the Aroostook
and the other on the Rio Grande, and holding up the star-spangled
banner amid the wreck of matter and the crush of worlds, may point
with bewildering scorn of the punier efforts of enslaved Europe. . . .
We hope soon to encounter our author among those higher walks
of literature in which he is evidently capable of achieving enduring
fame. Already we should be inclined to assign him a high position
in the bright galaxy of our American bards.

From the Saltriver Pilot and Flag of Freedom.

A volume in bad grammar and worse taste. . . . While the pieces
here collected were confined to their appropriate sphere in the corners of obscure newspapers, we considered them wholly beneath
contempt, but, as the author has chosen to come forward in this
public manner, he must expect the lash he so richly merits. . . .
Contemptible slanders. . . . Vilest Billingsgate. . . . Has raked all the
gutters of our language. . . . The most pure, upright, and consistent
politicians not safe from his malignant venom. . . . General Cushing
comes in for a share of his vile calumnies. . . . The *Reverend* Homer
Wilbur is a disgrace to his cloth. . . .

From the World-Harmonic-Æolian-Attachment.

Speech is silver : silence is golden. No utterance more Orphic than
this. While, therefore, as highest author, we reverence him whose
works continue heroically unwritten, we have also our hopeful word
for those who with pen (from wing of goose loud-cackling, or seraph

God-commissioned) record the thing that is revealed. . . . . Under mask of quaintest irony, we detect here the deep, storm-tost (nigh shipwracked) soul, thunder-scarred, semiarticulate, but ever climbing hopefully toward the peaceful summits of an Infinite Sorrow. . . . Yes, thou poor, forlorn Hosea, with Hebrew fire-flaming soul in thee, for thee also this life of ours has not been without its aspects of heavenliest pity and laughingest mirth. Conceivable enough! Through coarse Thersites-cloak, we have revelation of the heart, wild-glowing, world-clasping, that is in him. Bravely he grapples with the life-problem as it presents itself to him, uncombed, shaggy, careless of the " nicer proprieties," inexpert of " elegant diction," yet with voice audible enough to whoso hath ears, up there on the gravelly side-hills, or down on the splashy, Indiarubber-like salt-marshes of native Jaalam. To this soul also the *Necessity of Creating* somewhat has unveiled its awful front. If not Œdipuses and Electras and Alcestises, then in God's name Birdofredum Sawins! These also shall get born into the world, and filch (if so need) a Zingali subsistence therein, these lank, omnivorous Yankees of his. He shall paint the Seen, since the Unseen will not sit to him. Yet in him also are Nibelungen-lays, and Iliads, and Ulysses-wanderings, and Divine Comedies,—if only once he could come at them! Therein lies much, nay all; for what truly is this which we name *All*, but that which we do *not* possess? . . . Glimpses also are given us of an old father Ezekiel, not without paternal pride, as is the wont of such. A brown, parchment-hided old man of the geoponic or bucolic species, gray-eyed, we fancy, *queued* perhaps, with much weather-cunning and plentiful September-gale memories, bidding fair in good time to become the Oldest Inhabitant. After such hasty apparition, he vanishes and is seen no more. . . . Of " Rev. Homer Wilbur, A. M., Pastor of the First Church in Jaalam," we have small care to speak here. Spare touch in him of his Melesigenes namesake, save, haply, the—blindness! A tolerably caliginose, nephelegeretous elderly gentleman, with infinite faculty of sermonizing, muscularized by long practice, and excellent digestive apparatus, and, for the rest, wellmeaning enough, and with small private illuminations (somewhat tallowy, it is to be feared) of his own. To him, there, " Pastor of the First Church in Jaalam," our Hosea presents himself as a quite inexplicable Sphinx-riddle. A rich poverty of Latin and Greek,—so far is clear enough, even to eyes peering myopic through horn-lensed editorial spectacles,—but naught farther ? O purblind, well-meaning, altogether fuscous Melesigenes-Wilbur, there are things in him incommunicable by stroke of birch ! Did it ever enter that old bewildered head of thine that there was the *Possibility of the Infinite* in him ? To thee, quite wingless (and even featherless) biped, has not so much even as a dream of wings ever come ? "Talented young parishioner " ? Among the Arts whereof thou art *Magister*, does that of *seeing* happen to be one ? Unhappy *Artium Magister !* Somehow a Nemean lion, fulvous, torrid-eyed, dry-nursed in broad-howling sand-wildernesses of a sufficiently rare spirit-Libya (it may be supposed) has got whelped among the sheep. Already he stands wild-glaring, with feet clutching the ground as with oak-roots, gathering for a Remus-spring over the walls of thy little fold. In Heaven's name, go not near him with that flybite crook of thine ! In good time, thou painful preacher, thou wilt go to the appointed place of departed Artillery-Election Sermons, Right-Hands of Fellowship, and Results of Councils, gathered to thy spiritual fathers with much Latin of the Epitaphial sort ; thou, too, shalt have thy reward ; but on him the Eumenides have looked, not Xantippes of the pit, snake-tressed, finger-threatening, but radiantly calm as on antique gems ; for him paws impatient the winged courser of the gods, champing unwelcome bit ; him the starry deeps, the empyrean glooms, and far-flashing splendors await.

From the Onion Grove Phœnix.

A talented young townsman of ours, recently returned from a Continental tour, and who is already favorably known to our readers by his sprightly letters from abroad which have graced our columns, called at our office yesterday. We learn from him, that, having enjoyed the distinguished privilege, while in Germany, of an introduction to the celebrated Von Humbug, he took the opportunity to present that eminent man with a copy of the " Biglow Papers." The next morning he received the following note, which he has kindly furnished us for publication. We prefer to print it *verbatim,* knowing that our readers will readily forgive the few errors into which the illustrious writer has fallen, through ignorance of our language.

"HIGH-WORTHY MISTER!

" I shall also now especially happy starve, because I have more or less a work one those aboriginal Red-Men seen in which have I so deaf an interest ever taken fullworthy on the self shelf with our Gottsched to be upset.

"Pardon my in the English-speech unpractice !

"VON HUMBUG."

He also sent with the above note a copy of his famous work on " Cosmetics," to be presented to Mr. Biglow ; but this was taken from our friend by the English custom-house officers, probably through a petty national spite. No doubt, it has by this time found its way into the British Museum. We trust this outrage will be exposed in all our American papers. We shall do our best to bring it to the notice of the State Department. Our numerous readers will share in the pleasure we experience at seeing our young and vigorous national literature thus encouragingly patted on the head by this venerable and world-renowned German. We love to see these reciprocations of good-feeling between the different branches of the great Anglo-Saxon race.

[The following genuine "notice" having met my eye, I gladly insert a portion of it here, the more especially as it contains one of Mr. Biglow's poems not elsewhere printed.—H.W.]

From the Jaalam Independent Blunderbuss.

. . . But, while we lament to see our young townsman thus mingling in the heated contests of party politics, we think we detect in him the presence of talents which, if properly directed, might give an innocent pleasure to many. As a proof that he is competent to the production of other kinds of poetry, we copy for our readers a short fragment of a pastoral by him, the manuscript of which was loaned us by a friend. The title of it is " The Courtin'."

Homer's silhouette of Huldy possesses a quiet charm and is, in its minor way, a genuine artistic success. The Rev. Mr. Wilbur recognized the limitation of the silhouette, however, when he decided not to include in The Biglow Papers *his own portrait, "a profile (entirely black)," because it was "wanting in expression."*

Zekle crep' up, quite unbeknown,
An' peeked in thru the winder,

An' there sot Huldy all alone,
'ith no one nigh to hender.

Agin' the chimbly crooknecks hung,
An' in amongst 'em rusted
The ole queen's arm thet gran'ther Young
Fetched back frum Concord busted.

The wannut logs shot sparkles out
Towards the pootiest, bless her !
An' leetle fires danced all about
The chiny on the dresser.

The very room, coz she wuz in,
Looked warm frum floor to ceilin',
An' she looked full ez rosy agin
Ez th' apples she wuz peelin'.

She heerd a foot an' knowed it, tu,
Araspin' on the scraper,—
All ways to once her feelins flew
Like sparks in burnt-up paper.

He kin' o' l'itered on the mat,
Some doubtfle o' the seekle ;
His heart kep' goin' pitypat,
But hern went pity Zekle.

An' yet she gin her cheer a jerk
Ez though she wished him furder,
An' on her apples kep' to work
Ez ef a wager spurred her.

"You want to see my Pa, I spose ? "
"Wal, no ; I come designin'—"
"To see my Ma ? She 's sprinklin' clo'es
Agin tomorrow's i'nin'."

He stood a spell on one foot fust
Then stood a spell on tother,

14

An' on which one he felt the wust
He couldn't ha' told ye, nuther.

Sez he, "I'd better call agin ; "
Sez she, " think likely, *Mister ;* "
The last word pricked him like a pin,
An'—wal, he up and kist her.

When Ma bimeby upon 'em slips,
Huldy sot pale ez ashes,
All kind o' smily round the lips
An' teary round the lashes.

Her blood riz quick, though, like the tide
Down to the Bay o' Fundy,
An' all I know is they wuz cried
In meetin', come nex Sunday.

Satis multis sese emptores futuros libri professis, Georgius Nichols, Cantabrigiensis, opus emittet de parte gravi sed adhuc neglecta historiæ naturalis, cum titulo sequenti, videlicet :

Conatus ad Delineationem naturalem nonnihil perfectiorem Scarabæi Bombilatoris, vulgo dicti HUMBUG, ab HOMERO WILBUR, Artium Magistro, Societatis historico-naturalis Jaalamensis Præside, (Secretario, Socioque (eheu !) singulo,) multarumque aliarum Societatum eruditarum (sive ineruditarum) tam domesticarum quam transmarinarum Socio—forsitan futuro.

PROEMIUM.

LECTORI BENEVOLO S.

Toga scholastica nondum deposita, quum systemata varia entomologica, a viris ejus scientiæ cultoribus studiosissimis summa diligentia ædificata, penitus indagâssem, non fuit quin luctuose omnibus in iis, quamvis aliter laude dignissimis, hiatum magni momenti perciperem. Tunc, nescio quo motu superiore impulsus, aut qua captus dulcedine operis, ad eum implendum (Curtius alter) me solemniter devovi. Nec ab isto labore, δαιμονίως imposito, abstinui antequam tractatulum sufficienter inconcinnum lingua vernacula perfeceram. Inde, juveniliter tumefactus, et barathro ineptiæ τῶν βιβλιοπωλῶν (necnon " Publici Legentis ") nusquam explorato, me composuisse quod quasi placentas præfervidas (ut sic dicam) homines ingurgitarent credidi. Sed, quum huic et alio bibliopolæ MSS. mea submisissem et nihil solidius responsione valde negativa in Musæum meum retulissem, horror ingens atque misericordia, ob crassitudinem Lambertianam in cerebris homunculorum istius muneris cœlesti quadam ira infixam, me invasere. Extemplo mei solius impensis librum edere decrevi, nihil omnino dubitans quin "Mundus Scientificus" (ut aiunt) crumenam meam ampliter repleret. Nullam, attamen, ex agro illo meo parvulo segetem demessui, præter gaudium vacuum bene de Republica merendi. Iste panis meus pretiosus super aquas literarias fæculentas præfidenter jactus, quasi Harpyiarum quarundam (scilicet bibliopolarum istorum facinorosorum supradictorum) tactu rancidus, intra perpaucos dies mihi domum rediit. Et, quum ipse tali victu ali non tolerarem, primum in mentem venit pistori (typographo nempe) nihilominus solvendum esse. Animum non idcirco demisi, imo æque ac pueri naviculas suas penes se lino retinent (eo ut e recto cursu delapsas ad ripam retrahant), sic ego Argô meam chartaceam fluctibus laborantem a quæsitu velleris aurei, ipse potius tonsus pelleque exutus, mente solida revocavi. Metaphoram ut mutem, boomarangam meam a scopo aberrantem retraxi, dum majore vi, occasione ministrante, adversus Fortunam intorquerem. Ast mihi, talia volventi, et, sicut Saturnus ille παιδοβόρος, liberos intellectus mei depascere fidenti, casus miserandus, nec antea inauditus, supervenit. Nam, ut ferunt Scythas pietatis causa et parsimoniæ, parentes suos mortuos devorâsse, sic filius hic meus primogenitus, Scythis ipsis minus mansuetus, patrem vivum totum et calcitrantem exsorbere enixus est. Nec tamen hac de causa sobolem meam esurientem exheredavi. Sed famem istam pro valido testimonio virilitatis roborisque potius habui, cibumque ad eam satiandam, salva paterna mea carne, petii. Et quia bilem illam scaturientem ad æs etiam concoquendum idoneam esse estimabam, unde æs alienum, ut minoris pretii, haberem, circumspexi. Rebus ita se habentibus, ab avunculo meo Johanne Doolittle, Armigero, impetravi ut pecunias necessarias suppeditaret, ne opus esset mihi universitatem relinquendi antequam ad gradum primum in artibus pervenissem. Tunc ego, salvum facere patronum meum munificum maxime cupiens, omnes libros primæ editionis operis mei non venditos una cum privilegio in omne ævum ejusdem imprimendi et edendi avunculo meo dicto pigneravi. Ex illo die, atro lapide notando, curae vociferantes familiæ singulis annis crescentis eo usque insultabant ut nunquam tam carum pignus e vinculis istis aheneis solvere possem.

Avunculo vero nuper mortuo, quum inter alios consanguineos testamenti ejus lectionem audiendi causa advenissem, erectis auribus verba talia sequentia accepi : — " Quoniam persuasum habeo meum dilectum nepotem Homerum, longa et intima rerum angustarum domi experientia, aptissimum esse qui divitias tueatur, beneficenterque ac prudenter iis divinis creditis utatur,—ergo, motus hisce cogitationibus, exque amore meo in illum magno, do, legoque nepoti caro meo supranominato omnes singularesque istas possessiones nec ponderabiles nec computabiles meas quæ sequuntur, scilicet: quingentos libros quos mihi pigneravit dictus Homerus, anno lucis 1792, cum privilegio edendi et repetendi opus istud 'scientificum' (quod dicunt) suum, si sic elegerit. Tamen D. O. M. precor oculos Homeri nepotis mei ita aperiat eumque moveat, ut libros istos in bibliotheca unius e plurimis castellis suis Hispaniensibus tuto abscondat."

His verbis (vix credibilibus) auditis, cor meum in pectore exsultavit. Deinde, quoniam tractatus Anglice scriptus spem auctoris fefellerat, quippe quum studium Historiæ Naturalis in Republica nostra inter factionis strepitum languescat, Latine versum edere statui, et eo potius quia nescio quomodo disciplina academica et duo diplomata proficiant, nisi quod peritos linguarum omnino mortuarum (et damnandarum, ut dicebat iste πανοῦργος Gulielmus Cobbett) nos faciant.

Et mihi adhuc superstes est tota illa editio prima, quam quasi crepaculum per quod dentes caninos dentibam retineo.

NOTICES OF INDEPENDENT PRESS

OPERIS SPECIMEN.

(Ad exemplum Johannis Physiophili speciminis Monachologiæ.)

12. S. B. *Militaris,* Wilbur. *Carnifex,* Jablonsk. *Profanus,* Desfont.

[Male hancce speciem *Cyclopem* Fabricius vocat, ut qui singulo oculo ad quod sui interest distinguitur. Melius vero Isaacus Outis nullum inter S. milit. S. que Belzebul (Fabric. 152) discrimen esse defendit.] Habitat civitat. Americ. austral.

Aureis lineis splendidus ; plerumque tamen sordidus, utpote lanienas valde frequentans, fœtore sanguinis allectus. Amat quoque insuper septa apricari, neque inde, nisi maxima conatione, detruditur. *Candidatus* ergo populariter vocatus. Caput cristam quasi pennarum ostendit. Pro cibo vaccam publicam callide mulget; abdomen enorme ; facultas suctus haud facile estimanda. Otiosus, fatuus ; ferox nihilominus, semperque dimicare paratus. Tortuose repit.

Capite sæpe maxima cum cura dissecto, ne illud rudimentum etiam cerebri commune omnibus prope insectis detegere poteram. Unam de hoc S. milit. rem singularem notavi ; nam S. Guineens. (Fabric. 143) servos facit, et idcirco a multis summa in reverentia habitus, quasi scintillas rationis pæne humanæ demonstrans.

24. S. B. *Criticus,* Wilbur. *Zoilus,* Fabric. *Pygmæus,* Carlsen.

[Stultissime Johannes Stryx cum S. punctato (Fabric. 64–109) confundit. Specimina quamplurima scrutationi microscopicæ subjeci, nunquam tamen unum ulla indicia puncti cujusvis prorsus ostendentem inveni.]

Præcipue formidolosus, insectatusque, in proxima rima anonyma sese abscondit, *we, we,* creberrime stridens. Ineptus, segnipes.

Habitat ubique gentium ; in sicco ; nidum suum terebratione indefessa ædificans. Cibus. Libros depascit ; siccos præcipue seligens, et forte succidum

The Biglow Papers.

MELIBŒUS-HIPPONAX.

THE

𝔅iglow 𝔓apers,

EDITED,

WITH AN INTRODUCTION, NOTES,

GLOSSARY, AND COPIOUS INDEX,

BY

HOMER WILBUR, A. M.,

PASTOR OF THE FIRST CHURCH IN JAALAM, AND (PROSPECTIVE) MEMBER
OF MANY LITERARY, LEARNED AND SCIENTIFIC SOCIETIES,
(for which see page 25.)

The ploughman's whistle, or the trivial flute,
Finds more respect than great Apollo's lute.
Quarles's Emblems, B. II. E. 8.

Margaritas, munde porcine, calcâsti: en, siliquas accipe.
Jac. Car. Fil. ad Pub. Leg. § I.

CAMBRIDGE:

PUBLISHED BY GEORGE NICHOLS.

1848.

Note to Title-Page.

It will not have escaped the attentive eye, that I have, on the title-page, omitted those honorary appendages to the editorial name which not only add greatly to the value of every book, but whet and exacerbate the appetite of the reader. For not only does he surmise that an honorary membership of literary and scientific societies implies a certain amount of necessary distinction on the part of the recipient of such decorations, but he is willing to trust himself more entirely to an author who writes under the fearful responsibility of involving the reputation of such bodies as the *S. Archæol. Dahom.*, or the *Acad. Lit. et Scient. Kamtschat.* I cannot but think that the early editions of Shakspeare and Milton would have met with more rapid and general acceptance, but for the barrenness of their respective title-pages ; and I believe, that, even now, a publisher of the works of either of those justly distinguished men would find his account in procuring their admission to the membership of learned bodies on the Continent,—a proceeding no whit more incongruous than the reversal of the judgment against Socrates, when he was already more than twenty centuries beyond the reach of antidotes, and when his memory had acquired a deserved respectability. I conceive that it was a feeling of the importance of this precaution which induced Mr. Locke to style himself " Gent." on the title-page of his Essay, as who should say to his readers that they could receive his metaphysics on the honor of a gentleman.

Nevertheless, finding, that, without descending to a smaller size of type than would have been compatible with the dignity of the several societies to be named, I could not compress my intended list within the limits of a single page, and thinking, moreover, that the act would carry with it an air of decorous modesty, I have chosen to take the reader aside, as it were, into my private closet, and there not only exhibit to him the diplomas which I already possess, but also to furnish him with a prophetic vision of those which I may, without undue presumption, hope for, as not beyond the reach of human ambition and attainment. And I am the rather induced to this from the fact, that my name has been unaccountably dropped from the last triennial catalogue of our beloved *Alma Mater.* Whether this is to be attributed to the difficulty of Latinizing any of those honorary adjuncts (with a complete list of which I took care to furnish the proper persons nearly a year beforehand), or whether it had its origin in any more culpable motives, I forbear to consider in this place, the matter being in course of painful investigation. But, however this may be, I felt the omission the more keenly, as I had, in expectation of the new catalogue, enriched the library of the Jaalam Athenæum with the old one then in my possession, by which means it has come about that my children will be deprived of a never-wearying winter-evening's amusement in looking out the name of their parent in that distinguished roll. Those harmless innocents had at least committed no —— but I forbear, having intrusted my reflections and animadversions on this painful topic to the safe-keeping of my private diary, intended for posthumous publication. I state this fact here, in order that certain nameless individuals, who are, perhaps, overmuch congratulating themselves upon my silence, may know that a rod is in pickle which the vigorous hand of a justly incensed posterity will apply to their memories.

The careful reader will note, that, in the list which I have prepared, I have included the names of several Cisatlantic societies to which a place is not commonly assigned in processions of this nature. I have ventured to do this, not only to encourage native ambition and genius, but also because I have never been able to perceive in what way distance (unless we suppose them at the end of a lever) could increase the weight of learned bodies. As far as I have been able to extend my researches among such stuffed specimens as occasionally reach America, I have discovered no generic difference between the antipodal *Fogrum Japonicum* and the *F. Americanum* sufficiently common in our own immediate neighbourhood. Yet, with a becoming deference to the popular belief, that distinctions of this sort are enhanced in value by every additional mile they travel, I have intermixed the names of some tolerably distant literary and other associations with the rest.

I add here, also, an advertisement, which, that it may be the

NOTE TO TITLE-PAGE

more readily understood by those persons especially interested therein, I have written in that curtailed and otherwise maltreated canine Latin, to the writing and reading of which they are accustomed.

OMNIB. PER TOT. ORB. TERRAR. CATALOG.
ACADEM. EDD.

Minim. gent. diplom. ab inclytiss. acad. vest. orans, vir. honorand. operosiss., at sol. ut sciat. quant. glor. nom. meum (dipl. fort. concess.) catal. vest. temp. futur. affer., ill. subjec., addit. omnib. titul. honorar. qu. adh. non tant. opt. quam probab. put.
₊ *Litt. Uncial. distinx. ut Præs. S. Hist. Nat. Jaal.*

HOMERUS WILBUR, Mr., Episc. Jaalam. S. T. D. 1850, et Yal. 1849, et Neo-Cæs. et Brun. et Gulielm. 1852, et Gul. et Mar. et Bowd. et Georgiop. et Viridimont. et Columb. Nov. Ebor. 1853, et Amherst. et Watervill. et S. Jarlath. Hib. et S. Mar. et S. Joseph. et S. And. Scot. 1854, et Nashvill. et Dart. et Dickins. et Concord. et Wash. et Columbian. et Charlest. et Jeff. et Dubl. et Oxon. et Cantab. et cæt. 1855, P. U. N. C. H. et J. U. D. Gott. et Osnab. et Heidelb. 1860, et Acad. BORE US. Berolin. Soc. et SS. RR. Lugd. Bat. et Patav. et Lond. et Edinb. et Ins. Feejee. et Null. Terr. et Pekin. Soc. Hon. et S. H. S. et S. P. A. et A. A. S. et S. Humb. Univ. et S. Omn. Rer. Quarund. q. Aliar. Promov. Passamaquod. et H. P. C. et I. O. H. et A. Δ. Φ. et II. K. P. et Φ. B. K. et Peucin. et Erosoph. et Philadelph. et Frat. in Unit. et Σ. T. et S. Archæolog. Athen. et Acad. Scient. et Lit. Panorm. et SS. R. H. Matrit. et Beeloochist. et Caffrar. et Caribb. et M. S. Reg. Paris. et S. Am. Antiserv. Soc. Hon. et P. D. Gott. et LL.D. 1852, et D. C. L. et Mus. Doc. Oxon. 1860, et M. M. S. S. et M. D. 1854, et Med. Fac. Univ. Harv. Soc. et S. pro Convers. Pollywog. Soc. Hon. et Higgl. Piggl. et LL. B. 1853, et S. pro Christianiz. Moschet. Soc., et SS. Ante-Diluv. ubiq. Gent. Soc. Hon. et Civit. Cleric. Jaalam. et S. pro Diffus. General. Tenebr. Secret. Corr.

Introduction.

When, more than three years ago, my talented young parishioner, Mr. Biglow, came to me and submitted to my animadversions the first of his poems which he intended to commit to the more hazardous trial of a city newspaper, it never so much as entered my imagination to conceive that his productions would ever be gathered into a fair volume, and ushered into the august presence of the reading public by myself. So little are we short-sighted mortals able to predict the event! I confess that there is to me a quite new satisfaction in being associated (though only as sleeping partner) in a book which can stand by itself in an independent unity on the shelves of libraries. For there is always this drawback from the pleasure of printing a sermon, that, whereas the queasy stomach of this generation will not bear a discourse long enough to make a separate volume, those religious and godly-minded children (those Samuels, if I may call them so) of the brain must at first lie buried in an undistinguished heap, and then get such resurrection as is vouchsafed to them, mummy-wrapt with a score of others in a cheap binding, with no other mark of distinction than the word " *Miscellaneous* " printed upon the back. Far be it from me to claim any credit for the quite unexpected popularity which I am pleased to find these bucolic strains have attained unto. If I know myself, I am measurably free from the itch of vanity ; yet I may be allowed to say that I was not backward to recognize in them a certain wild, puckery, acidulous (sometimes even verging toward that point which, in our rustic phrase, is termed *shut-eye*) flavor, not wholly unpleasing, nor unwholesome, to palates cloyed with the sugariness of tamed and cultivated fruit. It may be, also, that some touches of my own, here and there, may have led to their wider acceptance, albeit solely from my larger experience of literature and authorship.*

* The reader curious in such matters may refer (if he can find them) to "A Sermon preached on the Anniversary of the Dark Day," "An Artil-

I was, at first, inclined to discourage Mr. Biglow's attempts, as knowing that the desire to poetize is one of the diseases naturally incident to adolescence, which, if the fitting remedies be not at once and with a bold hand applied, may become chronic, and render one, who might else have become in due time an ornament of the social circle, a painful object even to nearest friends and relatives. But thinking, on a further experience, that there was a germ of promise in him which required only culture and the pulling up of weeds from about it, I thought it best to set before him the acknowledged examples of English composition in verse, and leave the rest to natural emulation. With this view, I accordingly lent him some volumes of Pope and Goldsmith, to the assiduous study of which he promised to devote his evenings. Not long afterward, he brought me some verses written upon that model, a specimen of which I subjoin, having changed some phrases of less elegancy, and a few rhymes objectionable to the cultivated ear. The poem consisted of childish reminiscences, and the sketches which follow will not seem destitute of truth to those whose fortunate education began in a country village. And, first, let us hang up his charcoal portrait of the school-dame.

> "Propt on the marsh, a dwelling now, I see
> The humble school-house of my A, B, C,
> Where well-drilled urchins, each behind his tire,
> Waited in ranks the wished command to fire,
> Then all together, when the signal came,
> Discharged their *a-b abs* against the dame.
> Daughter of Danaus, who could daily pour
> In treacherous pipkins her Pierian store,
> She, 'mid the volleyed learning firm and calm,
> Patted the furloughed ferule on her palm,
> And, to our wonder, could divine at once
> Who flashed the pan, and who was downright dunce.

lery Election Sermon," "A Discourse on the Late Eclipse," "Dorcas, a Funeral Sermon on the Death of Madam Submit Tidd, Relict of the late Experience Tidd, Esq.," &c., &c.

There young Devotion learned to climb with ease
The gnarly limbs of Scripture family-trees,
And he was most commended and admired
Who soonest to the topmost twig perspired ;
Each name was called as many various ways
As pleased the reader's ear on different days,
So that the weather, or the ferule's stings,
Colds in the head, or fifty other things,
Transformed the helpless Hebrew thrice a week
To guttural Pequot or resounding Greek,
The vibrant accent skipping here and there,
Just as it pleased invention or despair ;
No controversial Hebraist was the Dame ;
With or without the points pleased her the same ;
If any tyro found a name too tough,
And looked at her, pride furnished skill enough ;
She nerved her larynx for the desperate thing,
And cleared the five-barred syllables at a spring.

Ah, dear old times ! there once it was my hap,
Perched on a stool, to wear the long-eared cap ;
From books degraded, there I sat at ease,
A drone, the envy of compulsory bees ;
Rewards of merit, too, full many a time,
Each with its woodcut and its moral rhyme,
And pierced half-dollars hung on ribbons gay
About my neck (to be restored next day)
I carried home, rewards as shining then
As those that deck the lifelong pains of men,
More solid than the redemanded praise
With which the world beribbons later days.

Ah, dear old times ! how brightly ye return !
How, rubbed afresh, your phosphor traces burn !
The ramble schoolward through dewsparkling meads ;
The willow-wands turned Cinderella steeds ;
The impromptu pinbent hook, the deep remorse
O'er the chance-captured minnow's inchlong corse ;

The pockets, plethoric with marbles round,
That still a space for ball and pegtop found,
Nor satiate yet, could manage to confine
Horsechestnuts, flagroot, and the kite's wound twine,
Nay, like the prophet's carpet could take in,
Enlarging still, the popgun's magazine ;
The dinner carried in the small tin pail,
Shared with some dog, whose most beseeching tail
And dripping tongue and eager ears belied
The assumed indifference of canine pride ;
The caper homeward, shortened if the cart
Of neighbor Pomeroy, trundling from the mart,
O'ertook me,—then, translated to the seat
I praised the steed, how staunch he was and fleet,
While the bluff farmer, with superior grin,
Explained where horses should be thick, where thin,
And warned me (joke he always had in store)
To shun a beast that four white stockings wore.
What a fine natural courtesy was his !
His nod was pleasure, and his full bow bliss ;
How did his well-thumbed hat, with ardor rapt,
Its curve decorous to each rank adapt !
How did it graduate with a courtly ease
The whole long scale of social differences,
Yet so gave each his measure running o'er,
None thought his own was less, his neighbor's more ;
The squire was flattered, and the pauper knew
Old times acknowledged 'neath the threadbare blue !
Dropped at the corner of the embowered lane,
Whistling I wade the knee-deep leaves again,
While eager Argus, who has missed all day
The sharer of his condescending play,
Comes leaping onward with a bark elate
And boisterous tail to greet me at the gate ;
That I was true in absence to our love
Let the thick dog's-ears in my primer prove."

I add only one further extract, which will possess a melancholy interest to all such as have endeavoured to glean the materials of Revolutionary history from the lips of aged persons, who took a part in the actual making of it, and, finding the manufacture profitable, continued the supply in an adequate proportion to the demand.

> "Old Joe is gone, who saw hot Percy goad
> His slow artillery up the Concord road,
> A tale which grew in wonder, year by year,
> As, every time he told it, Joe drew near
> To the main fight, till, faded and grown gray,
> The original scene to bolder tints gave way ;
> Then Joe had heard the foe's scared double-quick
> Beat on stove drum with one uncaptured stick,
> And, ere death came the lengthening tale to lop,
> Himself had fired, and seen a red-coat drop ;
> Had Joe lived long enough, that scrambling fight
> Had squared more nearly with his sense of right,
> And vanquished Percy, to complete the tale,
> Had hammered stone for life in Concord jail."

I do not know that the foregoing extracts ought not to be called my own rather than Mr. Biglow's, as, indeed, he maintained stoutly that my file had left nothing of his in them. I should not, perhaps, have felt entitled to take so great liberties with them, had I not more than suspected an hereditary vein of poetry in myself, a very near ancestor having written a Latin poem in the Harvard *Gratulatio* on the accession of George the Third. Suffice it to say, that, whether not satisfied with such limited approbation as I could conscientiously bestow, or from a sense of natural inaptitude, certain it is that my young friend could never be induced to any further essays in this kind. He affirmed that it was to him like writing in a foreign tongue,—that Mr. Pope's versification was like the regular ticking of one of Willard's clocks, in which one could fancy, after long listening, a certain kind of rhythm or tune, but which yet was only a poverty-stricken *tick, tick,* after all,—and that he had never seen a sweet-water on a trellis growing so fairly, or in forms so pleasing to his eye, as a fox-grape over a scrub-oak in a swamp. He added I know not what, to the effect that the sweet-water would only be the more disfigured by having its leaves starched and ironed out, and that Pegāsus (so he called him) hardly looked right with his mane and tail in curl-papers. These and other such opinions I did not long strive to eradicate, attributing them rather to a defective education and senses untuned by too long familiarity with purely natural objects, than to a perverted moral sense. I was the more inclined to this leniency since sufficient evidence was not to seek, that his verses, wanting as they certainly were in classic polish and point, had somehow taken hold of the public ear in a surprising manner. So, only setting him right as to the quantity of the proper name Pegasus, I left him to follow the bent of his natural genius.

Yet could I not surrender him wholly to the tutelage of the pagan (which, literally interpreted, signifies village) muse without yet a further effort for his conversion, and to this end I resolved that whatever of poetic fire yet burned in myself, aided by the assiduous bellows of correct models, should be put in requisition. Accordingly, when my ingenious young parishioner brought to my study a copy of verses which he had written touching the acquisition of territory resulting from the Mexican war, and the folly of leaving the question of slavery or freedom to the adjudication of chance, I did myself indite a short fable or apologue after the manner of Gay and Prior, to the end that he might see how easily even such subjects as he treated of were capable of a more refined style and more elegant expression. Mr. Biglow's production was as follows:

THE TWO GUNNERS,

A FABLE.

Two fellers, Isrel named and Joe,
One Sundy mornin' 'greed to go
Agunnin' soon'z the bells wuz done
And meetin' finally begun,
So'st no one wouldn't be about
Ther Sabbath-breakin' to spy out.

Joe didn't want to go a mite ;
He felt ez though 'twarnt skeercely right,
But, when his doubts he went to speak on,
Isrel he up and called him Deacon,
An' kep' apokin' fun like sin
An' then arubbin' on it in,
Till Joe, less skeered o' doin' wrong
Than bein' laughed at, went along.

Past noontime they went trampin' round
An' nary thing to pop at found,
Till, fairly tired o' their spree,
They leaned their guns agin a tree,
An' jest ez they wuz settin' down
To take their noonin', Joe looked roun'
And see (acrost lots in a pond
That warn't more'n twenty rod beyond,)
A goose that on the water sot
Ez ef awaitin' to be shot.

Isrel he ups and grabs his gun ;
Sez he, " By ginger, here's some fun ! "
"Don't fire," sez Joe, " it aint no use,
Thet's Deacon Peleg's tame wil'-goose ; "
Sez Isrel, " I don't care a cent,
I've sighted an' I'll let her went ; "
Bang! went queen's-arm, ole gander flopped
His wings a spell, an' quorked, an' dropped.

Sez Joe, " I wouldn't ha' been hired
At that poor critter to ha' fired,
But, sence it's clean gin up the ghost,
We'll hev the tallest kind o' roast ;
I guess our waistbands 'll be tight
'Fore it comes ten o'clock ternight."

" I won't agree to no such bender,"
Sez Isrel, " keep it tell it's tender ;
'Taint wuth a snap afore it's ripe."

Sez Joe, "I'd jest ez lives eat tripe ;
You *air* a buster ter suppose
I'd eat what makes me hol' my nose !"

So they disputed to an' fro
Till cunnin' Isrel sez to Joe,
"Don't le's stay here an' play the fool,
Le's wait till both on us git cool,
Jest for a day or two le's hide it
An' then toss up an' so decide it."
"Agreed !" sez Joe, an' so they did,
An' the ole goose wuz safely hid.

Now 'twuz the hottest kind o' weather,
An' when at last they come together,
It didn't signify which won,
Fer all the mischief hed ben done :
The goose wuz there, but, fer his soul,
Joe wouldn't ha' tetched it with a pole ;
But Isrel kind o' liked the smell on't
An' made *his* dinner very well on't.

My own humble attempt was in manner and form following, and
I print it here, I sincerely trust, out of no vain-glory, but solely with
the hope of doing good.

LEAVING THE MATTER OPEN.

A TALE.

BY HOMER WILBUR, A. M.

Two brothers once, an illmatched pair,
Together dwelt (no matter where,)
To whom an Uncle Sam, or some one,
Had left a house and farm in common :
The two in principles and habits
Were different as rats from rabbits ;
Stout farmer North, with frugal care,

Laid up provision for his heir,
Not scorning with hard sunbrowned hands
To scrape acquaintance with his lands ;
Whatever thing he had to do
He did, and made it pay him, too ;
He sold his waste stone by the pound,
His drains made waterwheels spin round,
His ice in summer-time he sold,
His wood brought profit when 'twas cold,
He dug and delved from morn till night,
Strove to make profit square with right,
Lived on his means, cut no great dash,
And paid his debts in honest cash.

On tother hand, his brother South
Lived very much from hand to mouth,
Played gentleman, nursed dainty hands,
Borrowed North 's money on his lands,
And culled his morals and his graces
From cockpits, barrooms, fights, and races :
His sole work in the farming line
Was keeping droves of long-legged swine,
Which brought great bothers and expenses
To North in looking after fences,
And, when they happened to break through,
Cost him both time and temper too,
For South insisted it was plain
He ought to drive them home again,
And North consented to the work
Because he loved to buy cheap pork.

Meanwhile, South 's swine increasing fast,
His farm became too small at last,
So, having thought the matter over,
And feeling bound to live in clover
And never pay the clover 's worth,
He said one day to brother North,—

"Our families are both increasing,
And, though we labor without ceasing,
Our produce soon will be too scant
To keep our children out of want ;
They who wish fortune to be lasting
Must be both prudent and forecasting ;
We soon shall need more land ; a lot
I know, that cheaply can be bo't ;
You lend the cash, I'll buy the acres,
And we'll be equally partakers."

Poor North, whose Anglo-Saxon blood
Gave him a hankering after mud,
Wavered a moment, then consented,
And, when the cash was paid, repented ;
To make the new land worth a pin,
Thought he, it must be all fenced in,
For, if South 's swine once get the run on 't
No kind of farming can be done on 't ;
If that don't suit the other side,
'Tis best we instantly divide.

But somehow South could ne'er incline
This way or that to run the line,
And always found some new pretence
'Gainst setting the division fence ;
At last he said,—

                              " For peace's sake,
Liberal concessions I will make ;
Though I believe, upon my soul,
I've a just title to the whole,
I'll make an offer which I call
Gen'rous,—we'll have no fence at all ;
Then both of us, whene'er we choose,
Can take what part we want to use ;
If you should chance to need it first,
Pick you the best, I'll take the worst."

"Agreed ! " cried North ; thought he, this fall
With wheat and rye I'll sow it all,
In that way I shall get the start,
And South may whistle for his part ;
So thought, so done, the field was sown,
And, winter having come and gone,
Sly North walked blithely forth to spy
The progress of his wheat and rye ;
Heavens, what a sight! his brother 's swine
Had asked themselves all out to dine,
Such grunting, munching, rooting, shoving,
The soil seemed all alive and moving,
As for his grain, such work they'd made on't,
He couldn't spy a single blade on't.

Off in a rage he rushed to South,
"My wheat and rye"—grief choked his mouth ;
"Pray don't mind me," said South, " but plant
All of the new land that you want ; "
"Yes, but your hogs," cried North ;

                        " The grain
Won't hurt them," answered South again ;
"But they destroy my crop ; "

                          " No doubt ;
'Tis fortunate you've found it out ;
Misfortunes teach, and only they,
You must not sow it in their way ; "
"Nay, you," says North, " must keep them out ; "
"Did I create them with a snout ? "
Asked South demurely, " as agreed,
The land is open to your seed,
And would you fain prevent my pigs
From running there their harmless rigs ?
God knows I view this compromise
With not the most approving eyes;
I gave up my unquestioned rights

For sake of quiet days and nights,
I offered then, you know 'tis true,
To cut the piece of land in two."
"Then cut it now," growls North ;

                "Abate
Your heat," says South, "'tis now too late ;
I offered you the rocky corner,
But you, of your own good the scorner,
Refused to take it ; I am sorry ;
No doubt you might have found a quarry,
Perhaps a gold-mine, for aught I know,
Containing heaps of native rhino ;
You can't expect me to resign
My rights "—

    "But where," quoth North, " are mine ? "
"*Your* rights," says tother, "well, that's funny,
I bought the land "—

             "*I* paid the money ; "
"That," answered South, " is from the point,
The ownership, you'll grant, is joint ;
I'm sure my only hope and trust is
Not law so much as abstract justice,
Though, you remember, 'twas agreed
That so and so—consult the deed ;
Objections now are out of date,
They might have answered once, but Fate
Quashes them at the point we've got to ;
Obsta principiis, that's my motto."

So saying, South began to whistle
And looked as obstinate as gristle,
While North went homeward, each brown paw
Clenched like a knot of natural law,
And all the while, in either ear,
Heard something clicking wondrous clear.

To turn now to other matters, there are two things upon which it should seem fitting to dilate somewhat more largely in this place,— the Yankee character and the Yankee dialect. And, first, of the Yankee character, which has wanted neither open maligners, nor even more dangerous enemies in the persons of those unskilful painters who have given to it that hardness, angularity, and want of proper perspective, which, in truth, belonged, not to their subject, but to their own niggard and unskilful pencil.

New England was not so much the colony of a mother country, as a Hagar driven forth into the wilderness. The little self-exiled band which came hither in 1620 came, not to seek gold, but to found a democracy. They came that they might have the privilege to work and pray, to sit upon hard benches and listen to painful preachers as long as they would, yea, even unto thirty-seventhly, if the spirit so willed it. And surely, if the Greek might boast his Thermopylæ, where three hundred men fell in resisting the Persian, we may well be proud of our Plymouth Rock, where a handful of men, women, and children not merely faced, but vanquished, winter, famine, the wilderness, and the yet more invincible *storge* that drew them back to the green island far away. These found no lotus growing upon the surly shore, the taste of which could make them forget their little native Ithaca; nor were they so wanting to themselves in faith as to burn their ship, but could see the fair west wind belly the homeward sail, and then turn unrepining to grapple with the terrible Unknown.

As Want was the prime foe these hardy exodists had to fortress themselves against, so it is little wonder if that traditional feud be long in wearing out of the stock. The wounds of the old warfare were long ahealing, and an east wind of hard times puts a new ache into every one of them. Thrift was the first lesson in their hornbook, pointed out, letter after letter, by the lean finger of the hard schoolmistress, Necessity. Neither were those plump, rosy-gilled Englishmen that came hither, but a hard-faced, atrabilious, earnest-eyed race, stiff from long wrestling with the Lord in prayer, and who had taught Satan to dread the new Puritan hug. Add two hundred years' influence of soil, climate, and exposure, with its necessary result of idiosyncrasies, and we have the present Yankee, full of expedients, half-master of all trades, inventive in all but the beautiful, full of shifts, not yet capable of comfort, armed at all points against the old enemy Hunger, longanimous, good at patching, not so careful for what is best as for what will *do*, with a clasp to his purse and a button to his pocket, not skilled to build against Time, as in old countries, but against sore-pressing Need, accustomed to move the world with no ποῦ στῶ but his own two feet, and no lever but his own long forecast. A strange hybrid, indeed, did circumstance beget, here in the New World, upon the old Puritan stock, and the earth never before saw such mystic-practicalism, such niggard-geniality, such calculating-fanaticism, such cast-iron-enthusiasm, such sourfaced-humor, such close-fisted-generosity. This new *Græculus esuriens* will make a living out of any thing. He will invent new trades as well as tools. His brain is his capital, and he will get education at all risks. Put him on Juan Fernandez, and he would make a spelling-book first, and a salt-pan afterward. *In cœlum, jusseris, ibit,*—or the other way either,—it is all one, so any thing is to be got by it. Yet, after all, thin, speculative Jonathan is more like the Englishman of two centuries ago than John Bull himself is. He has lost somewhat in solidity, has become fluent and adaptable, but more of the original groundwork of character remains. He feels more at home with Fulke Greville, Herbert of Cherbury, Quarles, George Herbert, and Browne, than with his modern English cousins. He is nearer than John, by at least a hundred years, to Naseby, Marston Moor, Worcester, and the time when, if ever, there were true Englishmen. John Bull has suffered the idea of the Invisible to be very much fattened out of him. Jonathan is conscious still that he lives in the world of the Unseen as well as of the Seen. To move John, you must make your fulcrum of solid beef and pudding; an abstract idea will do for Jonathan.

*** TO THE INDULGENT READER.

My friend, the Reverend Mr. Wilbur, having been seized with a dangerous fit of illness, before this Introduction had passed through the press, and being incapacitated for all literary exertion, sent to me his notes, memoranda, &c., and requested me to fashion them into some shape more fitting for the general eye. This, owing to the fragmentary and disjointed state of his manuscripts, I have felt wholly unable to do ; yet, being unwilling that the reader should be deprived of such parts of his lucubrations as seemed more finished, and not well discerning how to segregate these from the rest, I have concluded to send them all to the press precisely as they are.

CO LU M B U S   N Y E,
Pastor of a Church in Bungtown Corner.

It remains to speak of the Yankee dialect. And, first, it may be premised, in a general way, that any one much read in the writings of the early colonists need not be told that the far greater share of the words and phrases now esteemed peculiar to New England, and local there, were brought from the mother country. A person familiar with the dialect of certain portions of Massachusetts will not fail to recognize, in ordinary discourse, many words now noted in English vocabularies as archaic, the greater part of which were in common use about the time of the King James translation of the Bible. Shakspeare stands less in need of a glossary to most New Englanders than to many a native of the Old Country. The peculiarities of our speech, however, are rapidly wearing out. As there is no country where reading is so universal and newspapers are so multitudinous, so no phrase remains long local, but is transplanted in the mail-bags to every remotest corner of the land. Consequently our dialect approaches nearer to uniformity than that of any other nation.

The English have complained of us for coining new words. Many of those so stigmatized were old ones by them forgotten, and all make now an unquestioned part of the currency, wherever English is spoken. Undoubtedly, we have a right to make new words, as they are needed by the fresh aspects under which life presents itself here in the New World ; and, indeed, wherever a language is alive, it grows. It might be questioned whether we could not establish a stronger title to the ownership of the English tongue than the mother-islanders themselves. Here, past all question, is to be its great home and centre. And not only is it already spoken here by

greater numbers, but with a far higher popular average of correct-
ness, than in Britain. The great writers of it, too, we might claim
as ours, were ownership to be settled by the number of readers and
lovers.

As regards the provincialisms to be met with in this volume, I
may say that the reader will not find one which is not (as I believe)
either native or imported with the early settlers, nor one which I
have not, with my own ears, heard in familiar use. In the metrical
portion of the book, I have endeavoured to adapt the spelling as
nearly as possible to the ordinary mode of pronunciation. Let the
reader who deems me over-particular remember this caution of
Martial : —

> " Quem recitas, meus est, O Fidentine, libellus ;
> Sed male cum recitas, incipit esse tuus."

A few further explanatory remarks will not be impertinent.

I shall barely lay down a few general rules for the reader's
guidance.

1. The genuine Yankee never gives the rough sound to the r
when he can help it, and often displays considerable ingenuity in
avoiding it even before a vowel.

2. He seldom sounds the final g, a piece of self-denial, if we consider his partiality for nasals. The same of the final d, as han' and
stan' for hand and stand.

3. The h in such words as while, when, where, he omits altogether.

4. In regard to a, he shows some inconsistency, sometimes giving a close and obscure sound, as hev for have, hendy for handy, ez
for as, thet for that, and again giving it the broad sound it has in
father, as hânsome for handsome.

5. To the sound ou he prefixes an e (hard to exemplify otherwise
than orally).

The following passage in Shakspeare he would recite thus : —

> "Neow is the winta uv eour discontent
> Med glorious summa by this sun o' Yock,

An' all the cleouds thet leowered upun eour heouse
In the deep buzzum o' the oshin buried ;
Neow air eour breows beound 'ith victorious wreaths ;
Eour breused arms hung up fer monimunce ;
Eour starn alarums chănged to merry meetins,
Eour dreffle marches to delighfle masures.
Grim-visaged war heth smeuthed his wrinkled front,
An' neow, instid o' mountin' barebid steeds
To fright the souls o' ferfle edverseries,
He capers nimly in a lady's chămber,
To the lascivious pleasin' uv a loot."

6. *Au*, in such words as *daughter* and *slaughter*, he pronounces *ah*.

7. To the dish thus seasoned add a drawl *ad libitum*.

[Mr. Wilbur's notes here become entirely fragmentary.—C. N.]

a. Unable to procure a likeness of Mr. Biglow, I thought the curious reader might be gratified with a sight of the editorial effigies. And here a choice between two was offered,—the one a profile (entirely black) cut by Doyle, the other a portrait painted by a native artist of much promise. The first of these seemed wanting in expression, and in the second a slight obliquity of the visual organs has been heightened (perhaps from an over-desire of force on the part of the artist) into too close an approach to actual *strabismus*. This slight divergence in my optical apparatus from the ordinary model—however I may have been taught to regard it in the light of a mercy rather than a cross, since it enabled me to give as much of directness and personal application to my discourses as met the wants of my congregation, without risk of offending any by being supposed to have him or her in my eye (as the saying is)—seemed yet to Mrs. Wilbur a sufficient objection to the engraving of the aforesaid painting. We read of many who either absolutely refused to allow the copying of their features, as especially did Plotinus and Agesilaus among the ancients, not to mention the more modern instances of Scioppius, Palæottus, Pinellus, Velserus, Gataker, and others, or were indifferent thereto, as Cromwell.

β. Yet was Cæsar desirous of concealing his baldness. *Per contra*, my Lord Protector's carefulness in the matter of his wart might be cited. Men generally more desirous of being *improved* in their portraits than characters. Shall probably find very unflattered likenesses of ourselves in Recording Angel's gallery.

γ. Whether any of our national peculiarities may be traced to our use of stoves, as a certain closeness of the lips in pronunciation, and a smothered smoulderingness of disposition, seldom roused to open flame? An unrestrained intercourse with fire probably conducive to generosity and hospitality of soul. Ancient Mexicans used stoves, as the friar Augustin Ruiz reports, Hakluyt, III., 468,—but Popish priests not always reliable authority.

To-day picked my Isabella grapes. Crop injured by attacks of rose-bug in the spring. Whether Noah was justifiable in preserving this class of insects ?

δ. Concerning Mr. Biglow's pedigree. Tolerably certain that there was never a poet among his ancestors. An ordination hymn attributed to a maternal uncle, but perhaps a sort of production not demanding the creative faculty.

His grandfather a painter of the grandiose or Michael Angelo school. Seldom painted objects smaller than houses or barns, and these with uncommon expression.

ε. Of the Wilburs no complete pedigree. The crest said to be a *wild boar*, whence, perhaps, the name.(?) A connection with the Earls of Wilbraham (*quasi* wild boar ham) might be made out. This suggestion worth following up. In 1677, John W. m. Expect ——, had issue, 1. John, 2. Haggai, 3. Expect, 4. Ruhamah, 5. Desire.

> "Hear lyes yᵉ bodye of Mrs Expect Wilber,
> Yᵉ crewell salvages they kil'd her
> Together wᵗʰ other Christian soles eleaven,
> October yᵉ ix daye, 1707.

Yᵉ stream of Jordan sh' as crost ore
And now expeacts me on yᵉ other shore :
I live in hope her soon to join ;
Her earthlye yeeres were forty and nine."
From Gravestone in Pekusset, North Parish.

This is unquestionably the same John who afterward (1711)
married Tabitha Hagg or Ragg.

But if this were the case, she seems to have died early; for only
three years after, namely, 1714, we have evidence that he married
Winifred, daughter of Lieutenant Tipping.

He seems to have been a man of substance, for we find him in
1696 conveying " one undivided eightieth part of a salt-meadow " in
Yabbok, and he commanded a sloop in 1702.

Those who doubt the importance of genealogical studies *fuste
potius quam argumento erudiendi.*

I trace him as far as 1723, and there lose him. In that year he
was chosen selectman.

No gravestone. Perhaps overthrown when new hearse-house was
built, 1802.

He was probably the son of John, who came from Bilham Comit.
Salop. circa 1642.

This first John was a man of considerable importance, being
twice mentioned with the honorable prefix of *Mr.* in the town records. Name spelt with two *l*-s.

"Hear lyeth yᵉ bod [*stone unhappily broken.*]
    Mr. Ihon Willber [Esq.] [*I inclose this in brackets as doubtful.
        To me it seems clear.*]
    Ob't die [*illegible; looks like xviii.*] . . . . . iii [*prob.* 1693.]
        .   .   .   .   .   paynt
        .   .   .   .   deseased seinte :
    A friend and [fath]er untoe all yᵉ opreast,
    Hee gave yᵉ wicked familists noe reast,
    When Sat[an bl]ewe his Antinomian blaste,
    Wee clong to [Willber as a steadf]ast maste.
    [A]gaynst yᵉ horrid Qua[kers] . . . . . "

It is greatly to be lamented that this curious epitaph is mutilated. It is said that the sacrilegious British soldiers made a target of this stone during the war of Independence. How odious an animosity which pauses not at the grave ! How brutal that which spares not the monuments of authentic history ! This is not improbably from the pen of Rev. Moody Pyram, who is mentioned by Hubbard as having been noted for a silver vein of poetry. If his papers be still extant, a copy might possibly be recovered.

Contents.

No. I.

A Letter

FROM MR. EZEKIEL BIGLOW OF JAALAM

TO THE HON. JOSEPH T. BUCKINGHAM,

EDITOR OF THE BOSTON COURIER,

INCLOSING A POEM OF HIS SON,

MR. HOSEA BIGLOW.

JAYLEM, june 1846.

MISTER EDDYTER : —Our Hosea wuz down to Boston last week, and he see a cruetin Sarjunt a struttin round as popler as a hen with 1 chicking, with 2 fellers a drummin and fifin arter him like all nater. the sarjunt he thout Hosea hedn't gut his i teeth cut cos he looked a kindo's though he'd jest com down, so he cal'lated to hook him in, but Hosy woodn't take none o' his sarse for all he hed much as 20 Rooster's tales stuck onto his hat and eenamost enuf brass a bobbin up and down on his shoulders and figureed onto his coat and trousis, let alone wut nater hed sot in his featers, to make a 6 pounder out on.

wal, Hosea he com home considerabal riled, and arter I 'd gone to bed I heern Him a thrashin round like a short-tailed Bull in fli-time. The old Woman ses she to me ses she, Zekle, ses she, our Hosee's gut the chollery or suthin anuther ses she, don't you Bee skeered, ses I, he's oney amakin pottery* ses i, he's ollers on hand at that ere busynes like Da & martin, and shure enuf, cum mornin, Hosy he cum down stares full chizzle, hare on eend and cote tales flyin, and sot rite of to go reed his varses to Parson Wilbur bein he haint aney grate shows o' book larnin himself, bimeby he cum back and sed the parson wuz dreffle tickled with 'em as i hoop you will Be, and said they wuz True grit.

Hosea ses taint hardly fair to call 'em hisn now, cos the parson kind o' slicked off sum o' the last varses, but he told Hosee he didn't want to put his ore in to tetch to the Rest on 'em, bein they

---

* *Aut insanit, aut versos facit.*—H.W.

wuz verry well As thay wuz, and then Hosy ses he sed suthin a nuther about Simplex Mundishes or sum sech feller, but I guess Hosea kind o' didn't hear him, for I never hearn o' nobody o' that name in this villadge, and I've lived here man and boy 76 year cum next tater diggin, and thair aint no wheres a kitting spryer 'n I be.

If you print 'em I wish you'd jest let folks know who hosy's father is, cos my ant Keziah used to say it's nater to be curus ses she, she aint livin though and he's a likely kind o' lad.

ᴇᴢᴇᴋɪᴇʟ ʙɪɢʟᴏᴡ.

THRASH away, you 'll *hev* to rattle
  On them kittle drums o' yourn,—
'Taint a knowin' kind o' cattle
  Thet is ketched with mouldy corn ;
Put in stiff, you fifer feller,
  Let folks see how spry you be,—
Guess you 'll toot till you are yeller
  'Fore you git ahold o' me !

Thet air flag 's a leetle rotten,
  Hope it aint your Sunday's best ;—
Fact ! it takes a sight o' cotton
  To stuff out a soger's chest :
Sence we farmers hev to pay fer 't,
  Ef you must wear humps like these,
Sposin' you should try salt hay fer 't,
  It would du ez slick ez grease.

'T would n't suit them Southun fellers,
  They 're a dreffle graspin' set,
We must ollers blow the bellers
  Wen they want their irons het ;
May be it 's all right ez preachin',
  But *my* narves it kind o' grates,
Wen I see the overreachin'
  O' them nigger-drivin' States.

Them thet rule us, them slave-traders,
   Haint they cut a thunderin' swarth,
(Helped by Yankee renegaders,)
   Thru the vartu o' the North !
We begin to think it 's nater
   To take sarse an' not be riled ; —
Who 'd expect to see a tater
   All on eend at bein' biled ?

Ez fer war, I call it murder, —
   There you hev it plain an' flat ;
I don't want to go no furder
   Than my Testyment fer that ;
God hez sed so plump an' fairly,
   It 's ez long ez it is broad,
An' you 've gut to git up airly
   Ef you want to take in God.

'Taint your eppyletts an' feathers
   Make the thing a grain more right ;
'Taint afollerin' your bell-wethers
   Will excuse ye in His sight ;
Ef you take a sword an' dror it,
   An' go stick a feller thru,
Guv'ment aint to answer for it,
   God 'll send the bill to you.

Wut 's the use o' meetin-goin'
   Every Sabbath, wet or dry,
Ef it 's right to go amowin'
   Feller-men like oats an' rye ?
I dunno but wut it 's pooty
   Trainin' round in bobtail coats, —
But it 's curus Christian dooty
   This ere cuttin' folks's throats.

They may talk o' Freedom's airy
    Tell they 're pupple in the face,—
It 's a grand gret cemetary
    Fer the barthrights of our race ;
They jest want this Californy
    So 's to lug new slave-states in
To abuse ye, an' to scorn ye,
    An' to plunder ye like sin.

Aint it cute to see a Yankee
    Take sech everlastin' pains,
All to git the Devil's thankee,
    Helpin' on 'em weld their chains ?
Wy, it 's jest ez clear ez figgers,
    Clear ez one an' one make two,
Chaps thet make black slaves o' niggers
    Want to make wite slaves o' you.

Tell ye jest the eend I 've come to
    Arter cipherin' plaguy smart,
An' it makes a handy sum, tu,
    Any gump could larn by heart ;
Laborin' man an' laborin' woman
    Hev one glory an' one shame,
Ev'y thin' thet 's done inhuman
    Injers all on 'em the same.

'Taint by turnin' out to hack folks
    You 're agoin' to git your right,
Nor by lookin' down on black folks
    Coz you 're put upon by wite ;
Slavery aint o' nary color,
    'Taint the hide thet makes it wus,
All it keers fer in a feller
    'S jest to make him fill its pus.

Want to tackle *me* in, du ye ?
    I expect you 'll hev to wait ;

Wen cold lead puts daylight thru ye
    You 'll begin to kal'late ;
'Spose the crows wun't fall to pickin'
    All the carkiss from your bones,
Coz you helped to give a lickin'
    To them poor half-Spanish drones ?

Jest go home an' ask our Nancy
    Wether I 'd be sech a goose
Ez to jine ye,—guess you 'd fancy
    The etarnal bung wuz loose !
She wants me fer home consumption,
    Let alone the hay 's to mow,—
Ef you 're arter folks o' gumption,
    You 've a darned long row to hoe.

Take them editors thet 's crowin'
    Like a cockerel three months old,—
Don't ketch any on 'em goin',
    Though they *be* so blasted bold ;
Aint they a prime lot o' fellers ?
    'Fore they think on 't guess they 'll sprout,
(Like a peach thet's got the yellers,)
    With the meanness bustin' out.

Wal, go 'long to help 'em stealin'
    Bigger pens to cram with slaves,
Help the men thet 's ollers dealin'
    Insults on your fathers' graves ;
Help the strong to grind the feeble,
    Help the many agin the few,
Help the men thet call your people
    Witewashed slaves an' peddlin' crew !

Massachusetts, God forgive her,
    She 's akneelin' with the rest,
She, thet ough' to ha' clung fer ever
    In her grand old eagle-nest ;

She thet ough' to stand so fearless
  Wile the wracks are round her hurled,
Holdin' up a beacon peerless
  To the oppressed of all the world !

Haint they sold your colored seamen ?
  Haint they made your env'ys wiz ?
Wut 'll make ye act like freemen ?
  Wut 'll git your dander riz ?
Come, I 'll tell ye wut I 'm thinkin'
  Is our dooty in this fix,
They 'd ha' done 't ez quick ez winkin'
  In the days o' seventy-six.

Clang the bells in every steeple,
  Call all true men to disown
The tradoocers of our people,
  The enslavers o' their own ;
Let our dear old Bay State proudly
  Put the trumpet to her mouth,
Let her ring this messidge loudly
  In the ears of all the South : —

"I 'll return ye good fer evil
  Much ez we frail mortils can,
But I wun't go help the Devil
  Makin' man the cus o' man ;
Call me coward, call me traiter,
  Jest ez suits your mean idees, —
Here I stand a tyrant-hater,
  An' the friend o' God an' Peace ! "

Ef I 'd *my* way I hed ruther
  We should go to work an' part, —
They take one way, we take t'other, —
  Guess it would n't break my heart ;

" The everlasting cuss he stuck his one prined pich-fork in me "

This and the four ink drawings that follow, all illustrating letters of Birdofredum Sawin, were made by the American comic artist Edward Windsor Kemble (1861–1933). Neither their date nor purpose is known, and they are published here for the first time.

Man hed ough' to put asunder
   Them thet God has noways jined ;
An' I should n't gretly wonder
   Ef there 's thousands o' my mind.

[The first recruiting sergeant on record I conceive to have been that individual who is mentioned in the Book of Job as *going to and fro in the earth, and walking up and down in it.* Bishop Latimer will have him to have been a bishop, but to me that other calling would appear more congenial. The sect of Cainites is not yet extinct, who esteemed the first-born of Adam to be the most worthy, not only because of that privilege of primogeniture, but inasmuch as he was able to overcome and slay his younger brother. That was a wise saying of the famous

Marquis Pescara to the Papal Legate, that *it was impossible for men to serve Mars and Christ at the same time*. Yet in time past the profession of arms was judged to be κατ' ἐξοχήν that of a gentleman, nor does this opinion want for strenuous upholders even in our day. Must we suppose, then, that the profession of Christianity was only intended for losels, or, at best, to afford an opening for plebeian ambition? Or shall we hold with that nicely metaphysical Pomeranian, Captain Vratz, who was Count Königsmark's chief instrument in the murder of Mr. Thynne, that the Scheme of Salvation has been arranged with an especial eye to the necessities of the upper classes, and that "God would consider *a gentleman* and deal with him suitably to the condition and profession he had placed him in"? It may be said of us all, *Exemplo plus quam ratione vivimus*. —H.W.]

No. II.

A Letter

FROM MR. HOSEA BIGLOW TO THE
HON. J. T. BUCKINGHAM, EDITOR OF THE BOSTON COURIER,
COVERING A LETTER FROM MR. B. SAWIN,
PRIVATE IN THE MASSACHUSETTS REGIMENT.

[This letter of Mr. Sawin's was not originally written in verse.
Mr. Biglow, thinking it peculiarly susceptible of metrical
adornment, translated it, so to speak, into his own vernacular
tongue. This is not the time to consider the question, whether
rhyme be a mode of expression natural to the human race. If
leisure from other and more important avocations be granted,
I will handle the matter more at large in an appendix to the
present volume. In this place I will barely remark, that I have
sometimes noticed in the unlanguaged prattlings of infants
a fondness for alliteration, assonance, and even rhyme, in
which natural predisposition we may trace the three degrees
through which our Anglo-Saxon verse rose to its culmination in
the poetry of Pope. I would not be understood as questioning
in these remarks that pious theory which supposes that children, if left entirely to themselves, would naturally discourse in
Hebrew. For this the authority of one experiment is claimed,
and I could, with Sir Thomas Browne, desire its establishment,
inasmuch as the acquirement of that sacred tongue would
thereby be facilitated. I am aware that Herodotus states the
conclusion of Psammeticus to have been in favor of a dialect of
the Phrygian. But, beside the chance that a trial of this importance would hardly be blessed to a Pagan monarch whose
only motive was curiosity, we have on the Hebrew side the
comparatively recent investigation of James the Fourth of
Scotland. I will add to this prefatory remark, that Mr. Sawin,
though a native of Jaalam, has never been a stated attendant
on the religious exercises of my congregation. I consider my

humble efforts prospered in that not one of my sheep hath ever
indued the wolf's clothing of war, save for the comparatively
innocent diversion of a militia training. Not that my flock are
backward to undergo the hardships of *defensive* warfare. They
serve cheerfully in the great army which fights even unto
death *pro aris et focis*, accoutred with the spade, the axe, the
plane, the sledge, the spelling-book, and other such effectual
weapons against want and ignorance and unthrift. I have
taught them (under God) to esteem our human institutions as
but tents of a night, to be stricken whenever Truth puts the
bugle to her lips and sounds a march to the heights of wider-
viewed intelligence and more perfect organization.—H.W.]

MISTER BUCKINUM, the follerin Billet was writ hum by a Yung feller
of our town that wuz cussed fool enuff to goe atrottin inter Miss
Chiff arter a Drum and fife. it ain't Nater for a feller to let on that
he's sick o' any bizness that He went intu off his own free will and
a Cord, but I rather cal'late he's middlin tired o' voluntearin By this
Time. I bleeve u may put dependunts on his statemence. For I never
heered nothin bad on him let Alone his havin what Parson Wilbur
cals a *pongshong* for cocktales, and he ses it wuz a soshiashun of
idees sot him agoin arter the Crootin Sargient cos he wore a cock-
tale onto his hat.

his Folks gin the letter to me and i shew it to parson Wilbur and
he ses it oughter Bee printed. send It to mister Buckinum, ses he,
i don't ollers agree with him, ses he, but by Time,* ses he, I *du* like
a feller that ain't a Feared.

I have intusspussed a Few refleckshuns hear and thair. We're
kind o' prest with Hayin.

Ewers respecfly

HOSEA BIGLOW.

* In relation to this expression, I cannot but think that Mr. Biglow has
been too hasty in attributing it to me. Though Time be a comparatively
innocent personage to swear by, and though Longinus in his discourse
Περὶ Ὕψους have commended timely oaths as not only a useful but sublime figure of speech, yet I have always kept my lips free from that abom-
ination. *Odi profanum vulgus,* I hate your swearing and hectoring fellows.—H.W.

THIS kind o' sogerin' aint a mite like our October trainin',
A chap could clear right out from there ef 't only looked like rainin'.
An' th' Cunnles, tu, could kiver up their shappoes with bandanners,
An' send the insines skootin' to the bar-room with their banners,
(Fear o' gittin' on 'em spotted,) an' a feller could cry quarter
Ef he fired away his ramrod arter tu much rum an' water.
Recollect wut fun we hed, you 'n I an' Ezry Hollis,
Up there to Waltham plain last fall, along o' the Cornwallis ?*
This sort o' thing aint *jest* like thet,—I wish thet I wuz furder,—†
Nimepunce a day fer killin' folks comes kind o' low fer murder,
(Wy I 've worked out to slarterin' some fer Deacon Cephas Billins,
An' in the hardest times there wuz I ollers tetched ten shillins,)
There 's sutthin' gits into my throat thet makes it hard to swaller,
It comes so nateral to think about a hempen collar ;
It 's glory,—but, in spite o' all my tryin' to git callous,
I feel a kind o' in a cart, aridin' to the gallus.
But wen it comes to *bein'* killed,—I tell ye I felt streaked
The fust time 'tever I found out wy baggonets wuz peaked ;
Here 's how it wuz : I started out to go to a fandango,
The sentinul he ups an' sez, " Thet 's furder 'an you can go."
" None o' your sarse," sez I ; sez he, " Stan' back ! " " Aint you a
        buster ? "
Sez I, " I 'm up to all thet air, I guess I 've ben to muster ;
I know wy sentinuls air sot ; you aint agoin' to eat us ;
Caleb haint no monopoly to court the seenoreetas ;
My folks to hum air full ez good ez hisn be, by golly ! "
An' so ez I wuz goin' by, not thinkin' wut would folly,
The everlastin' cus he stuck his one-pronged pitchfork in me
An' made a hole right thru my close ez ef I wuz an in'my.

Wal, it beats all how big I felt hoorawin' in ole Funnel
Wen Mister Bolles he gin the sword to our Leftenant Cunnle,
(It 's Mister Secondary Bolles,‡ thet writ the prize peace essay ;

* i hait the Site of a feller with a muskit as I du pizn But their *is* fun
to a cornwallis I aint agoin' to deny it.—H.B.
  † he means Not quite so fur i guess.—H.B.
  ‡ the ignerant creeter means Sekketary ; but he ollers stuck to his books
like cobbler's wax to an ile-stone.—H.B.

Kemble

" None er yer sarse." says I.

Birdofredom sawin

Thet 's wy he did n't list himself along o' us, I dessay,)
An' Rantoul, tu, talked pooty loud, but don't put *his* foot in it,
Coz human life 's so sacred thet he 's principled agin' it,—
Though I myself can 't rightly see it 's any wus achokin' on 'em
Than puttin' bullets thru their lights, or with a bagnet pokin' on 'em ;
How dreffle slick he reeled it off, (like Blitz at our lyceum
Ahaulin' ribbins from his chops so quick you skeercely see 'em,)
About the Anglo-Saxon race (an' saxons would be handy
To du the buryin' down here upon the Rio Grandy),
About our patriotic pas an' our star-spangled banner,
Our country's bird alookin' on an' singin' out hosanner,
An' how he (Mister B. himself) wuz happy fer Ameriky,—
I felt, ez sister Patience sez, a leetle mite histericky.
I felt, I swon, ez though it wuz a dreffle kind o' privilege
Atrampin' round thru Boston streets among the gutter's drivelage ;
I act'lly thought it wuz a treat to hear a little drummin',
An' it did bonyfidy seem millanyum wuz acomin'
Wen all on us got suits (darned like them wore in the state prison)
An' every feller felt ez though all Mexico wuz hisn.*

This 'ere 's about the meanest place a skunk could wal diskiver
(Saltillo 's Mexican, I b'lieve, fer wut we call Salt-river).
The sort o' trash a feller gits to eat doos beat all nater,
I 'd give a year's pay fer a smell o' one good bluenose tater ;
The country here thet Mister Bolles declared to be so charmin'
Throughout is swarmin' with the most alarmin' kind o' varmin'.
He talked about delishis froots, but then it wuz a wopper all,
The holl on't 's mud an' prickly pears, with here an' there a
        chapparal ;
You see a feller peekin' out, an', fust you know, a lariat

---

* it must be aloud that thare 's a streak o' nater in lovin' sho, but it
sartinly is 1 of the curusest things in nater to see a rispecktable dri goods
dealer (deekon off a chutch mayby) a riggin' himself out in the Weigh
they du and struttin' round in the Reign aspilin' his trowsis and makin'
wet goods of himself. Ef any thin 's foolisher and moor dicklus than
militerry gloary it is milishy gloary.—H.B.

Is round your throat an' you a copse, 'fore you can say, " Wut air
    ye at ? " *
You never see sech darned gret bugs (it may not be irrelevant
To say I 've seen a *scarabæus pilularius*† big ez a year old elephant,)
The rigiment come up one day in time to stop a red bug
From runnin' off with Cunnle Wright,—'t wuz jest a common
    cimex lectularius.

One night I started up on eend an' thought I wuz to hum agin,
I heern a horn, thinks I it 's Sol the fisherman hez come agin,
His bellowses is sound enough,—ez I 'm a livin' creeter,
I felt a thing go thru my leg,—'t wuz nothin' more 'n a skeeter !
Then there 's the yaller fever, tu, they call it here el vomito,—
(Come, thet wun't du, you landcrab there, I tell ye to le' *go* my toe !
My gracious ! it 's a scorpion thet 's took a shine to play with 't,
I dars n't skeer the tarnal thing fer fear he 'd run away with 't.)
Afore I come away from hum I hed a strong persuasion
Thet Mexicans worn't human beans,‡—an ourang outang nation,
A sort o' folks a chap could kill an' never dream on 't arter,
No more 'n a feller 'd dream o' pigs thet he hed hed to slarter ;
I 'd an idee thet they were built arter the darkie fashion all,
An' kickin' colored folks about, you know, 's a kind o' national ;
But wen I jined I worn't so wise ez thet air queen o' Sheby,
Fer, come to look at 'em, they aint much diff'rent from wut we be,
An' here we air ascrougin' 'em out o' thir own dominions,
Ashelterin' 'em, ez Caleb sez, under our eagle's pinions,
Wich means to take a feller up jest by the slack o' 's trowsis
An' walk him Spanish clean right out o' all his homes an' houses ;
Wal, it doos seem a curus way, but then hooraw fer Jackson !

* these fellers are verry proppilly called Rank Heroes, and the more
tha kill the ranker and more Herowick tha bekum.—H.B.
† it wuz " tumblebug "as he Writ it, but the parson put the Latten instid. i sed tother maid better meeter, but he said tha was eddykated peepl
to Boston and tha would n't stan' it no how. idnow as tha *wood* and idnow
as tha wood.—H.B.
‡ he means human beins, that 's wut he means. i spose he kinder
thought tha wuz human beans ware the Xisle Poles comes from.—H.B.

It must be right, fer Caleb sez it 's reg'lar Anglosaxon.
The Mex'cans don't fight fair, they say, they piz'n all the water,
An' du amazin' lots o' things thet is n't wut they ough' to ;
Bein' they haint no lead, they make their bullets out o' copper
An' shoot the darned things at us, tu, wich Caleb sez aint proper ;
He sez they 'd ough' to stan' right up an' let us pop 'em fairly,
(Guess wen he ketches 'em at thet he 'll hev to git up airly,)
Thet our nation 's bigger 'n theirn an' so its rights air bigger,
An' thet it 's all to make 'em free thet we air pullin' trigger,
Thet Anglo Saxondom's idee 's abreakin' 'em to pieces,
An' thet idee 's thet every man doos jest wut he damn pleases ;
Ef I don't make his meanin' clear, perhaps in some respex I can,
I know thet " every man " don't mean a nigger or a Mexican ;
An' there 's another thing I know, an' thet is, ef these creeturs,
Thet stick an Anglosaxon mask onto State-prison feeturs,
Should come to Jaalam Centre fer to argify an' spout on 't,
The gals 'ould count the silver spoons the minnit they cleared
      out on 't.

This goin' ware glory waits ye haint one agreeable feetur,
An' ef it worn't fer wakin' snakes, I 'd home agin short meter ;
O, would n't I be off, quick time, ef 't worn't thet I wuz sartin
They 'd let the daylight into me to pay me fer desartin !
I don't approve o' tellin' tales, but jest to you I may state
Our ossifers aint wut they wuz afore they left the Bay-state ;
Then it wuz " Mister Sawin, sir, you 're middlin' well now, be ye ?
Step up an' take a nipper, sir ; I 'm dreffle glad to see ye " ;
But now it 's " Ware 's my eppylet ? here, Sawin, step an' fetch it !
An' mind your eye, be thund'rin' spry, or, damn ye, you shall
      ketch it ! "
Wal, ez the Doctor sez, some pork will bile so, but by mighty,
Ef I hed some on 'em to hum, I 'd give 'em linkum vity,
I 'd play the rogue's march on their hides an' other music follerin'—
But I must close my letter here, fer one on 'em 's ahollerin',
These Anglosaxon ossifers,—wal, taint no use ajawin',
I 'm safe enlisted fer the war,
              Yourn,

                    BIRDOFREDOM SAWIN.

[Those have not been wanting (as, indeed, when hath Satan been to seek for attorneys ?) who have maintained that our late inroad upon Mexico was undertaken, not so much for the avenging of any national quarrel, as for the spreading of free institutions and of Protestantism. *Capita vix duabus Anticyris medenda!* Verily I admire that no pious sergeant among these new Crusaders beheld Martin Luther riding at the front of the host upon a tamed pontifical bull, as, in that former invasion of Mexico, the zealous Gomara (spawn though he were of the Scarlet Woman) was favored with a vision of St. James of Compostella, skewering the infidels upon his apostolical lance. We read, also, that Richard of the lion heart, having gone to Palestine on a similar errand of mercy, was divinely encouraged to cut the throats of such Paynims as refused to swallow the bread of life (doubtless that they might be thereafter incapacitated for swallowing the filthy gobbets of Mahound) by angels of heaven, who cried to the king and his knights,—*Seigneurs, tuez! tuez!* providentially using the French tongue, as being the only one understood by their auditors. This would argue for the pantoglottism of these celestial intelligences, while, on the other hand, the Devil, *teste* Cotton Mather, is unversed in certain of the Indian dialects. Yet must he be a semeiologist the most expert, making himself intelligible to every people and kindred by signs ; no other discourse, indeed, being needful, than such as the mackerel-fisher holds with his finned quarry, who, if other bait be wanting, can by a bare bit of white rag at the end of a string captivate those foolish fishes. Such piscatorial persuasion is Satan cunning in. Before one he trails a hat and feather, or a bare feather without a hat ; before another, a Presidential chair, or a tide-waiter's stool, or a pulpit in the city, no matter what. To us, dangling there over our heads, they seem junkets dropped out of the seventh heaven, sops dipped in nectar, but, once in our mouths, they are all one, bits of fuzzy cotton.

This, however, by the way. It is time now *revocare gradum.* While so many miracles of this sort, vouched by eyewitnesses, have encouraged the arms of Papists, not to speak of Echetlæus at Marathon and those *Dioscuri* (whom we must conclude imps of the pit) who sundry times captained the pagan Roman soldiery, it is strange that our first American crusade was not in some such wise also signalized. Yet it is said that the Lord hath manifestly prospered our armies. This opens the question, whether, when our hands are strengthened to make great slaughter of our enemies, it be absolutely and demonstratively certain that this might is added to us from above, or whether some Potentate from an opposite quarter may not have a finger in it, as there are few pies into which his meddling digits are not thrust. Would the Sanctifier and Setter-apart of the seventh day have assisted in a victory gained on the Sabbath, as was one in the late war? Do we not know from Josephus, that, careful of His decree, a certain river in Judæa abstained from flowing on the day of Rest? Or has that day become less an object of his especial care since the year 1697, when so manifest a providence occurred to Mr. William Trowbridge, in answer to whose prayers, when he and all on shipboard with him were starving, a dolphin was sent daily, "which was enough to serve 'em; only on *Saturdays* they still catched a couple, and on the *Lord's Days* they could catch none at all"? Haply they might have been permitted, by way of mortification, to take some few sculpins (those banes of the salt-water angler), which unseemly fish would, moreover, have conveyed to them a symbolical reproof for their breach of the day, being known in the rude dialect of our mariners as *Cape Cod Clergymen.*

It has been a refreshment to many nice consciences to know that our Chief Magistrate would not regard with eyes of approval the (by many esteemed) sinful pastime of dancing, and I own myself to be so far of that mind, that I could not but set my face against this Mexican Polka, though danced to the Presidential piping with a Gubernatorial second. If ever the country should be seized with another such mania *pro propagandâ fide,* I think it would be wise to fill our bombshells with alternate copies of the Cambridge Platform and the Thirty-nine Articles, which would produce a mixture of the highest ex-

plosive power, and to wrap every one of our cannon-balls in a
leaf of the New Testament, the reading of which is denied to
those who sit in the darkness of Popery. Those iron evangelists
would thus be able to disseminate vital religion and Gospel
truth in quarters inaccessible to the ordinary missionary. I have
seen lads, unimpregnate with the more sublimated punctilious-
ness of Walton, secure pickerel, taking their unwary *siesta*
beneath the lily-pads too nigh the surface, with a gun and small
shot. Why not, then, since gunpowder was unknown in the
time of the Apostles (not to enter here upon the question
whether it were discovered before that period by the Chinese),
suit our metaphor to the age in which we live and say *shooters*
as well as *fishers* of men?

I do much fear that we shall be seized now and then with a
Protestant fervor, as long as we have neighbour Naboths whose
wallowings in Papistical mire excite our horror in exact proportion to the size and desirableness of their vineyards. Yet I
rejoice that some earnest Protestants have been made by this
war,—I mean those who protested against it. Fewer they were
than I could wish, for one might imagine America to have
been colonized by a tribe of those nondescript African animals
the Aye-Ayes, so difficult a word is *No* to us all. There is some
malformation or defect of the vocal organs, which either pre-
vents our uttering it at all, or gives it so thick a pronunciation
as to be unintelligible. A mouth filled with the national pudding,
or watering in expectation thereof, is wholly incompetent to
this refractory monosyllable. An abject and herpetic Public
Opinion is the Pope, the Anti-Christ, for us to protest against
e corde cordium. And by what College of Cardinals is this our
God's-vicar, our binder and looser, elected? Very like, by the
sacred conclave of Tag, Rag, and Bobtail, in the gracious
atmosphere of the grog-shop. Yet it is of this that we must all be
puppets. This thumps the pulpit-cushion, this guides the editor's pen, this wags the senator's tongue. This decides what
Scriptures are canonical, and shuffles Christ away into the
Apocrypha. According to that sentence fathered upon Solon,

" This here's about the meanest place a skunk could
well diskiver "

Birdofredom Sawin

Οὕτω δημόσιον κακὸν ἔρχεται οἴκαδ᾽ ἑκάστῳ. This unclean spirit is skilful to assume various shapes. I have known it to enter my own study and nudge my elbow of a Saturday, under the semblance of a wealthy member of my congregation. It were a great blessing, if every particular of what in the sum we call popular sentiment could carry about the name of its manufacturer stamped legibly upon it. I gave a stab under the fifth rib to that pestilent fallacy,—"Our country, right or wrong," —by tracing its original to a speech of Ensign Cilley at a dinner of the Bungtown Fencibles.—H.W.]

No. III.

What Mr. Robinson Thinks.

[A few remarks on the following verses will not be out of place. The satire in them was not meant to have any personal, but only a general, application. Of the gentleman upon whose letter they were intended as a commentary Mr. Biglow had never heard, till he saw the letter itself. The position of the satirist is oftentimes one which he would not have chosen, had the election been left to himself. In attacking bad principles, he is obliged to select some individual who has made himself their exponent, and in whom they are impersonate, to the end that what he says may not, through ambiguity, be dissipated *tenues in auras*. For what says Seneca? *Longum iter per præcepta, breve et efficace per exempla.* A bad principle is comparatively harmless while it continues to be an abstraction, nor can the general mind comprehend it fully till it is printed in that large type which all men can read at sight, namely, the life and character, the sayings and doings, of particular persons. It is one of the cunningest fetches of Satan, that he never exposes himself directly to our arrows, but, still dodging behind this neighbour or that acquaintance, compels us to wound him through them, if at all. He holds our affections as hostages, the while he patches up a truce with our conscience.

Meanwhile, let us not forget that the aim of the true satirist is not to be severe upon persons, but only upon falsehood, and, as Truth and Falsehood start from the same point, and sometimes even go along together for a little way, his business is to follow the path of the latter after it diverges, and to show her floundering in the bog at the end of it. Truth is quite beyond the reach of satire. There is so brave a simplicity in her, that she can no more be made ridiculous than an oak or a pine. The danger of the satirist is, that continual use may deaden his sensibility to the force of language. He becomes more and more liable to strike harder than he knows or intends. He may be careful to put on his boxing-gloves, and yet forget, that, the older they grow, the more plainly may the knuckles inside be felt. Moreover, in the heat of contest, the eye is insensibly drawn to the crown of victory, whose tawdry tinsel glitters through that dust of the ring which obscures Truth's wreath of simple leaves. I have sometimes thought that my young friend, Mr. Biglow, needed a monitory hand laid on his arm,—*aliquid sufflaminandus erat.* I have never thought it good husbandry to water the tender plants of reform with *aqua fortis,* yet, where so much is to do in the beds, he were a sorry gardener who should wage a whole day's war with an iron scuffle on those ill weeds that make the garden-walks of life unsightly, when a sprinkle of Attic salt will wither them up. *Est ars etiam maledicendi,* says Scaliger, and truly it is a hard thing to say where the graceful gentleness of the lamb merges in downright sheepishness. We may conclude with worthy and wise Dr. Fuller, that "one may be a lamb in private wrongs, but in hearing general affronts to goodness they are asses which are not lions."—H.W.]

GUVENER B. is a sensible man ;
  He stays to his home an' looks arter his folks ;
He draws his furrer ez straight ez he can,
    An' into nobody's tater-patch pokes ;—
        But John P.
        Robinson he
    Sez he wunt vote fer Guvener B.

My ! aint it terrible ? Wut shall we du ?
  We can't never choose him, o' course,—thet's flat ;
Guess we shall hev to come round, (don't you ?)
    An' go in fer thunder an' guns, an' all that ;
        Fer John P.
        Robinson he
    Sez he wunt vote fer Guvener B.

Gineral C. is a dreffle smart man :
  He 's ben on all sides thet give places or pelf ;

The rigiment come up one day
        in time to stop a red bug,
from runnin off with Cunnle Wright "

                        Birdofredom Sawin

But consistency still wuz a part of his plan,—
    He 's ben true to *one* party,—an' thet is himself ;—
            So John P.
            Robinson he
        Sez he shall vote fer Gineral C.

Gineral C. he goes in fer the war ;
    He don't vally princerple more 'n an old cud ;
Wut did God make us raytional creeturs fer,
    But glory an' gunpowder, plunder an' blood ?
        So John P.
        Robinson he
    Sez he shall vote fer Gineral C.

We were gittin' on nicely up here to our village,
    With good old idees o' wut 's right an' wut aint,
We kind o' thought Christ went agin war an' pillage,
    An' thet eppyletts worn't the best mark of a saint ;
        But John P.
        Robinson he
    Sez this kind o' thing 's an exploded idee.

The side of our country must ollers be took,
    An' Presidunt Polk, you know, *he* is our country ;
An' the angel thet writes all our sins in a book
    Puts the *debit* to him, an' to us the *per contry ;*
        An' John P.
        Robinson he
    Sez this is his view o' the thing to a T.

Parson Wilbur he calls all these argimunts lies ;
    Sez they 're nothin' on airth but jest *fee, faw, fum ;*
An' thet all this big talk of our destinies
    Is half on it ign'ance, an' t'other half rum ;
        But John P.
        Robinson he
    Sez it aint no sech thing; an', of course, so must we.

Parson Wilbur sez *he* never heerd in his life
    Thet th' Apostles rigged out in their swaller-tail coats,
An' marched round in front of a drum an' a fife,
    To git some on 'em office, an' some on 'em votes ;
        But John P.
        Robinson he
    Sez they did n't know everythin' down in Judee.

Wal, it's a marcy we've gut folks to tell us
    The rights an' the wrongs o' these matters, I vow,—
God sends country lawyers, an' other wise fellers,
    To start the world's team wen it gits in a slough ;
        Fer John P.
        Robinson he
    Sez the world 'll go right, ef he hollers out Gee !

[The attentive reader will doubtless have perceived in the foregoing poem an allusion to that pernicious sentiment,—"Our
country, right or wrong." It is an abuse of language to call a
certain portion of land, much more, certain personages elevated
for the time being to high station, our country. I would not
sever nor loosen a single one of those ties by which we are
united to the spot of our birth, nor minish by a tittle the respect
due to the Magistrate. I love our own Bay State too well to do
the one, and as for the other, I have myself for nigh forty years
exercised, however unworthily, the function of Justice of the
Peace, having been called thereto by the unsolicited kindness
of that most excellent man and upright patriot, Caleb Strong.
Patriæ fumus igne alieno luculentior is best qualified with
this,—*Ubi libertas, ibi patria.* We are inhabitants of two worlds,
and owe a double, but not a divided, allegiance. In virtue of
our clay, this little ball of earth exacts a certain loyalty of us,
while, in our capacity as spirits, we are admitted citizens of an
invisible and holier fatherland. There is a patriotism of the
soul whose claim absolves us from our other and terrene fealty.
Our true country is that ideal realm which we represent to
ourselves under the names of religion, duty, and the like. Our
terrestrial organizations are but far-off approaches to so fair
a model, and all they are verily traitors who resist not any
attempt to divert them from this their original intendment.
When, therefore, one would have us to fling up our caps and
shout with the multitude,—"*Our country, however bounded !*"
he demands of us that we sacrifice the larger to the less, the
higher to the lower, and that we yield to the imaginary claims
of a few acres of soil our duty and privilege as liegemen of
Truth. Our true country is bounded on the north and the south,

on the east and the west, by Justice, and when she oversteps that invisible boundary-line by so much as a hair's-breadth, she ceases to be our mother, and chooses rather to be looked upon *quasi noverca.* That is a hard choice, when our earthly love of country calls upon us to tread one path and our duty points us to another. We must make as noble and becoming an election as did Penelope between Icarius and Ulysses. Veiling our faces, we must take silently the hand of Duty to follow her.

Shortly after the publication of the foregoing poem, there appeared some comments upon it in one of the public prints which seemed to call for animadversion. I accordingly addressed to Mr. Buckingham, of the Boston Courier, the following letter.

"JAALAM, November 4, 1847.

"*To the Editor of the Courier :*

"RESPECTED SIR,—Calling at the post-office this morning, our worthy and efficient postmaster offered for my perusal a paragraph in the Boston Morning Post of the 3d instant, wherein certain effusions of the pastoral muse are attributed to the pen of Mr. James Russell Lowell. For aught I know or can affirm to the contrary, this Mr. Lowell may be a very deserving person and a youth of parts (though I have seen verses of his which I could never rightly understand); and if he be such, he, I am certain, as well as I, would be free from any proclivity to appropriate to himself whatever of credit (or discredit) may honestly belong to another. I am confident, that, in penning these few lines, I am only forestalling a disclaimer from that young gentleman, whose silence hitherto, when rumor pointed to himward, has excited in my bosom mingled emotions of sorrow and surprise. Well may my young parishioner, Mr. Biglow, exclaim with the poet,

'Sic vos non vobis' &c. ;

though, in saying this, I would not convey the impression that he is a proficient in the Latin tongue,—the tongue, I might add, of a Horace and a Tully.

"Mr. B. does not employ his pen, I can safely say, for any lucre of worldly gain, or to be exalted by the carnal plaudits of men, *digito monstrari*, &c. He does not wait upon Providence for mercies, and in his heart mean *merces*. But I should esteem myself as verily deficient in my duty (who am his friend and in some unworthy sort his spiritual *fidus Achates*, &c.), if I did not step forward to claim for him whatever measure of applause might be assigned to him by the judicious.

"If this were a fitting occasion, I might venture here a brief dissertation touching the manner and kind of my young friend's poetry. But I dubitate whether this abstruser sort of speculation (though enlivened by some apposite instances from Aristophanes) would sufficiently interest your oppidan readers. As regards their satirical tone, and their plainness of speech, I will only say, that, in my pastoral experience, I have found that the Arch-Enemy loves nothing better than to be treated as a religious, moral, and intellectual being, and that there is no *apage Sathanas !* so potent as ridicule. But it is a kind of weapon that must have a button of good-nature on the point of it.

"The productions of Mr. B. have been stigmatized in some quarters as unpatriotic ; but I can vouch that he loves his native soil with that hearty, though discriminating, attachment which springs from an intimate social intercourse of many years' standing. In the ploughing season, no one has a deeper share in the well-being of the country than he. If Dean Swift were right in saying that he who makes two blades of grass grow where one grew before confers a greater benefit on the state than he who taketh a city, Mr. B. might exhibit a fairer claim to the Presidency than General Scott himself. I think that some of those disinterested lovers of the hard-handed democracy, whose fingers have never touched any thing rougher than the dollars of our common country, would hesitate to compare palms with him. It would do your heart good, respected Sir, to see that young man mow. He cuts a cleaner and wider swarth than any in this town.

"But it is time for me to be at my Post. It is very clear that my young friend's shot has struck the lintel, for the Post is shaken (Amos ix. 1). The editor of that paper is a strenuous advocate of the Mexican war, and a colonel, as I am given to understand. I presume, that, being necessarily absent in Mexico, he has left his journal in some less judicious hands. At any rate, the Post has been too swift on this occasion. It could hardly have cited a more incontrovertible line from any poem than that which it has selected for animadversion, namely,—

'We kind o' thought Christ went agin war an' pillage.'

"If the Post maintains the converse of this proposition, it can hardly be considered as a safe guide-post for the moral and religious portions of its party, however many other excellent qualities of a post it may be blessed with. There is a sign in London on which is painted,—'The Green Man.' It would do very well as a portrait of any individual who should support so unscriptural a thesis. As regards the language of the line in question, I am bold to say that He who readeth the hearts of men will not account any dialect unseemly which conveys a sound and pious sentiment. I could wish that such sentiments were more common, however uncouthly expressed. Saint Ambrose affirms, that *veritas a quocunque* (why not, then, *quomodocunque*?) *dicatur, a spiritu sancto est.* Digest also this of Baxter :—'The plainest words are the most profitable oratory in the weightiest matters.'

"When the paragraph in question was shown to Mr. Biglow, the only part of it which seemed to give him any dissatisfaction was that which classed him with the Whig party. He says, that, if resolutions are a nourishing kind of diet, that party must be in a very hearty and flourishing condition ; for that they have quietly eaten more good ones of their own baking than he could have conceived to be possible without repletion. He has been for some years past (I regret to say) an ardent opponent of those sound doctrines of protective policy which form so prominent a portion of the creed of that party. I confess, that, in some discussions which I have had with him on this point in my study, he has displayed a vein of obstinacy which I had not hitherto detected in his composition. He is also (*horresco*

referens) infected in no small measure with the peculiar notions of a print called the Liberator, whose heresies I take every
proper opportunity of combating, and of which, I thank God,
I have never read a single line.

"I did not see Mr. B.'s verses until they appeared in print,
and there *is* certainly one thing in them which I consider highly
improper. I allude to the personal references to myself by name.
To confer notoriety on an humble individual who is laboring
quietly in his vocation, and who keeps his cloth as free as he
can from the dust of the political arena (though *væ mihi si non
evangelizavero*), is no doubt an indecorum. The sentiments
which he attributes to me I will not deny to be mine. They were
embodied, though in a different form, in a discourse preached
upon the last day of public fasting, and were acceptable to my
entire people (of whatever political views), except the postmaster, who dissented *ex officio*. I observe that you sometimes
devote a portion of your paper to a religious summary. I should
be well pleased to furnish a copy of my discourse for insertion
in this department of your instructive journal. By omitting the
advertisements, it might easily be got within the limits of a single number, and I venture to insure you the sale of some scores
of copies in this town. I will cheerfully render myself responsible for ten. It might possibly be advantageous to issue it as an
extra. But perhaps you will not esteem it an object, and I will
not press it. My offer does not spring from any weak desire of
seeing my name in print; for I can enjoy this satisfaction at
any time by turning to the Triennial Catalogue of the University, where it also possesses that added emphasis of Italics with
which those of my calling are distinguished.

"I would simply add, that I continue to fit ingenuous youth
for college, and that I have two spacious and airy sleeping
apartments at this moment unoccupied. *Ingenuas didicisse*,
&c. Terms, which vary according to the circumstances of the
parents, may be known on application to me by letter, post
paid. In all cases the lad will be expected to fetch his own
towels. This rule, Mrs. W. desires me to add, has no exceptions.

"Respectfully, your obedient servant,
               "HOMER WILBUR, A. M.

"P.S. Perhaps the last paragraph may look like an attempt to obtain the insertion of my circular gratuitously. If it should appear to you in that light, I desire that you would erase it, or charge for it at the usual rates, and deduct the amount from the proceeds in your hands from the sale of my discourse, when it shall be printed. My circular is much longer and more explicit, and will be forwarded without charge to any who may desire it. It has been very neatly executed on a letter sheet, by a very deserving printer, who attends upon my ministry, and is a creditable specimen of the typographic art. I have one hung over my mantelpiece in a neat frame, where it makes a beautiful and appropriate ornament, and balances the profile of Mrs. W., cut with her toes by the young lady born without arms.

"H.W."

I have in the foregoing letter mentioned General Scott in connection with the Presidency, because I have been given to understand that he has blown to pieces and otherwise caused to be destroyed more Mexicans than any other commander. His claim would therefore be deservedly considered the strongest. Until accurate returns of the Mexican killed, wounded, and maimed be obtained, it will be difficult to settle these nice points of precedence. Should it prove that any other officer has been more meritorious and destructive than General S., and has thereby rendered himself more worthy of the confidence and support of the conservative portion of our community, I shall cheerfully insert his name, instead of that of General S., in a future edition. It may be thought, likewise, that General S. has invalidated his claims by too much attention to the decencies of apparel, and the habits belonging to a gentleman. These abstruser points of statesmanship are beyond my scope. I wonder not that successful military achievement should attract the admiration of the multitude. Rather do I rejoice with wonder to behold how rapidly this sentiment is losing its hold upon the popular mind. It is related of Thomas Warton, the second of that honored name who held the office of Poetry Professor at Oxford, that, when one wished to find

him, being absconded, as was his wont, in some obscure ale-
house, he was counselled to traverse the city with a drum
and fife, the sound of which inspiring music would be sure to
draw the Doctor from his retirement into the street. We are all
more or less bitten with this martial insanity. *Nescio quâ
dulcedine . . . . . cunctos ducit.* I confess to some infection of
that itch myself. When I see a Brigadier-General maintaining
his insecure elevation in the saddle under the severe fire of
the training-field, and when I remember that some military
enthusiasts, through haste, inexperience, or an over-desire to
lend reality to those fictitious combats, will sometimes discharge their ramrods, I cannot but admire, while I deplore, the
mistaken devotion of those heroic officers. *Semel insanivimus
omnes.* I was myself, during the late war with Great Britain,
chaplain of a regiment, which was fortunately never called to
active military duty. I mention this circumstance with regret
rather than pride. Had I been summoned to actual warfare,
I trust that I might have been strengthened to bear myself after
the manner of that reverend father in our New England Israel,
Dr. Benjamin Colman, who, as we are told in Turell's life of
him, when the vessel in which he had taken passage for
England was attacked by a French privateer, "fought like a
philosopher and a Christian, ... and prayed all the while he
charged and fired." As this note is already long, I shall not
here enter upon a discussion of the question, whether Chris-
tians may lawfully be soldiers. I think it sufficiently evident,
that, during the first two centuries of the Christian era, at
least, the two professions were esteemed incompatible. Consult
Jortin on this head.—H.W.]

No. IV.

Remarks of Increase D. O'Phace, Esquire,

AT AN EXTRUMPERY CAUCUS IN STATE STREET,
REPORTED BY MR. H. BIGLOW.

[The ingenious reader will at once understand that no such speech as the following was ever *totidem verbis* pronounced. But there are simpler and less guarded wits, for the satisfying of which such an explanation may be needful. For there are certain invisible lines, which as Truth successively overpasses, she becomes Untruth to one and another of us, as a large river, flowing from one kingdom into another, sometimes takes a new name, albeit the waters undergo no change, how small soever. There is, moreover, a truth of fiction more veracious than the truth of fact, as that of the Poet, which represents to us things and events as they ought to be, rather than servilely copies them as they are imperfectly imaged in the crooked and smoky glass of our mundane affairs. It is this which makes the speech of Antonius, though originally spoken in no wider a forum than the brain of Shakspeare, more historically valuable than that other which Appian has reported, by as much as the understanding of the Englishman was more comprehensive than that of the Alexandrian. Mr. Biglow, in the present instance, has only made use of a license assumed by all the historians of antiquity, who put into the mouths of various characters such words as seem to them most fitting to the occasion and to the speaker. If it be objected that no such oration could ever have been delivered, I answer, that there are few assemblages for speech-making which do not better deserve the title of *Parliamentum Indoctorum* than did the sixth Parliament of Henry the Fourth, and that men still continue to have as much faith in the Oracle of Fools as ever Pantagruel had. Howell, in his letters, recounts a merry tale of

a certain ambassador of Queen Elizabeth, who, having written
two letters, one to her Majesty and the other to his wife, directed them at cross-purposes, so that the Queen was beducked
and bedeared and requested to send a change of hose, and the
wife was beprincessed and otherwise unwontedly besuper-
latived, till the one feared for the wits of her ambassador, and
the other for those of her husband. In like manner it may be
presumed that our speaker has misdirected some of his
thoughts, and given to the whole theatre what he would have
wished to confide only to a select auditory at the back of the
curtain. For it is seldom that we can get any frank utterance
from men, who address, for the most part, a Buncombe either
in this world or the next. As for their audiences, it may be
truly said of our people, that they enjoy one political institution
in common with the ancient Athenians : I mean a certain
profitless kind of *ostracism*, wherewith, nevertheless, they seem
hitherto well enough content. For in Presidential elections,
and other affairs of the sort, whereas I observe that the *oysters*
fall to the lot of comparatively few, the *shells* (such as the
privileges of voting as they are told to do by the *ostrivori* aforesaid, and of huzzaing at public meetings) are very liberally
distributed among the people, as being their prescriptive and
quite sufficient portion.

The occasion of the speech is supposed to be Mr. Palfrey's
refusal to vote for the Whig candidate for the Speakership.
—H.W.]

No ? Hez he ? He haint, though ? Wut ? Voted agin him ?
Ef the bird of our country could ketch him, she 'd skin him ;
I seem 's though I see her, with wrath in each quill,
Like a chancery lawyer, afilin' her bill,
An' grindin' her talents ez sharp ez all nater,
To pounce like a writ on the back o' the traiter.
Forgive me, my friends, ef I seem to be het,
But a crisis like this must with vigor be met ;
Wen an Arnold the star-spangled banner bestains,
Holl Fourth o' Julys seem to bile in my veins.

Who ever 'd ha' thought sech a pisonous rig
Would be run by a chap thet wuz chose fer a Wig ?
" We knowed wut his princerples wuz 'fore we sent him " ?
Wut wuz ther in them from this vote to pervent him ?
A marciful Providunce fashioned us holler
O' purpose thet we might our princerples swaller ;
It can hold any quantity on 'em, the belly can,
An' bring 'em up ready fer use like the pelican,
Or more like the kangaroo, who (wich is stranger)
Puts her family into her pouch wen there 's danger.
Aint princerple precious ? then, who 's goin' to use it
Wen there 's resk o' some chap's gittin' up to abuse it ?
I can't tell the wy on 't, but nothin' is so sure
Ez thet princerple kind o' gits spiled by exposure ;*
A man thet lets all sorts o' folks git a sight on 't
Ough' to hev it all took right away, every mite on 't ;
Ef he can't keep it all to himself wen it 's wise to,
He aint one it 's fit to trust nothin' so nice to.

Besides, ther 's a wonderful power in latitude
To shift a man's morril relations an' attitude ;
Some flossifers think thet a fakkilty 's granted
The minnit it 's proved to be thoroughly wanted,
Thet a change o' demand makes a change o' condition,
An' thet everythin' 's nothin' except by position ;
Ez, fer instance, thet rubber-trees fust begun bearin'
Wen p'litikle conshunces come into wearin',—

* The speaker is of a different mind from Tully, who, in his recently
discovered tractate *De Republicâ*, tells us,—*Nec vero habere virtutem
satis est, quasi artem aliquam, nisi utare*, and from our Milton, who says,
—" I cannot praise a fugitive and cloistered virtue, unexercised and un-
breathed, that never sallies out and sees her adversary, but slinks out of
the race where that immortal garland is to be run for, *not without dust
and heat.*"—*Areop.* He had taken the words out of the Roman's mouth,
without knowing it, and might well exclaim with Donatus (if St. Jerome's tutor may stand sponsor for a curse), *Pereant qui ante nos nostra
dixerint !*—H.W.

Thet the fears of a monkey, whose holt chanced to fail,
Drawed the vertibry out to a prehensile tail ;
So, wen one 's chose to Congriss, ez soon ez he 's in it,
A collar grows right round his neck in a minnit,
An' sartin it is thet a man cannot be strict
In bein' himself, wen he gits to the Deestrict,
Fer a coat thet sets wal here in ole Massachusetts,
Wen it gits on to Washinton, somehow askew sets.

Resolves, do you say, o' the Springfield Convention ?
Thet 's percisely the pint I was goin' to mention ;
Resolves air a thing we most gen'ally keep ill,
They 're a cheap kind o' dust fer the eyes o' the people ;
A parcel o' delligits jest git together
An' chat fer a spell o' the crops an' the weather,
Then, comin' to order, they squabble awile
An' let off the speeches they 're ferful 'll spile ;
Then—Resolve,—Thet we wunt hev an inch o' slave territory ;
Thet Presidunt Polk's holl perceedins air very tory ;
Thet the war is a damned war, an' them thet enlist in it
Should hev a cravat with a dreffle tight twist in it ;
Thet the war is a war fer the spreadin' o' slavery ;
Thet our army desarves our best thanks fer their bravery ;
Thet we 're the original friends o' the nation,
All the rest air a paltry an' base fabrication ;
Thet we highly respect Messrs. A, B, an' C,
An' ez deeply despise Messrs. E, F, an' G.
In this way they go to the eend o' the chapter,
An' then they bust out in a kind of a raptur
About their own vartoo, an' folks's stone-blindness
To the men thet 'ould actilly do 'em a kindness,—
The American eagle, the Pilgrims thet landed,
Till on ole Plymouth Rock they git finally stranded.
Wal, the people they listen an' say, "Thet 's the ticket ;
Ez fer Mexico, t'aint no great glory to lick it,
But 't would be a darned shame to go pullin' o' triggers

To extend the aree of abusin' the niggers."

So they march in percessions, an' git up hooraws,
An' tramp thru the mud fer the good o' the cause,
An' think they 're a kind o' fulfillin' the prophecies,
Wen they 're on'y jest changin' the holders of offices ;
Ware A sot afore, B is comf'tably seated,
One humbug 's victor'ous, an' t'other defeated.
Each honnable doughface gits jest wut he axes,
An' the people—their annooal soft sodder an' taxes.

Now, to keep unimpaired all these glorious feeturs
Thet characterize morril an' reasonin' creeturs,
Thet give every paytriot all he can cram,
Thet oust the untrustworthy Presidunt Flam,
An' stick honest Presidunt Sham in his place,
To the manifest gain o' the holl human race,
An' to some indervidgewals on 't in partickler,
Who love Public Opinion an' know how to tickle her,—
I say thet a party with gret aims like these
Must stick jest ez close ez a hive full o' bees.

I 'm willin' a man should go tollable strong
Agin wrong in the abstract, fer thet kind o' wrong
Is ollers unpop'lar an' never gits pitied,
Because it 's a crime no one never committed ;
But he mus' n't be hard on partickler sins,
Coz then he'll be kickin' the people's own shins ;
On'y look at the Demmercrats, see wut they 've done
Jest simply by stickin' together like fun ;
They 've sucked us right into a mis'able war
Thet no one on airth aint responsible for ;
They 've run us a hunderd cool millions in debt,
(An' fer Demmercrat Horners ther 's good plums left yet) ;
They talk agin tayriffs, but act fer a high one,
An' so coax all parties to build up their Zion ;
To the people they 're ollers ez slick ez molasses,

An' butter their bread on both sides with The Masses,
Half o' whom they 've persuaded, by way of a joke,
Thet Washinton's mantelpiece fell upon Polk.

Now all o' these blessins the Wigs might enjoy,
Ef they 'd gumption enough the right means to imploy ;*
Fer the silver spoon born in Dermoc'acy's mouth
Is a kind of a scringe thet they hev to the South ;
Their masters can cuss 'em an' kick 'em an' wale 'em,
An' they notice it less 'an the ass did to Balaam ;
In this way they screw into second-rate offices
Wich the slaveholder thinks 'ould substract too much off his ease ;
The file-leaders, I mean, du, fer they, by their wiles,
Unlike the old viper, grow fat on their files.
Wal, the Wigs hev been tryin' to grab all this prey frum 'em
An' to hook this nice spoon o' good fortin' away frum 'em,
An' they might ha' succeeded, ez likely ez not,
In lickin' the Demmercrats all round the lot,
Ef it warn't thet, while all faithful Wigs were their knees on,
Some stuffy old codger would holler out,—" Treason !
You must keep a sharp eye on a dog thet hez bit you once,
An' *I* aint agoin' to cheat my constitoounts,"—
Wen every fool knows thet a man represents
Not the fellers thet sent him, but them on the fence,—
Impartially ready to jump either side
An' make the fust use of a turn o' the tide,—
The waiters on Providunce here in the city,
Who compose wut they call a State Centerl Committy.
Constitoounts air hendy to help a man in,
But arterwards don't weigh the heft of a pin.
Wy, the people can't all live on Uncle Sam's pus,
So they 've nothin' to du with 't fer better or wus ;
It 's the folks thet air kind o' brought up to depend on 't
Thet hev any consarn in 't, an' thet is the end on 't.

* That was a pithy saying of Persius, and fits our politicians without a
wrinkle,—*Magister artis, ingeniique largitor venter.*—H.W.

Now here wuz New England ahevin' the honor
Of a chance at the Speakership showered upon her ; —
Do you say, — " She don't want no more Speakers, but fewer ;
She 's hed plenty o' them, wut she wants is a *doer*" ?
Fer the matter o' thet, it 's notorous in town
Thet her own representatives du her quite brown.
But thet 's nothin' to du with it ; wut right hed Palfrey
To mix himself up with fanatical small fry ?
Warn't we gittin' on prime with our hot an' cold blowin',
Acondemnin' the war wilst we kep' it agoin' ?
We 'd assumed with gret skill a commandin' position,
On this side or thet, no one could n't tell wich one,
So, wutever side wipped, we 'd a chance at the plunder
An' could sue fer infringin' our paytented thunder ;
We were ready to vote fer whoever wuz eligible,
Ef on all pints at issoo he 'd stay unintelligible.
Wal, sposin' we hed to gulp down our perfessions,
We were ready to come out next mornin' with fresh ones ;
Besides, ef we did, 't was our business alone,
Fer could n't we du wut we would with our own ?
An' ef a man can, wen pervisions hev riz so,
Eat up his own words, it 's a marcy it is so.

Wy, these chaps frum the North, with back-bones to 'em, darn 'em,
'Ould be wuth more 'an Gennle Tom Thumb is to Barnum ;
Ther 's enough thet to office on this very plan grow,
By exhibitin' how very small a man can grow ;
But an M. C. frum here ollers hastens to state he
Belongs to the order called invertebraty,
Wence some gret filologists judge primy fashy
Thet M. C. is M. T. by paronomashy ;
An' these few exceptions air *loosus naytury*
Folks 'ould put down their quarters to stare at, like fury.

It 's no use to open the door o' success,
Ef a member can bolt so fer nothin' or less ;
Wy, all o' them grand constitootional pillers

Our fore-fathers fetched with 'em over the billers,
Them pillers the people so soundly hev slep' on,
Wile to slav'ry, invasion, an' debt they were swep' on,
Wile our Destiny higher an' higher kep' mountin',
(Though I guess folks 'll stare wen she hends her account in,)
Ef members in this way go kickin' agin 'em,
They wunt hev so much ez a feather left in 'em.

An', ez fer this Palfrey,* we thought wen we 'd gut him in,
He 'd go kindly in wutever harness we put him in ;
Supposin' we *did* know thet he wuz a peace man ?
Doos he think he can be Uncle Sammle's policeman,
An' wen Sam gits tipsy an' kicks up a riot,
Lead him off to the lockup to snooze till he 's quiet ?
Wy, the war is a war thet true paytriots can bear, ef
It leads to the fat promised land of a tayriff ;
We don't go an' fight it, nor aint to be driv on,
Nor Demmercrats nuther, thet hev wut to live on ;
Ef it aint jest the thing thet 's well pleasin' to God,
It makes us thought highly on elsewhere abroad ;
The Rooshian black eagle looks blue in his eerie
An' shakes both his heads wen he hears o' Monteery ;
In the Tower Victory sets, all of a fluster,
An' reads, with locked doors, how we won Cherry Buster ;
An' old Philip Lewis—thet come an' kep' school here
Fer the mere sake o' scorin' his ryalist ruler
On the tenderest part of our kings *in futuro*—
Hides his crown underneath an old shut in his bureau,
Breaks off in his brags to a suckle o' merry kings,
How he often hed hided young native Amerrikins,
An', turnin' quite faint in the midst of his fooleries,
Sneaks down stairs to bolt the front door o' the Tooleries.†

* There is truth yet in this of Juvenal,—
    " Dat veniam corvis, vexat censura columbas."—H.W.

    † Jortin is willing to allow of other miracles besides those recorded in
Holy Writ, and why not of other prophecies ? It is granting too much to

You say,—" We 'd ha' scared 'em by growin' in peace,
A plaguy sight more then by bobberies like these " ?
Who is it dares say thet " our naytional eagle
Wun't much longer be classed with the birds thet air regal,
Coz theirn be hooked beaks, an' she, arter this slaughter,
'll bring back a bill ten times longer 'n she 'd ough' to" ?
Wut 's your name ? Come, I see ye, you up-country feller,
You 've put me out severil times with your beller ;
Out with it ! Wut ? Biglow ? I say nothin' furder,
Thet feller would like nothin' better 'n a murder ;
He 's a traiter, blasphemer, an' wut ruther worse is,
He puts all his ath'ism in dreffle bad verses ;
Socity aint safe till sech monsters air out on it,
Refer to the Post, ef you hev the least doubt on it ;
Wy, he goes agin war, agin indirect taxes,
Agin sellin' wild lands 'cept to settlers with axes,
Agin holdin' o' slaves, though he knows it 's the corner
Our libbaty rests on, the mis'able scorner !
In short, he would wholly upset with his ravages
All thet keeps us above the brute critters an' savages,
An' pitch into all kinds o' briles an' confusions

Satan to suppose him, as divers of the learned have done, the inspirer of
the ancient oracles. Wiser, I esteem it, to give chance the credit of the
successful ones. What is said here of Louis Philippe was verified in some
of its minute particulars within a few months' time. Enough to have
made the fortune of Delphi or Hammon, and no thanks to Beelzebub
neither! That of Seneca in Medea will suit here : —

> " Rapida fortuna ac levis,
> Præcepsque regno eripuit, exsilio dedit."

Let us allow, even to richly deserved misfortune, our commiseration,
and be not over-hasty meanwhile in our censure of the French people,
left for the first time to govern themselves, remembering that wise sentence of Æschylus,—

> "Απας δὲ τραχὺς ὅστις ἂν νέον κρατῇ.

H.W.

The holl of our civerlized, free institutions ;
He writes fer thet ruther unsafe print, the Courier,
An' likely ez not hez a squintin' to Foorier ;
I 'll be ——, thet is, I mean I 'll be blest,
Ef I hark to a word frum so noted a pest ;
I shan't talk with *him*, my religion 's too fervent.—
Good mornin', my friends, I 'm your most humble servant.

[Into the question, whether the ability to express ourselves in articulate language has been productive of more good or evil, I shall not here enter at large. The two faculties of speech and of speech-making are wholly diverse in their natures. By the first we make ourselves intelligible, by the last unintelligible, to our fellows. It has not seldom occurred to me (noting how in our national legislature every thing runs to talk, as lettuces, if the season or the soil be unpropitious, shoot up lankly to seed, instead of forming handsome heads) that Babel was the first Congress, the earliest mill erected for the manufacture of gabble. In these days, what with Town Meetings, School Committees, Boards (lumber) of one kind and another, Congresses, Parliaments, Diets, Indian Councils, Palavers, and the like, there is scarce a village which has not its factories of this description driven by (milk-and-)water power. I cannot conceive the confusion of tongues to have been the curse of Babel, since I esteem my ignorance of other languages as a kind of Martello-tower, in which I am safe from the furious bombardments of foreign garrulity. For this reason I have ever preferred the study of the dead languages, those primitive formations being Ararats upon whose silent peaks I sit secure and watch this new deluge without fear, though it rain figures (*simulacra*, semblances) of speech forty days and nights together, as it not uncommonly happens. Thus is my coat, as it were, without buttons by which any but a vernacular wild bore can seize me. Is it not possible that the Shakers may intend to convey a quiet reproof and hint, in fastening their outer garments with hooks and eyes ?

This reflection concerning Babel, which I find in no Commentary, was first thrown upon my mind when an excellent deacon of my congregation (being infected with the Second Advent delusion) assured me that he had received a first instalment of the gift of tongues as a small earnest of larger possessions in the like kind to follow. For, of a truth, I could not reconcile it with my ideas of the Divine justice and mercy that the single wall which protected people of other languages from the incursions of this otherwise well-meaning propagandist should be broken down.

In reading Congressional debates, I have fancied, that, after the subsidence of those painful buzzings in the brain which result from such exercises, I detected a slender residuum of valuable information. I made the discovery that *nothing* takes longer in the saying than any thing else, for, as *ex nihilo nihil fit*, so from one polypus *nothing* any number of similar ones may be produced. I would recommend to the attention of *vivâ voce* debaters and controversialists the admirable example of the monk Copres, who, in the fourth century, stood for half an hour in the midst of a great fire, and thereby silenced a Manichæan antagonist who had less of the salamander in him. As for those who quarrel in print, I have no concern with them here, since the eyelids are a Divinely-granted shield aginst all such. Moreover, I have observed in many modern books that the printed portion is becoming gradually smaller, and the number of blank or fly-leaves (as they are called) greater. Should this fortunate tendency of literature continue, books will grow more valuable from year to year, and the whole Serbonian bog yield to the advances of firm arable land.

The sagacious Lacedæmonians hearing that Tesephone had bragged that he could talk all day long on any given subject, made no more ado, but forthwith banished him, whereby they supplied him a topic and at the same time took care that his experiment upon it should be tried out of ear-shot.

I have wondered, in the Representatives' Chamber of our own Commonwealth, to mark how little impression seemed to be produced by that emblematic fish suspended over the heads of the members. Our wiser ancestors, no doubt, hung it there as being the animal which the Pythagoreans reverenced for its silence, and which certainly in that particular does not so well merit the epithet *cold-blooded*, by which naturalists distinguish it, as certain bipeds, afflicted with ditch-water on the brain, who take occasion to tap themselves in Faneuil Halls, meeting-houses, and other places of public resort.—H.W.]

No. V.

The Debate in the Sennit.

SOT TO A NUSRY RHYME.

[The incident which gave rise to the debate satirized in the
following verses was the unsuccessful attempt of Drayton and
Sayres to give freedom to seventy men and women, fellow-
beings and fellow-Christians. Had Tripoli, instead of Washington, been the scene of this undertaking, the unhappy leaders
in it would have been as secure of the theoretic as they now
are of the practical part of martyrdom. I question whether the
Dey of Tripoli is blessed with a District Attorney so benighted
as ours at the seat of government. Very fitly is he named Key,
who would allow himself to be made the instrument of locking
the door of hope against sufferers in such a cause. Not all the
waters of the ocean can cleanse the vile smutch of the jailer's
fingers from off that little Key. *Ahenea clavis*, a brazen Key
indeed!

Mr. Calhoun, who is made the chief speaker in this bur-
lesque, seems to think that the light of the nineteenth century
is to be put out as soon as he tinkles his little cow-bell curfew.
Whenever slavery is touched, he sets up his scarecrow of
dissolving the Union. This may do for the North, but I should
conjecture that something more than a pumpkin-lantern is
required to scare manifest and irretrievable Destiny out of her
path. Mr. Calhoun cannot let go the apron-string of the Past.
The Past is a good nurse, but we must be weaned from her
sooner or later, even though, like Plotinus, we should run home
from school to ask the breast, after we are tolerably well-grown
youths. It will not do for us to hide our faces in her lap, whenever the strange Future holds out her arms and asks us to
come to her.

But we are all alike. We have all heard it said, often enough,
that little boys must not play with fire ; and yet, if the matches

be taken away from us and put out of reach upon the shelf, we must needs get into our little corner, and scowl and stamp and threaten the dire revenge of going to bed without our supper. The world shall stop till we get our dangerous plaything again. Dame Earth, meanwhile, who has more than enough household matters to mind, goes bustling hither and thither as a hiss or a sputter tells her that this or that kettle of hers is boiling over, and before bedtime we are glad to eat our porridge cold, and gulp down our dignity along with it.

Mr. Calhoun has somehow acquired the name of a great statesman, and, if it be great statesmanship to put lance in rest and run a tilt at the Spirit of the Age with the certainty of being next moment hurled neck and heels into the dust amid universal laughter, he deserves the title. He is the Sir Kay of our modern chivalry. He should remember the old Scandinavian mythus. Thor was the strongest of gods, but he could not wrestle with Time, nor so much as lift up a fold of the great snake which bound the universe together; and when he smote the Earth, though with his terrible mallet, it was but as if a leaf had fallen. Yet all the while it seemed to Thor that he had only been wrestling with an old woman, striving to lift a cat, and striking a stupid giant on the head.

And in old times, doubtless, the giants *were* stupid, and there was no better sport for the Sir Launcelots and Sir Gawains than to go about cutting off their great blundering heads with enchanted swords. But things have wonderfully changed. It is the giants, now-a-days, that have the science and the intelligence, while the chivalrous Don Quixotes of Conservatism still cumber themselves with the clumsy armour of a by-gone age. On whirls the restless globe through unsounded time, with its cities and its silences, its births and funerals, half light, half shade, but never wholly dark, and sure to swing round into the happy morning at last. With an involuntary smile, one sees Mr. Calhoun letting slip his pack-thread cable with a crooked pin at the end of it to anchor South Carolina upon the bank and shoal of the Past.—H.W.]

THE BIGLOW PAPERS

TO MR. BUCKENAM.

MR. EDITER, As i wuz kinder prunin round, in a little nussry sot out a year or 2 a go, the Dbait in the sennit cum inter my mine An so i took & Sot it to wut I call a nussry rime. I hev made sum onnable Gentlemun speak thut dident speak in a Kind uv Poetikul lie sense the seeson is dreffle backerd up This way

ewers as ushul

HOSEA BIGLOW.

"HERE we stan' on the Constitution, by thunder !
It 's a fact o' wich ther 's bushils o' proofs ;
Fer how could we trample on 't so, I wonder,
    Ef 't worn't thet it 's ollers under our hoofs ? "
    Sez John C. Calhoun, sez he ;
        " Human rights haint no more
        Right to come on this floor,
    No more 'n the man in the moon," sez he.

" The North haint no kind o' bisness with nothin',
    An' you 've no idee how much bother it saves ;
We aint none riled by their frettin' an' frothin',
    We 're *used* to layin' the string on our slaves,"
    Sez John C. Calhoun, sez he ;—
        Sez Mister Foote,
        " I should like to shoot
    The holl gang, by the gret horn spoon ! " sez he.

" Freedom's Keystone is Slavery, thet ther 's no doubt on,
    It 's sutthin' thet 's—wha' d' ye call it ?—divine,—
An' the slaves thet we ollers *make* the most out on
    Air them north o' Mason an' Dixon's line,"
    Sez John C. Calhoun, sez he ;—
        " Fer all thet," sez Mangum,
        " 'T would be better to hang 'em,
    An' so git red on 'em soon," sez he.

"The mass ough' to labor an' we lay on soffies,
    Thet's the reason I want to spread Freedom's aree ;
It puts all the cunninest on us in office,
    An' reelises our Maker's orig'nal idee,"
        Sez John C. Calhoun, sez he ; —
            "Thet's ez plain," sez Cass,
            "Ez thet some one's an ass,
        It's ez clear ez the sun is at noon," sez he.

"Now don't go to say I'm the friend of oppression,
    But keep all your spare breath fer coolin' your broth,
Fer I ollers hev strove (at least thet's my impression)
    To make cussed free with the rights o' the North,"
        Sez John C. Calhoun, sez he ; —
            "Yes," sez Davis o' Miss.,
            "The perfection o' bliss
        Is in skinnin' thet same old coon," sez he.

"Slavery's a thing thet depends on complexion,
    It's God's law thet fetters on black skins don't chafe ;
Ef brains wuz to settle it (horrid reflection !)
    Wich of our onnable body'd be safe ? "
        Sez John C. Calhoun, sez he ; —
            Sez Mister Hannegan,
            Afore he began agin,
        "Thet exception is quite oppertoon," sez he.

"Gen'nle Cass, Sir, you need n't be twitchin' your collar,
    Your merit's quite clear by the dut on your knees,
At the North we don't make no distinctions o' color ;
    You can all take a lick at our shoes wen you please,"
        Sez John C. Calhoun, sez he ; —
            Sez Mister Jarnagin,
            "They wunt hev to larn agin,
        They all on 'em know the old toon," sez he.

" The slavery question aint no ways bewilderin'.
  North an' South hev one int'rest, it 's plain to a glance ;
No'thern men, like us patriarchs, don't sell their childrin,
  But they *du* sell themselves, ef they git a good chance,"
    Sez John C. Calhoun, sez he ; —
      Sez Atherton here,
      " This is gittin' severe,
    I wish I could dive like a loon," sez he.

" It 'll break up the Union, this talk about freedom,
  An' your fact'ry gals (soon ez we split) 'll make head,
An' gittin' some Miss chief or other to lead 'em,
  'll go to work raisin' permiscoous Ned,"
    Sez John C. Calhoun, sez he ; —
      " Yes, the North," sez Colquitt,
      " Ef we Southeners all quit,
    Would go down like a busted balloon," sez he.

" Jest look wut is doin', wut annyky 's brewin'
  In the beautiful clime o' the olive an' vine,
All the wise aristoxy 's a tumblin' to ruin,
  An' the sankylots drorin' an' drinkin' their wine,"
    Sez John C. Calhoun, sez he ; —
      " Yes," sez Johnson, " in France
      They 're beginnin' to dance
    Beelzebub's own rigadoon," sez he.

" The South 's safe enough, it don't feel a mite skeery,
  Our slaves in their darkness an' dut air tu blest
Not to welcome with proud hallylugers the ery
  Wen our eagle kicks yourn from the naytional nest,"
    Sez John C. Calhoun, sez he ; —
      " O," sez Westcott o' Florida,
      " Wut treason is horrider
    Then our priv'leges tryin' to proon ? " sez he.

" It 's 'coz they 're so happy, thet, wen crazy sarpints
  Stick their nose in our bizness, we git so darned riled ;
We think it 's our dooty to give pooty sharp hints,
  Thet the last crumb of Edin on airth shan't be spiled,"
    Sez John C. Calhoun, sez he ;—
      " Ah," sez Dixon H. Lewis,
      " It perfectly true is
  Thet slavery 's airth's grettest boon," sez he.

[It was said of old time, that riches have wings ; and, though
this be not applicable in a literal strictness to the wealth of
our patriarchal brethren of the South, yet it is clear that their
possessions have legs, and an unaccountable propensity for
using them in a northerly direction. I marvel that the grand
jury of Washington did not find a true bill against the North
Star for aiding and abetting Drayton and Sayres. It would have
been quite of a piece with the intelligence displayed by the
South on other questions connected with slavery. I think that
no ship of state was ever freighted with a more veritable Jonah
than this same domestic institution of ours. Mephistopheles
himself could not feign so bitterly, so satirically sad a sight as
this of three millions of human beings crushed beyond help
or hope by this one mighty argument,—*Our fathers knew no
better !* Nevertheless, it is the unavoidable destiny of Jonahs to
be cast overboard sooner or later. Or shall we try the experiment
of hiding our Jonah in a safe place, that none may lay hands
on him to make jetsam of him ? Let us, then, with equal fore-
thought and wisdom, lash ourselves to the anchor, and await,
in pious confidence, the certain result. Perhaps our suspicious
passenger is no Jonah after all, being black. For it is well
known that a superintending Providence made a kind of sand-
wich of Ham and his descendants, to be devoured by the
Caucasian race.

In God's name, let all, who hear nearer and nearer the hungry moan of the storm and the growl of the breakers, speak
out ! But, alas ! we have no right to interfere. If a man pluck an
apple of mine, he shall be in danger of the justice ; but if he

steal my brother, I must be silent. Who says this? Our Constitution, consecrated by the callous consuetude of sixty years,
and grasped in triumphant argument by the left hand of him
whose right hand clutches the clotted slave-whip. Justice,
venerable with the undethronable majesty of countless æons,
says,—SPEAK! The Past, wise with the sorrows and desolations
of ages, from amid her shattered fanes and wolf-housing pal-
aces, echoes,—SPEAK! Nature, through her thousand trumpets
of freedom, her stars, her sunrises, her seas, her winds, her
cataracts, her mountains blue with cloudy pines, blows jubilant
encouragement, and cries,—SPEAK! From the soul's trembling
abysses the still, small voice not vaguely murmurs,—SPEAK!
But, alas! the Constitution and the Honorable Mr. Bagowind,
M. C., say,—BE DUMB!

It occurs to me to suggest, as a topic of inquiry in this connection, whether, on that momentous occasion when the goats
and the sheep shall be parted, the Constitution and the Honorable Mr. Bagowind, M. C., will be expected to take their places
on the left as our hircine vicars.

> *Quid sum miser tunc dicturus?*
> *Quem patronum rogaturus?*

There is a point where toleration sinks into sheer baseness and
poltroonery. The toleration of the worst leads us to look on
what is barely better as good enough, and to worship what is
only moderately good. Woe to that man, or that nation, to whom
mediocrity has become an ideal!

Has our experiment of self-government succeeded, if it
barely manage to *rub and go*? Here, now, is a piece of barba-
rism which Christ and the nineteenth century say shall cease,
and which Messrs. Smith, Brown, and others say shall *not*
cease. I would by no means deny the eminent respectability of
these gentlemen, but I confess, that, in such a wrestling-match,
I cannot help having my fears for them.

> *Discite justitiam, moniti, et non temnere divos.*

H.W.]

No. VI.

The Pious Editor's Creed.

[At the special instance of Mr. Biglow, I preface the following satire with an extract from a sermon preached during the past summer, from Ezekiel xxxiv. 2 : —"Son of man, prophesy against the shepherds of Israel." Since the Sabbath on which this discourse was delivered, the editor of the "Jaalam Independent Blunderbuss" has unaccountably absented himself from our house of worship.

"I know of no so responsible position as that of the public journalist. The editor of our day bears the same relation to his time that the clerk bore to the age before the invention of printing. Indeed, the position which he holds is that which the clergyman should hold even now. But the clergyman chooses to walk off to the extreme edge of the world, and to throw such seed as he has clear over into that darkness which he calls the Next Life. As if *next* did not mean *nearest,* and as if any life were nearer than that immediately present one which boils and eddies all around him at the caucus, the ratification meeting, and the polls ! Who taught him to exhort men to prepare for eternity, as for some future era of which the present forms no integral part ? The furrow which Time is even now turning runs through the Everlasting, and in that must he plant, or nowhere. Yet he would fain believe and teach that we are *going* to have more of eternity than we have now. This *going* of his is like that of the auctioneer, on which *gone* follows before we have made up our minds to bid,—in which manner, not three months back, I lost an excellent copy of Chappelow on Job. So it has come to pass that the preacher, instead of being a living force, has faded into an emblematic figure at christenings, weddings, and funerals. Or, if he exercise any other function, it is as keeper and feeder of certain theologic dogmas, which, when occasion offers, he unkennels with a *staboy!* "to bark and bite as 't is their nature to," whence that reproach of *odium theologicum* has arisen.

"Meanwhile, see what a pulpit the editor mounts daily, sometimes with a congregation of fifty thousand within reach of his voice, and never so much as a nodder, even, among them! And from what a Bible can he choose his text,—a Bible which needs no translation, and which no priestcraft can shut and clasp from the laity,—the open volume of the world, upon which, with a pen of sunshine or destroying fire, the inspired Present is even now writing the annals of God! Methinks the editor who should understand his calling, and be equal thereto, would truly deserve that title of ποιμὴν λαῶν, which Homer bestows upon princes. He would be the Moses of our nineteenth century, and whereas the old Sinai, silent now, is but a common mountain stared at by the elegant tourist and crawled over by the hammering geologist, he must find his tables of the new law here among factories and cities in this Wilderness of Sin (Numbers xxxiii. 12) called Progress of Civilization, and be the captain of our Exodus into the Canaan of a truer social order.

"Nevertheless, our editor will not come so far within even the shadow of Sinai as Mahomet did, but chooses rather to construe Moses by Joe Smith. He takes up the crook, not that the sheep may be fed, but that he may never want a warm woollen suit and a joint of mutton.

Immemor, O, fidei, pecorumque oblite tuorum!

For which reason I would derive the name *editor* not so much from *edo*, to publish, as from *edo*, to eat, that being the peculiar profession to which he esteems himself called. He blows up the flames of political discord for no other occasion than that he may thereby handily boil his own pot. I believe there are two thousand of these mutton-loving shepherds in the United States, and of these, how many have even the dimmest perception of their immense power, and the duties consequent thereon? Here and there, haply, one. Nine hundred and ninety-nine labor to impress upon the people the great principles of

Tweedledum, and other nine hundred and ninety-nine preach
with equal earnestness the gospel according to *Tweedledee.*"
—H.W.]

I DU believe in Freedom's cause,
    Ez fur away ez Payris is ;
I love to see her stick her claws
    In them infarnal Phayrisees ;
It 's wal enough agin a king
    To dror resolves an' triggers,—
But libbaty 's a kind o' thing
    Thet don't agree with niggers.

I du believe the people want
    A tax on teas an' coffees,
Thet nothin' aint extravygunt,—
    Purvidin' I 'm in office ;
Fer I hev loved my country sence
    My eye-teeth filled their sockets,
An' Uncle Sam I reverence,
    Partic'larly his pockets.

I du believe in *any* plan
    O' levyin' the taxes,
Ez long ez, like a lumberman,
    I git jest wut I axes ;
I go free trade thru thick an' thin,
    Because it kind o' rouses
The folks to vote,—an' keeps us in
    Our quiet custom-houses.

I du believe it 's wise an' good
    To sen' out furrin missions,
Thet is, on sartin understood
    An' orthodox conditions ;—
I mean nine thousan' dolls. per ann.,
    Nine thousan' more fer outfit,

An' me to recommend a man
  The place 'ould jest about fit.

I du believe in special ways
  O' prayin' an' convartin' ;
The bread comes back in many days,
  An' buttered, tu, fer sartin ;—
I mean in preyin' till one busts
  On wut the party chooses,
An' in convartin' public trusts
  To very privit uses.

I du believe hard coin the stuff
  Fer 'lectioneers to spout on ;
The people 's ollers soft enough
  To make hard money out on ;
Dear Uncle Sam pervides fer his,
  An' gives a good-sized junk to all,—
I don't care how hard money is,
  Ez long ez mine 's paid punctooal.

I du believe with all my soul
  In the gret Press's freedom,
To pint the people to the goal
  An' in the traces lead 'em ;
Palsied the arm thet forges yokes
  At my fat contracts squintin',
An' withered be the nose thet pokes
  Inter the gov'ment printin' !

I du believe thet I should give
  Wut 's his'n unto Cæsar,
Fer it 's by him I move an' live,
  Frum him my bread an' cheese air ;
I du believe thet all o' me
  Doth bear his souperscription,—

Will, conscience, honor, honesty,
　An' things o' thet description.

I du believe in prayer an' praise
　To him thet hez the grantin'
O' jobs,—in every thin' thet pays,
　But most of all in CANTIN' ;
This doth my cup with marcies fill,
　This lays all thought o' sin to rest,—
I *don't* believe in princerple,
　But, O, I *du* in interest.

I du believe in bein' this
　Or thet, ez it may happen
One way or t'other hendiest is
　To ketch the people nappin' ;
It aint by princerples nor men
　My preudunt course is steadied,—
I scent wich pays the best, an' then
　Go into it baldheaded.

I du believe thet holdin' slaves
　Comes nat'ral tu a Presidunt,
Let 'lone the rowdedow it saves
　To hev a wal-broke precedunt ;
Fer any office, small or gret,
　I could n't ax with no face,
'uthout I 'd ben, thru dry an' wet,
　Th' unrizzest kind o' doughface.

I du believe wutever trash
　'll keep the people in blindness,—
Thet we the Mexicans can thrash
　Right inter brotherly kindness,
Thet bombshells, grape, an' powder 'n' ball
　Air good-will's strongest magnets,

Thet peace, to make it stick at all,
  Must be druv in with bagnets.

In short, I firmly du believe
  In Humbug generally,
Fer it's a thing thet I perceive
  To hev a solid vally ;
This heth my faithful shepherd ben,
  In pasturs sweet heth led me,
An' this 'll keep the people green
  To feed ez they hev fed me.

[I subjoin here another passage from my before-mentioned discourse.

"Wonderful, to him that has eyes to see it rightly, is the newspaper. To me, for example, sitting on the critical front bench of the pit, in my study here in Jaalam, the advent of my weekly journal is as that of a strolling theatre, or rather of a puppet-show, on whose stage, narrow as it is, the tragedy, comedy, and farce of life are played in little. Behold the whole huge earth sent to me hebdomadally in a brown-paper wrapper !

"Hither, to my obscure corner, by wind or steam, on horse-back or dromedary-back, in the pouch of the Indian runner, or clicking over the magnetic wires, troop all the famous performers from the four quarters of the globe. Looked at from a point of criticism, tiny puppets they seem all, as the editor sets up his booth upon my desk and officiates as showman. Now I can truly see how little and transitory is life. The earth appears almost as a drop of vinegar, on which the solar microscope of the imagination must be brought to bear in order to make out any thing distinctly. That animalcule there, in the pea-jacket, is Louis Philippe, just landed on the coast of England. That other, in the gray surtout and cocked hat, is Napoleon Bonaparte Smith, assuring France that she need apprehend no interference from him in the present alarming juncture. At that spot, where you seem to see a speck of something in motion, is an immense mass-meeting. Look sharper, and you will see a mite brandishing his mandibles in an excited manner. That is the great Mr. Soandso, defining his position amid tumultuous and irrepressible cheers. That infinitestimal creature, upon whom some score of others, as minute as he, are gazing in open-mouthed admiration, is a famous philosopher, expounding to a select audience their capacity for the Infinite. That scarce discernible pufflet of smoke and dust is a revolution. That speck there is a reformer, just arranging the lever with which he is to move the world. And lo, there creeps forward the shadow of a skeleton that blows one breath between its grinning teeth, and all our distinguished actors are whisked off the slippery stage into the dark Beyond.

"Yes, the little show-box has its solemner suggestions. Now and then we catch a glimpse of a grim old man, who lays down a scythe and hour-glass in the corner while he shifts the scenes. There, too, in the dim back-ground, a weird shape is ever delving. Sometimes he leans upon his mattock, and gazes, as a coach whirls by, bearing the newly married on their wedding jaunt, or glances carelessly at a babe brought home from christening. Suddenly (for the scene grows larger and larger as we look) a bony hand snatches back a performer in the midst of his part, and him, whom yesterday two infinities (past and future) would not suffice, a handful of dust is enough to cover and silence for ever. Nay, we see the same fleshless fingers opening to clutch the showman himself, and guess, not without a shudder, that they are lying in wait for spectator also.

"Think of it : for three dollars a year I buy a season-ticket to this great Globe Theatre, for which God would write the dramas (only that we like farces, spectacles, and the tragedies of Apollyon better), whose scene-shifter is Time, and whose curtain is rung down by Death.

"Such thoughts will occur to me sometimes as I am tearing off the wrapper of my newspaper. Then suddenly that otherwise too often vacant sheet becomes invested for me with a strange kind of awe. Look ! deaths and marriages, notices of inventions, discoveries, and books, lists of promotions, of killed, wounded, and missing, news of fires, accidents, of sudden wealth and as sudden poverty ;—I hold in my hand the ends of myriad invisible electric conductors, along which tremble the joys, sorrows, wrongs, triumphs, hopes, and despairs of as many men and women everywhere. So that upon that mood of mind which seems to isolate me from mankind as a spectator of their puppet-pranks, another supervenes, in which I feel that I, too, unknown and unheard of, am yet of some import to my fellows. For, through my newspaper here, do not families take pains to send me, an entire stranger, news of a death among them ? Are not here two who would have me know of their marriage ? And, strangest of all, is not this singular person anxious to have me informed that he has received a fresh sup- ply of Dimitry Bruisgins ? But to none of us does the Present continue miraculous (even if for a moment discerned as such). We glance carelessly at the sunrise, and get used to Orion and the Pleiades. The wonder wears off, and to-morrow this sheet (Acts x. 11, 12), in which a vision was let down to me from Heaven, shall be the wrappage to a bar of soap or the platter for a beggar's broken victuals."—H.W.]

No. VII.

A Letter

FROM A CANDIDATE FOR THE PRESIDENCY
IN ANSWER TO SUTTIN QUESTIONS PROPOSED
BY MR. HOSEA BIGLOW, INCLOSED IN A NOTE
FROM MR. BIGLOW TO S. H. GAY, ESQ.,
EDITOR OF THE NATIONAL ANTI-SLAVERY STANDARD.

[Curiosity may be said to be the quality which preëminently distinguishes and segregates man from the lower animals. As we trace the scale of animated nature downward, we find this faculty (as it may truly be called) of the mind diminished in the savage, and wellnigh extinct in the brute. The first object which civilized man proposes to himself I take to be the finding out whatsoever he can concerning his neighbours. *Nihil humanum a me alienum puto;* I am curious about even John Smith. The desire next in strength to this (an opposite pole, indeed, of the same magnet) is that of communicating the unintelligence we have carefully picked up.

Men in general may be divided into the inquisitive and the communicative. To the first class belong Peeping Toms, eavesdroppers, navel-contemplating Brahmins, metaphysicians, travellers, Empedocleses, spies, the various societies for promoting Rhinothism, Columbuses, Yankees, discoverers, and men of science, who present themselves to the mind as so many marks of interrogation wandering up and down the world, or sitting in studies and laboratories. The second class I should again subdivide into four. In the first subdivision I would rank those who have an itch to tell us about themselves,—as keepers of diaries, insignificant persons generally, Montaignes, Horace Walpoles, autobiographers, poets. The second includes those who are anxious to impart information concerning other people,—as historians, barbers, and such. To the third belong those who labor to give us intelligence about nothing at all,—

as novelists, political orators, the large majority of authors, preachers, lecturers, and the like. In the fourth come those who are communicative from motives of public benevolence,—as finders of mares'-nests and bringers of ill news. Each of us two-legged fowls without feathers embraces all these subdivisions in himself to a greater or less degree, for none of us so much as lays an egg, or incubates a chalk one, but straightway the whole barn-yard shall know it by our cackle or our cluck. *Omnibus hoc vitium est.* There are different grades in all these classes. One will turn his telescope toward a back-yard, another toward Uranus ; one will tell you that he dined with Smith, another that he supped with Plato.In one particular, all men may be considered as belonging to the first grand division, inasmuch as they all seem equally desirous of discovering the mote in their neighbour's eye.

To one or another of these species every human being may safely be referred. I think it beyond a peradventure that Jonah prosecuted some inquiries into the digestive apparatus of whales, and that Noah sealed up a letter in an empty bottle, that news in regard to him might not be wanting in case of the worst. They had else been super or subter human. I conceive, also, that, as there are certain persons who continually peep and pry at the key-hole of that mysterious door through which, sooner or later, we all make our exits, so there are doubtless ghosts fidgeting and fretting on the other side of it, because they have no means of conveying back to this world the scraps of news they have picked up in that. For there is an answer ready somewhere to every question, the great law of *give and take* runs through all nature, and if we see a hook, we may be sure that an eye is waiting for it. I read in every face I meet a standing advertisement of information wanted in regard to A. B., or that the friends of C. D. can hear something to his disadvantage by application to such a one.

It was to gratify the two great passions of asking and answering that epistolary correspondence was first invented. Letters (for by this usurped title epistles are now commonly known) are of several kinds. First, there are those which are not letters at all,—as letters patent, letters dimissory, letters inclosing bills, letters of administration, Pliny's letters, letters of diplomacy, of Cato, of Mentor, of Lords Lyttelton, Chester-field, and Orrery, of Jacob Behmen, Seneca (whom St. Jerome includes in his list of sacred writers), letters from abroad, from sons in college to their fathers, letters of marque, and letters generally, which are in no wise letters of mark. Second, are real letters, such as those of Gray, Cowper, Walpole, Howel, Lamb, D. Y., the first letters from children (printed in staggering capitals), Letters from New York, letters of credit, and others, interesting for the sake of the writer or the thing written. I have read also letters from Europe by a gentleman named Pinto, containing some curious gossip, and which I hope to see collected for the benefit of the curious. There are, besides, letters addressed to posterity,—as epitaphs, for example, written for their own monuments by monarchs, whereby we have lately become possessed of the names of several great conquerors and kings of kings, hitherto unheard of and still unpronounceable, but valuable to the student of the entirely dark ages. The letter of our Saviour to King Abgarus, that which St. Peter sent to King Pepin in the year of grace 755, that of the Virgin to the magistrates of Messina, that of the Sanhedrim of Toledo to Annas and Caiaphas, A.D. 35, that of Galeazzo Sforza's spirit to his brother Lodovico, that of St. Gregory Thaumaturgus to the D—l, and that of this last-mentioned active police-magistrate to a nun of Girgenti, I would place in a class by themselves, as also the letters of candidates, concerning which I shall dilate more fully in a note at the end of the following poem. At present, *sat prata biberunt.* Only, concerning the shape of letters, they are all either square or oblong, to which general figures circular letters and round-robins also conform themselves.—H.W.]

DEER SIR its gut to be the fashun now to rite letters to the candid 8s and i wus chose at a publick Meetin in Jaalam to du wut wus nessary fur that town. i writ to 271 ginerals and gut ansers to 209. tha air called candid 8s but I don't see nothin candid about em. this here 1 wich I send wus thought satty's factory. I dunno as it's ushle to print Poscrips, but as all the ansers i gut hed the saim, I sposed it wus best. times has gretly changed. Formaly to knock a man into a cocked hat wus to use him up, but now it ony gives him a chance fur the cheef madgustracy.—H.B.

DEAR SIR,—You wish to know my notions
    On sartin pints thet rile the land ;
There 's nothin' thet my natur *so* shuns
    Ez bein' mum or underhand ;
I 'm a straight-spoken kind o' creetur
    Thet blurts right out wut 's in his head,
An' ef I 've one pecooler feetur,
    It is a nose thet wunt be led.

So, to begin at the beginnin',
    An' come direcly to the pint,
I think the country's underpinnin'
    Is some consid'ble out o' jint ;
I aint agoin' to try your patience
    By tellin' who done this or thet,
I don't make no insinooations,
    I jest let on I smell a rat.

Thet is, I mean, it seems to me so,
    But, ef the public think I 'm wrong,
I wunt deny but wut I be so,—
    An', fact, it don't smell very strong ;
My mind 's tu fair to lose its balance
    An' say wich party hez most sense ;
There may be folks o' greater talence
    Thet can't set stiddier on the fence.

I 'm an eclectic ; ez to choosin'
    'Twixt this an' thet, I 'm plaguy lawth ;
I leave a side thet looks like losin',
    But (wile there 's doubt) I stick to both ;

I stan' upon the Constitution,
    Ez preudunt statesmun say, who 've planned
A way to git the most profusion
    O' chances ez to *ware* they 'll stand.

Ez fer the war, I go agin it,—
    I mean to say I kind o' du,—
Thet is, I mean thet, bein' in it,
    The best way wuz to fight it thru ;
Not but wut abstract war is horrid,
    I sign to thet with all my heart,—
But civlyzation *doos* git forrid
    Sometimes upon a powder-cart.

About thet darned Proviso matter
    I never hed a grain o' doubt,
Nor I aint one my sense to scatter
    So 'st no one could n't pick it out ;
My love fer North an' South is equil,
    So I 'll jest answer plump an' frank,
No matter wut may be the sequil,—
    Yes, Sir, I *am* agin a Bank.

Ez to the answerin' o' questions,
    I 'm an off ox at bein' druv,
Though I aint one thet ary test shuns
    'll give our folks a helpin' shove ;
Kind o' permiscoous I go it
    Fer the holl country, an' the ground
I take, ez nigh ez I can show it,
    Is pooty gen'ally all round.

I don't appruve o' givin' pledges ;
    You 'd ough' to leave a feller free,
An' not go knockin' out the wedges
    To ketch his fingers in the tree ;

Pledges air awfle breachy cattle
   Thet preudunt farmers don't turn out,—
Ez long 'z the people git their rattle,
   Wut is there fer 'm to grout about ?

Ez to the slaves, there 's no confusion
   In *my* idees consarnin' them,—
I think they air an Institution,
   A sort of—yes, jes so,—ahem :
Do *I* own any ? Of my merit
   On thet pint you yourself may jedge ;
All is, I never drink no sperit,
   Nor I haint never signed no pledge.

Ez to my princerples, I glory
   In hevin' nothin' o' the sort ;
I aint a Wig, I aint a Tory,
   I 'm jest a canderdate, in short ;
Thet 's fair an' square an' parpendicler,
   But, ef the Public cares a fig
To hev me an' thin' in particler,
   Wy, I 'm a kind o' peri-wig.

P. S.

Ez we 're a sort o' privateerin',
   O' course, you know, it 's sheer an' sheer,
An' there is sutthin' wuth your hearin'
   I 'll mention in *your* privit ear ;
Ef you git *me* inside the White House,
   Your head with ile I 'll kin' o' 'nint
By gittin' *you* inside the Light-house
   Down to the eend o' Jaalam Pint.

An', ez the North hez took to brustlin'
   At bein' scrouged frum off the roost,

I'll tell ye wut'll save all tusslin'
    An' give our side a harnsome boost,—
Tell 'em thet on the Slavery question
    I 'm RIGHT, although to speak I 'm lawth ;
This gives you a safe pint to rest on,
    An' leaves me frontin' South by North.

[And now of epistles candidatial, which are of two kinds,—
namely, letters of acceptance, and letters definitive of position.
Our republic, on the eve of an election, may safely enough be
called a republic of letters. Epistolary composition becomes
then an epidemic, which seizes one candidate after another,
not seldom cutting short the thread of political life. It has come
to such a pass, that a party dreads less the attacks of its opponents than a letter from its candidate. *Litera scripta manet,*
and it will go hard if something bad cannot be made of it.
General Harrison, it is well understood, was surrounded, during
his candidacy, with the *cordon sanitaire* of a vigilance committee. No prisoner in Spielberg was ever more cautiously
deprived of writing materials. The soot was scraped carefully
from the chimney-places ; outposts of expert rifle-shooters
rendered it sure death for any goose (who came clad in feathers) to approach within a certain limited distance of North
Bend ; and all domestic fowls about the premises were reduced
to the condition of Plato's original man. By these precautions
the General was saved. *Parva componere magnis,* I remember,
that, when party-spirit once ran high among my people, upon
occasion of the choice of a new deacon, I, having my prefer-
ences, yet not caring too openly to express them, made use of an
innocent fraud to bring about that result which I deemed most
desirable. My stratagem was no other than the throwing a
copy of the Complete Letter-Writer in the way of the candidate
whom I wished to defeat. He caught the infection, and addressed a short note to his constituents, in which the opposite
party detected so many and so grave improprieties, (he had
modelled it upon the letter of a young lady accepting a proposal
of marriage,) that he not only lost his election, but, falling

under a suspicion of Sabellianism and I know not what, (the widow Endive assured me that he was a Paralipomenon, to her certain knowledge,) was forced to leave the town. Thus it is that the letter killeth.

The object which candidates propose to themselves in writing is to convey no meaning at all. And here is a quite unsuspected pitfall into which they successively plunge headlong. For it is precisely in such cryptographies that mankind are prone to seek for and find a wonderful amount and variety of significance. *Omne ignotum pro mirifico.* How do we admire at the antique world striving to crack those oracular nuts from Delphi, Hammon, and elsewhere, in only one of which can I so much as surmise that any kernel had ever lodged; that, namely, wherein Apollo confessed that he was mortal. One Didymus is, moreover, related to have written six thousand books on the single subject of grammar, a topic rendered only more tenebrific by the labors of his successors, and which seems still to possess an attraction for authors in proportion as they can make nothing of it. A singular loadstone for theologians, also, is the Beast in the Apocalypse, whereof, in the course of my studies, I have noted two hundred and three several interpretations, each lethiferal to all the rest. *Non nostrum est tantas componere lites,* yet I have myself ventured upon a two hundred and fourth, which I embodied in a discourse preached on occasion of the demise of the late usurper, Napoleon Bonaparte, and which quieted, in a large measure, the minds of my people. It is true that my views on this important point were ardently controverted by Mr. Shearjashub Holden, the then preceptor of our academy, and in other particulars a very deserving and sensible young man, though possessing a somewhat limited knowledge of the Greek tongue. But his heresy struck down no deep root, and, he having been lately removed by the hand of Providence, I had the satisfaction of reaffirming my cherished sentiments in a sermon preached upon the Lord's day immediately succeeding his funeral. This might seem like taking an unfair advantage, did I not add that he had made provision in his last will (being celibate) for

the publication of a posthumous tractate in support of his
own dangerous opinions.

I know of nothing in our modern times which approaches so
nearly to the ancient oracle as the letter of a Presidential candidate. Now, among the Greeks, the eating of beans was strictly
forbidden to all such as had it in mind to consult those expert
amphibologists, and this same prohibition on the part of
Pythagoras to his disciples is understood to imply an abstinence
from politics, beans having been used as ballots. That other
explication, *quod videlicet sensus eo cibo obtundi existimaret*,
though supported *pugnis et calcibus* by many of the learned,
and not wanting the countenance of Cicero, is confuted by the
larger experience of New England. On the whole, I think it
safer to apply here the rule of interpretation which now generally obtains in regard to antique cosmogonies, myths, fables,
proverbial expressions, and knotty points generally, which is,
to find a common-sense meaning, and then select whatever can
be imagined the most opposite thereto. In this way we arrive
at the conclusion, that the Greeks objected to the questioning of
candidates. And very properly, if, as I conceive, the chief point
be not to discover what a person in that position is, or what
he will do, but whether he can be elected. *Vos exemplaria
Græca nocturna versate manu, versate diurna.*

But, since an imitation of the Greeks in this particular (the
asking of questions being one chief privilege of freemen) is
hardly to be hoped for, and our candidates will answer, whether
they are questioned or not, I would recommend that these
ante-electionary dialogues should be carried on by symbols, as
were the diplomatic correspondence of the Scythians and
Macrobii, or confined to the language of signs, like the famous
interview of Panurge and Goatsnose. A candidate might then
convey a suitable reply to all committees of inquiry by closing
one eye, or by presenting them with a phial of Egyptian darkness to be speculated upon by their respective constituencies.
These answers would be susceptible of whatever retrospective
construction the exigencies of the political campaign might
seem to demand, and the candidate could take his position on

either side of the fence with entire consistency. Or, if letters must be written, profitable use might be made of the Dighton rock hieroglyphic or the cuneiform script, every fresh decipherer of which is enabled to educe a different meaning, whereby a sculptured stone or two supplies us, and will probably continue to supply posterity, with a very vast and various body of authentic history. For even the briefest epistle in the ordinary chirography is dangerous. There is scarce any style so compressed that superfluous words may not be detected in it. A severe critic might curtail that famous brevity of Cæsar's by two thirds, drawing his pen through the supererogatory *veni* and *vidi*. Perhaps, after all, the surest footing of hope is to be found in the rapidly increasing tendency to demand less and less of qualification in candidates. Already have statesmanship, experience, and the possession (nay, the profession, even) of principles been rejected as superfluous, and may not the patriot reasonably hope that the ability to write will follow? At present, there may be death in pot-hooks as well as pots, the loop of a letter may suffice for a bow-string, and all the dreadful heresies of Antislavery may lurk in a flourish.—H.W.]

No. VIII.

A Second Letter
From B. Sawin, Esq.

[In the following epistle, we behold Mr. Sawin returning, a *miles emeritus*, to the bosom of his family. *Quantum mutatus!* The good Father of us all had doubtless intrusted to the keeping of this child of his certain faculties of a constructive kind. He had put in him a share of that vital force, the nicest economy of every minute atom of which is necessary to the perfect development of Humanity. He had given him a brain and heart, and so had equipped his soul with the two strong wings of knowledge and love, whereby it can mount to hang its nest under the eaves of heaven. And this child, so dowered, he had intrusted to the keeping of his vicar, the State. How stands the account of that stewardship? The State, or Society, (call her by what name you will,) had taken no manner of thought of him till she saw him swept out into the street, the pitiful leavings of last night's debauch, with cigar-ends, lemon-parings, tobacco-quids, slops, vile stenches, and the whole loathsome next-morning of the bar-room,—an own child of the Almighty God! I remember him as he was brought to be christened, a ruddy, rugged babe ; and now there he wallows, reeking, seething,—the dead corpse, not of a man, but of a soul, —a putrefying lump, horrible for the life that is in it. Comes the wind of heaven, that good Samaritan, and parts the hair upon his forehead, nor is too nice to kiss those parched, cracked lips ; the morning opens upon him her eyes full of pitying sunshine, the sky yearns down to him,—and there he lies fermenting. O sleep ! let me not profane thy holy name by calling that stertorous unconsciousness a slumber ! By and by comes along the State, God's vicar. Does she say,—"My poor, forlorn foster-child ! Behold here a force which I will make dig and plant and build for me"? Not so, but,—"Here is a recruit ready-made to my hand, a piece of destroying energy lying unprofitably idle." So she claps an ugly gray suit on him, puts a musket in his grasp, and sends him off, with Gubernatorial and other godspeeds, to do duty as a destroyer.

I made one of the crowd at the last Mechanics' Fair, and, with the rest, stood gazing in wonder at a perfect machine, with its soul of fire, its boiler-heart that sent the hot blood pulsing along the iron arteries, and its thews of steel. And while I was admiring the adaptation of means to end, the harmonious involutions of contrivance, and the never-bewildered complexity, I saw a grimed and greasy fellow, the imperious engine's lackey and drudge, whose sole office was to let fall, at intervals, a drop or two of oil upon a certain joint. Then my soul said within me, See there a piece of mechanism to which that other you marvel at is but as the rude first effort of a child,—a force which not merely suffices to set a few wheels in motion, but which can send an impulse all through the infinite future,—a contrivance, not for turning out pins, or stitching button-holes, but for making Hamlets and Lears. And yet this thing of iron shall be housed, waited on, guarded from rust and dust, and it shall be a crime but so much as to scratch it with a pin ; while the other, with its fire of God in it, shall be buffeted hither and thither, and finally sent carefully a thousand miles to be the target for a Mexican cannon-ball. Unthrifty Mother State ! My heart burned within me for pity and indignation, and I renewed this covenant with my own soul,—*In aliis mansuetus ero, at, in blasphemiis contra Christum, non ita.*—H.W.]

I SPOSE you wonder ware I be ;—I can't tell, fer the soul o' me,
Exackly ware I be myself,—meanin' by thet the holl o' me.
Wen I left hum, I hed two legs, an' they worn't bad ones neither,
(The scaliest trick they ever played wuz bringin' on me hither,)
Now one on 'em 's I dunno ware ;—they thought I wuz adyin',
An' sawed it off because they said 'twuz kin' o' mortifyin' ;
I 'm willin' to believe it wuz, an' yit I don't see nuther
Wy one should take to feelin' cheap a minnit sooner 'n t'other,
Sence both wuz equilly to blame ; but things is ez they be ;
It took on so they took it off, an' thet 's enough fer me :

There 's one good thing, though, to be said about my wooden new
    one,—
The liquor can't git into it ez 't used to in the true one ;
So it saves drink ; an' then, besides, a feller could n't beg
A gretter blessin' then to hev one ollers sober peg ;
It 's true a chap 's in want o' two fer follerin' a drum,
But all the march I 'm up to now is jest to Kingdom Come.

I 've lost one eye, but thet 's a loss it's easy to supply
Out o' the glory thet I 've gut, fer thet is all my eye ;
An' one is big enough, I guess, by diligently usin' it,
To see all I shall ever git by way o' pay fer losin' it ;
Off'cers, I notice, who git paid fer all our thumps an' kickins,
Du wal by keepin' single eyes arter the fattest pickins ;
So, ez the eye 's put fairly out, I 'll larn to go without it,
An' not allow *myself* to be no gret put out about it.
Now, le' me see, thet is n't all ; I used, 'fore leavin' Jaalam,
To count things on my finger-eends, but sutthin' seems to ail 'em :
Ware 's my left hand ? Oh, darn it, yes, I recollect wut 's come on 't ;
I haint no left arm but my right, an' thet 's gut jest a thumb on 't ;
It aint so hendy ez it wuz to cal'late a sum on 't.
I 've hed some ribs broke,—six (I b'lieve),—I haint kep' no account
    on 'em ;
Wen pensions git to be the talk, I 'll settle the amount on 'em.
An' now I 'm speakin' about ribs, it kin' o' brings to mind
One thet I could n't never break,—the one I lef' behind ;
Ef you should see her, jest clear out the spout o' your invention
An' pour the longest sweetnin' in about an annooal pension,
An' kin' o' hint (in case, you know, the critter should refuse to be
Consoled) I aint so 'xpensive now to keep ez wut I used to be ;
There 's one arm less, ditto one eye, an' then the leg thet 's wooden
Can be took off an' sot away wenever ther' 's a puddin'.

I spose you think I 'm comin' back ez opperlunt ez thunder,
With shiploads o' gold images an' varus sorts o' plunder ;
Wal, 'fore I vullinteered, I thought this country wuz a sort o'

Canaan, a reg'lar Promised Land flowin' with rum an' water,
Ware propaty growed up like time, without no cultivation,
An' gold wuz dug ez taters be among our Yankee nation,
Ware nateral advantages were pufficly amazin',
Ware every rock there wuz about with precious stuns wuz blazin',
Ware mill-sites filled the country up ez thick ez you could cram 'em,
An' desput rivers run about abeggin' folks to dam 'em ;
Then there were meetinhouses, tu, chockfull o' gold an' silver
Thet you could take, an' no one could n't hand ye in no bill fer ;—
Thet 's wut I thought afore I went, thet 's wut them fellers told us
Thet stayed to hum an' speechified an' to the buzzards sold us ;
I thought thet gold mines could be gut cheaper than Chiny asters,
An' see myself acomin' back like sixty Jacob Astors ;
But sech idees soon melted down an' did n't leave a grease-spot,
I vow my holl sheer o' the spiles would n't come nigh a V spot ;
Although, most anywares we 've ben, you need n't break no locks,
Nor run no kin' o' risks, to fill your pocket full o' rocks.

I 'xpect I mentioned in my last some o' the nateral feeturs
O' this all-fiered buggy hole in th' way o' awfle creeturs,
But I fergut to name (new things to speak on so abounded)
How one day you 'll most die o' thust, an' 'fore the next git drownded.
The clymit seems to me jest like a teapot made o' pewter
Our Preudence hed, thet would n't pour (all she could du) to suit
        her ;
Fust place the leaves 'ould choke the spout, so 's not a drop 'ould
        dreen out,
Then Prude 'ould tip an' tip an' tip, till the holl kit bust clean out,
The kiver-hinge-pin bein' lost, tea-leaves an' tea an' kiver
'ould all come down *kerswosh* ! ez though the dam bust in a river.
Jest so 't is here ; holl months there aint a day o' rainy weather,
An' jest ez th' officers 'ould be alayin' heads together
Ez t' how they 'd mix their drink at sech a milingtary deepot,—
'T 'ould pour ez though the lid wuz off the everlastin' teapot.
The consqunce is, thet I shall take, wen I 'm allowed to leave here,
One piece o' propaty along,—an' thet 's the shakin' fever ;
It 's reggilar employment, though, an' thet aint thought to harm one,

Nor 't aint so tiresome ez it wuz with t' other leg an' arm on ;
An' it 's a consolation, tu, although it doos n't pay,
To hev it said you 're some gret shakes in any kin' o' way.

'T worn't very long, I tell ye wut, I thought o' fortin-makin',—
One day a reg'lar shiver-de-freeze, an' next ez good ez bakin',—
One day abrilin' in the sand, then smoth'rin' in the mashes,—
Git up all sound, be put to bed a mess o' hacks an' smashes.
But then, thinks I, at any rate there 's glory to be hed,—
Thet 's an investment, arter all, thet may n't turn out so bad ;
But somehow, wen we 'd fit an' licked, I ollers found the thanks
Gut kin' o' lodged afore they come ez low down ez the ranks ;
The Gin'rals gut the biggest sheer, the Cunnles next, an' so on,—
We never gut a blasted mite o' glory ez I know on ;
An' spose we hed, I wonder how you 're goin' to contrive its
Division so 's to give a piece to twenty thousand privits ;
Ef you should multiply by ten the portion o' the brav'st one,
You would n't git more 'n half enough to speak of on a grave-stun ;
We git the licks,—we 're jest the grist thet 's put into War's hoppers ;
Leftenants is the lowest grade thet helps pick up the coppers.
It may suit folks thet go agin a body with a soul in 't,
An' aint contented with a hide without a bagnet hole in 't ;
But glory is a kin' o' thing I shan't pursue no furder,
Coz thet 's the off'cers parquisite,—yourn 's on'y jest the murder.

Wal, arter I gin glory up, thinks I at least there 's one
Thing in the bills we aint hed yit, an' thet 's the GLORIOUS FUN ;
Ef once we git to Mexico, we fairly may persume we
All day an' night shall revel in the halls o' Montezumy.
I 'll tell ye wut *my* revels wuz, an' see how you would like 'em ;
We never gut inside the hall : the nighest ever *I* come
Wuz stan'in' sentry in the sun (an', fact ! it *seemed* a cent'ry)
A ketchin' smells o' biled an' roast thet come out thru the entry,
An' hearin', ez I sweltered thru my passes an' repasses,
A rat-tat-too o' knives an' forks, a clinkty-clink o' glasses :
I can't tell off the bill o' fare the Gin'rals hed inside ;
All I know is, thet out o' doors a pair o' soles wuz fried,

An' not a hunderd miles away frum ware this child wuz posted,
A Massachusetts citizen wuz baked an' biled an' roasted ;
The on'y thing like revellin' thet ever come to me
Wuz bein' routed out o' sleep by thet darned revelee.

They say the quarrel 's settled now ; fer my part I 've some doubt
    on 't,
'T 'll take more fish-skin than folks think to take the rile clean out
    on 't ;
At any rate, I 'm so used up I can't do no more fightin',
The on'y chance thet 's left to me is politics or writin' ;
Now, ez the people 's gut to hev a milingtary man,
An' I aint nothin' else jest now, I 've hit upon a plan ;
The can'idatin' line, you know, 'ould suit me to a T.
An' ef I lose, 't wunt hurt my ears to lodge another flea ;
So I 'll set up ez can'idate fer any kin' o' office,
(I mean fer any thet includes good easy-cheers an' soffies ;
Fer ez tu runnin' fer a place ware work 's the time o' day,
You know thet's wut I never did,—except the other way ;)
Ef it 's the Presidential cheer fer wich I 'd better run,
Wut two legs anywares about could keep up with my one ?
There aint no kin' o' quality in can'idates, it 's said,
So useful ez a wooden leg,—except a wooden head ;
There 's nothin' aint so poppylar—(wy, it 's a parfect sin
To think wut Mexico hez paid fer Santy Anny's pin ;)—
Then I haint gut no princerples, an', sence I wuz knee-high,
I never *did* hev any gret, ez you can testify ;
I 'm a decided peace-man, tu, an' go agin the war,—
Fer now the holl on 't 's gone an' past, wut is there to go *for* ?
Ef, wile you 're 'lectioneerin' round, some curus chaps should beg
To know my views o' state affairs, jest answer WOODEN LEG !
Ef they aint settisfied with thet, an' kin' o' pry an' doubt
An' ax fer sutthin' deffynit, jest say ONE EYE PUT OUT !
Thet kin' o' talk I guess you 'll find 'll answer to a charm,
An' wen you 're druv tu nigh the wall, hol' up my missin' arm ;
Ef they should nose round fer a pledge, put on a vartoous look
An' tell 'em thet 's percisely wut I never gin nor—took !

Then you can call me " Timbertoes",—thet 's wut the people likes ;
Sutthin' combinin' morril truth with phrases sech ez strikes ;
Some say the people 's fond o' this, or thet, or wut you please,—
I tell ye wut the people want is jest correct idees ;
" Old Timbertoes", you see, 's a creed it 's safe to be quite bold on,
There 's nothin' in 't the other side can any ways git hold on ;
It 's a good tangible idee, a sutthin' to embody
Thet valooable class o' men who look thru brandy-toddy ;
It gives a Party Platform, tu, jest level with the mind
Of all right-thinkin', honest folks thet mean to go it blind ;
Then there air other good hooraws to dror on ez you need 'em,
Sech ez the ONE-EYED SLARTERER, the BLOODY BIRDOFREDUM ;
Them 's wut takes hold o' folks thet think, ez well ez o' the masses,
An' makes you sartin o' the aid o' good men of all classes.

There 's one thing I 'm in doubt about ; in order to be Presidunt,
It 's absolutely ne'ssary to be a Southern residunt ;
The Constitution settles thet, an' also thet a feller
Must own a nigger o' some sort, jetblack, or brown, or yeller.
Now I haint no objections agin particklar climes,
Nor agin ownin' anythin' (except the truth sometimes),
But, ez I haint no capital, up there among ye, may be,
You might raise funds enough fer me to buy a low-priced baby,
An' then, to suit the No'thern folks, who feel obleeged to say
They hate an' cuss the very thing they vote fer every day,
Say you 're assured I go full butt fer Libbaty's diffusion,
An' made the purchis on'y jest to spite the Institootion ;—
But, golly ! there 's the currier's hoss upon the pavement pawin' !
I 'll be more 'xplicit in my next.
                    Yourn,
                              BIRDOFREDUM SAWIN.

[We have now a tolerably fair chance of estimating how the
balance-sheet stands between our returned volunteer and
glory. Supposing the entries to be set down on both sides of the
account in fractional parts of one hundred, we shall arrive at
something like the following result : —

" An gold wuz dug as taters wuz"

Birdofredom Sawin

Cr.	B. SAWIN, Esq., in account with (BLANK) GLORY.			Dr.
By loss of one leg, . . .	20	To one 675th three cheers		
" do. one arm, . .	15	in Faneuil Hall, . . .		30
" do. four fingers, .	5	" do. do. on		
" do. one eye, . .	10	occasion of presenta-		
" the breaking of six ribs,	6	tion of sword to Colonel		
" having served under		Wright, ...		25
Colonel Cushing one		" one suit of gray clothes		
month, ...	44	(ingeniously unbecom-		
		ing), ...		15
		" musical entertain-		
		ments (drum and fife		
		six months), ...		5
		" one dinner after re-		
		turn, ...		1
		" chance of pension, .		1
		" privilege of drawing		
		long-bow during rest of		
		natural life, ...		23
	100			100

E. E.

It should appear that Mr. Sawin found the actual feast curiously the reverse of the bill of fare advertised in Faneuil Hall and other places. His primary object seems to have been the making of his fortune. *Quærenda pecunia primum, virtus post nummos.* He hoisted sail for Eldorado, and shipwrecked on Point Tribulation. *Quid non mortalia pectora cogis, auri sacra fames?* The speculation has sometimes crossed my mind, in that dreary interval of drought which intervenes between quarterly stipendiary showers, that Providence, by the creation of a money-tree, might have simplified wonderfully the sometimes perplexing problem of human life. We read of bread-trees, the butter for which lies ready-churned in Irish bogs. Milk-trees we are assured of in South America, and stout Sir

John Hawkins testifies to water-trees in the Canaries. Boot-trees
bear abundantly in Lynn and elsewhere; and I have seen, in
the entries of the wealthy, hat-trees with a fair show of fruit.
A family-tree I once cultivated myself, and found therefrom
but a scanty yield, and that quite tasteless and innutritious. Of
trees bearing men we are not without examples; as those in
the park of Louis the Eleventh of France. Who has forgotten,
moreover, that olive-tree, growing in the Athenian's back-
garden, with its strange uxorious crop, for the general propa-
gation of which, as of a new and precious variety, the philosopher Diogenes, hitherto uninterested in arboriculture, was
so zealous? In the *sylva* of our own Southern States, the fe-
males of my family have called my attention to the china-tree.
Not to multiply examples, I will barely add to my list the
birch-tree, in the smaller branches of which has been implanted
so miraculous a virtue for communicating the Latin and Greek
languages, and which may well, therefore, be classed among
the trees producing necessaries of life,—*venerabile donum
fatalis virgæ*. That money-trees existed in the golden age there
want not prevalent reasons for our believing. For does not the
old proverb, when it asserts that money does not grow on
every bush, imply *a fortiori* that there were certain bushes
which did produce it? Again, there is another ancient saw to
the effect that money is the *root* of all evil. From which two
adages it may be safe to infer that the aforesaid species of tree
first degenerated into a shrub, then absconded underground,
and finally, in our iron age, vanished altogether. In favorable
exposures it may be conjectured that a specimen or two survived to a great age, as in the garden of the Hesperides; and,
indeed, what else could that tree in the Sixth Æneid have
been, with a branch whereof the Trojan hero procured admission to a territory, for the entering of which money is a surer
passport than to a certain other more profitable and too foreign
kingdom? Whether these speculations of mine have any force
in them, or whether they will not rather, by most readers, be
deemed impertinent to the matter in hand, is a question which

I leave to the determination of an indulgent posterity. That
there were, in more primitive and happier times, shops where
money was sold,—and that, too, on credit and at a bargain,
—I take to be matter of demonstration. For what but a dealer
in this article was that Æolus who supplied Ulysses with motive
power for his fleet in bags? What that Ericus, King of Sweden,
who is said to have kept the winds in his cap? What, in more
recent times, those Lapland Nornas who traded in favorable
breezes? All which will appear the more clearly when we
consider, that, even to this day, *raising the wind* is proverbial
for raising money, and that brokers and banks were invented
by the Venetians at a later period.

And now for the improvement of this digression. I find a
parallel to Mr. Sawin's fortune in an adventure of my own.
For, shortly after I had first broached to myself the before-
stated natural-historical and archæological theories, as I was
passing, *hæc negotia penitus mecum revolvens,* through one of
the obscure suburbs of our New England metropolis, my eye
was attracted by these words upon a sign-board,—CHEAP
CASH-STORE. Here was at once the confirmation of my speculations, and the substance of my hopes. Here lingered the
fragment of a happier past, or stretched out the first tremulous
organic filament of a more fortunate future. Thus glowed the
distant Mexico to the eyes of Sawin, as he looked through the
dirty pane of the recruiting-office window, or speculated from
the summit of that mirage-Pisgah which the imps of the bottle
are so cunning to raise up. Already had my Alnaschar-fancy
(even during that first half-believing glance) expended in
various useful directions the funds to be obtained by pledging
the manuscript of a proposed volume of discourses. Already did
a clock ornament the tower of the Jaalam meeting-house, a
gift appropriately, but modestly, commemorated in the parish
and town records, both, for now many years, kept by myself.
Already had my son Seneca completed his course at the University. Whether, for the moment, we may not be considered as
actually lording it over those Baratarias with the viceroyalty

of which Hope invests us, and whether we are ever so warmly housed as in our Spanish castles, would afford matter of argument. Enough that I found that sign-board to be no other than a bait to the trap of a decayed grocer. Nevertheless, I bought a pound of dates (getting short weight by reason of immense flights of harpy flies who pursued and lighted upon their prey even in the very scales), which purchase I made, not only with an eye to the little ones at home, but also as a figurative reproof of that too frequent habit of my mind, which, forgetting the due order of chronology, will often persuade me that the happy sceptre of Saturn is stretched over this Astræa-forsaken nineteenth century.

Having glanced at the ledger of Glory under the title *Sawin, B.*, let us extend our investigations, and discover if that instructive volume does not contain some charges more personally interesting to ourselves. I think we should be more economical of our resources, did we thoroughly appreciate the fact, that, whenever Brother Jonathan seems to be thrusting his hand into his own pocket, he is, in fact, picking ours. I confess that the late *muck* which the country has been running has materially changed my views as to the best method of raising revenue. If, by means of direct taxation, the bills for every extraordinary outlay were brought under our immediate eye, so that, like thrifty housekeepers, we could see where and how fast the money was going, we should be less likely to commit extravagances. At present, these things are managed in such a hugger-mugger way, that we know not what we pay for ; the poor man is charged as much as the rich ; and, while we are saving and scrimping at the spigot, the government is drawing off at the bung. If we could know that a part of the money we expend for tea and coffee goes to buy powder and balls, and that it is Mexican blood which makes the clothes on our backs more costly, it would set some of us athinking. During the present fall, I have often pictured to myself a government official entering my study and handing me the following bill : —

WASHINGTON, Sept. 30, 1848.

REV. HOMER WILBUR to Uncle Samuel,   Dr.

To his share of work done in Mexico on partnership account,
sundry jobs, as below.

" killing, maiming, and wounding about 5,000 Mexicans, $2.00
" slaughtering one woman carrying water to wounded,   .   .10
" extra work on two different Sabbaths (one bombard-
    ment and one assault) whereby the Mexicans were
    prevented from defiling themselves with the idol-
    atries of high mass, ...   3.50
" throwing an especially fortunate and Protestant bomb-
    shell into the Cathedral at Vera Cruz, whereby sev-
    eral female Papists were slain at the altar, ...50
" his proportion of cash paid for conquered territory, .   . 1.75
"   do.   do.   for conquering   do., .   .   . 1.50
" manuring   do.   with new superior compost called
    " American Citizen," 50
" extending the area of freedom and Protestantism,   .   .   .01
" glory, ...01
                                                           ─────
                                                            $9.87

Immediate payment is requested.

N.B.   Thankful for former favors, U.S. requests a continuance
of patronage. Orders executed with neatness and despatch. Terms
as low as those of any other contractor for the same kind and style
of work.

I can fancy the official answering my look of horror with,—
"Yes, Sir, it looks like a high charge, Sir ; but in these days
slaughtering is slaughtering." Verily, I would that every one
understood that it was ; for it goes about obtaining money under
the false pretence of being glory. For me, I have an imagination
which plays me uncomfortable tricks. It happens to me sometimes to see a slaughterer on his way home from his day's
work, and forthwith my imagination puts a cocked-hat upon

his head and epaulettes upon his shoulders, and sets him up as a candidate for the Presidency. So, also, on a recent public occasion, as the place assigned to the "Reverend Clergy" is just behind that of "Officers of the Army and Navy" in processions, it was my fortune to be seated at the dinner-table over against one of these respectable persons. He was arrayed as (out of his own profession) only kings, court-officers, and footmen are in Europe, and Indians in America. Now what does my over-officious imagination but set to work upon him, strip him of his gay livery, and present him to me coatless, his trousers thrust into the tops of a pair of boots thick with clotted blood, and a basket on his arm out of which lolled a gore-smeared axe, thereby destroying my relish for the temporal mercies upon the board before me !—H.W.]

No. IX.

A Third Letter
From B. Sawin, Esq.

[Upon the following letter slender comment will be needful. In
what river Selemnus has Mr. Sawin bathed, that he has become
so swiftly oblivious of his former loves ? From an ardent and
(as befits a soldier) confident wooer of that coy bride, the
popular favor, we see him subside of a sudden into the (I trust
not jilted) Cincinnatus, returning to his plough with a goodly-
sized branch of willow in his hand ; figuratively returning,
however, to a figurative plough, and from no profound affection
for that honored implement of husbandry, (for which, indeed,
Mr. Sawin never displayed any decided predilection,) but in
order to be gracefully summoned therefrom to more congenial
labors. It should seem that the character of the ancient Dictator
had become part of the recognized stock of our modern political comedy, though, as our term of office extends to a qua-
drennial length, the parallel is not so minutely exact as could
be desired. It is sufficiently so, however, for purposes of scenic
representation. An humble cottage (if built of logs, the better)
forms the Arcadian back-ground of the stage. This rustic
paradise is labelled Ashland, Jaalam, North Bend, Marshfield,
Kinderhook, or Bâton Rouge, as occasion demands. Before
the door stands a something with one handle (the other painted
in proper perspective), which represents, in happy ideal vague-
ness, the plough. To this the defeated candidate rushes with
delirious joy, welcomed as a father by appropriate groups of
happy laborers, or from it the successful one is torn with
difficulty, sustained alone by a noble sense of public duty. Only
I have observed, that, if the scene be laid at Bâton Rouge or
Ashland, the laborers are kept carefully in the background,
and are heard to shout from behind the scenes in a singular
tone resembling ululation, and accompanied by a sound not
unlike vigorous clapping. This, however, may be artistically in
keeping with the habits of the rustic population of those lo-
calities. The precise connection between agricultural pursuits

and statesmanship I have not been able, after diligent inquiry, to discover. But, that my investigations may not be barren of all fruit, I will mention one curious statistical fact, which I consider thoroughly established, namely, that no real farmer ever attains practically beyond a seat in the General Court, however theoretically qualified for more exalted station.

It is probable that some other prospect has been opened to Mr. Sawin, and that he has not made this great sacrifice without some definite understanding in regard to a seat in the cabinet or a foreign mission. It may be supposed that we of Jaalam were not untouched by a feeling of villatic pride in beholding our townsman occupying so large a space in the public eye. And to me, deeply revolving the qualifications necessary to a candidate in these frugal times, those of Mr. S. seemed peculiarly adapted to a successful campaign. The loss of a leg, an arm, an eye, and four fingers, reduced him so nearly to the condition of a *vox et præterea nihil,* that I could think of nothing but the loss of his head by which his chance could have been bettered. But since he has chosen to balk our suffrages, we must content ourselves with what we can get, remembering *lactucas non esse dandas, dum cardui sufficiant.* —H.W.]

I SPOSE you recollect thet I explained my gennle views
In the last billet thet I writ, 'way down frum Veery Cruze,
Jest arter I 'd a kin' o' ben spontanously sot up
To run unannermously fer the Preserdential cup ;
O' course it worn't no wish o' mine, 't wuz ferflely distressin',
But poppiler enthusiasm gut so almighty pressin'
Thet, though like sixty all along I fumed an' fussed an' sorrerd,
There did n't seem no ways to stop their bringin' on me forrerd :
Fact is, they udged the matter so, I could n't help admittin'
The Father o' his Country's shoes no feet but mine 'ould fit in,
Besides the savin' o' the soles fer ages to succeed,
Seein' thet with one wannut foot, a pair 'd be more 'n I need ;
An', tell ye wut, them shoes 'll want a thund'rin' sight o' patchin',

Ef this ere fashion is to last we 've gut into o' hatchin'
A pair o' second Washintons fer every new election,—
Though, fur ez number one 's consarned, I don't make no objection.

I wuz agoin' on to say thet wen at fust I saw
The masses would stick to 't I wuz the Country's father-'n-law,
(They would ha' hed it *Father*, but I told 'em 't would n't du,
Coz thet wuz sutthin' of a sort they could n't split in tu,
An' Washinton hed hed the thing laid fairly to his door,
Nor dars n't say 't worn't hisn, much ez sixty year afore,)
But 't aint no matter ez to thet;—wen I wuz nomernated,
'T worn't natur but wut I should feel consid'able elated,
An' wile the hooraw o' the thing wuz kind o' noo an' fresh,
I thought our ticket would ha' caird the country with a resh.

Sence I 've come hum, though, an' looked round, I think I seem to
        find
Strong argimunts ez thick ez fleas to make me change my mind ;
It 's clear to any one whose brain ain't fur gone in a phthisis,
Thet hail Columby's happy land is goin' thru a crisis,
An' 't would n't noways du to hev the people's mind distracted
By bein' all to once by sev'ral pop'lar names attackted ;
'T would save holl haycartloads o' fuss an' three four months o' jaw,
Ef some illustrous paytriot should back out an' withdraw ;
So, ez I aint a crooked stick, jest like—like ole (I swow,
I dunno ez I know his name)—I 'll go back to my plough.

Wenever an Amerikin distinguished politishin
Begins to try et wut they call definin' his posishin,
Wal, I, fer one, feel sure he aint gut nothin' to define ;
It 's so nine cases out o' ten, but jest that tenth is mine ;
An' 't aint no more 'n is proper 'n' right in sech a sitooation
To hint the course you think 'll be the savin' o' the nation ;
To funk right out o' p'lit'cal strife aint thought to be the thing,
Without you deacon off the toon you want your folks should sing ;
So I edvise the noomrous friends thet 's in one boat with me

To jest up killock, jam right down their hellum hard a lee,
Haul the sheets taut, an', layin' out upon the Suthun tack,
Make fer the safest port they can, wich, I think, is Ole Zack.

Next thing you 'll want to know, I spose, wut argimunts I seem
To see thet makes me think this ere 'll be the strongest team ;
Fust place, I 've ben consid'ble round in bar-rooms an' saloons
Agethrin' public sentiment, 'mongst Demmercrats and Coons,
An' 't aint ve'y offen thet I meet a chap but wut goes in
Fer Rough an' Ready, fair an' square, hufs, taller, horns, an' skin ;
I don't deny but wut, fer one, ez fur ez I could see,
I didn't like at fust the Pheladelphy nomernee ;
I could ha' pinted to a man thet wuz, I guess, a peg
Higher than him,—a soger, tu, an' with a wooden leg ;
But every day with more an' more o' Taylor zeal I 'm burnin',
Seein' wich way the tide thet sets to office is aturnin' ;
Wy, in to Bellers's we notched the votes down on three sticks,—
'T wuz Birdofredum *one*, Cass *aught*, an' Taylor *twenty six*,
An', bein' the on'y canderdate thet wuz upon the ground,
They said 't wuz no more 'n right thet I should pay the drinks all
    round ;
Ef I 'd expected sech a trick, I would n't ha' cut my foot
By goin' an' votin' fer myself like a consumed coot ;
It did n't make no deff'rence, though ; I wish I may be cust,
Ef Bellers wuz n't slim enough to say he would n't trust !

Another pint thet influnces the minds o' sober jedges
Is thet the Gin'ral hez n't gut tied hand an' foot with pledges ;
He hez n't told ye wut he is, an' so there aint no knowin'
But wut he may turn out to be the best there is agoin' ;
This, at the on'y spot thet pinched, the shoe direcly eases,
Coz every one is free to 'xpect percisely wut he pleases :
I want freetrade ; you don't ; the Gin'ral is n't bound to neither ;—
I vote my way ; you, yourn ; an' both air sooted to a T there.
Ole Rough an' Ready, tu, 's a Wig, but without bein' ultry
(He 's like a holsome hayinday, thet 's warm, but is n't sultry) ;

He 's jest wut I should call myself, a kin' o' *scratch*, ez 't ware,
Thet aint exacly all a wig nor wholly your own hair ;
I 've ben a Wig three weeks myself, jest o' this mod'rate sort,
An' don't find them an' Demmercrats so deffrent ez I thought ;
They both act pooty much alike, an' push an' scrouge an' cus ;
They 're like two pickpockets in league fer Uncle Samwell's pus ;
Each takes a side, an' then they squeeze the ole man in between 'em,
Turn all his pockets wrong side out an' quick ez lightnin' clean 'em ;
To nary one on 'em I 'd trust a secon'-handed rail
No furder off 'an I could sling a bullock by the tail.

Webster sot matters right in thet air Mashfiel' speech o' his'n ;—
" Taylor," sez he, " aint nary ways the one thet I 'd a chizzen,
Nor he aint fittin' fer the place, an' like ez not he aint
No more 'n a tough ole bullethead, an' no gret of a saint ;
But then," sez he, " obsarve my pint, he 's jest ez good to vote fer
Ez though the greasin' on him worn't a thing to hire Choate fer ;
Aint it ez easy done to drop a ballot in a box
Fer one ez 't is fer t'other, fer the bulldog ez the fox ? "
It takes a mind like Dannel's, fact, ez big ez all ou' doors,
To find out thet it looks like rain arter it fairly pours ;
I 'gree with him, it aint so dreffle troublesome to vote
Fer Taylor arter all,—it 's jest to go an' change your coat ;
Wen he 's once greased, you 'll swaller him an' never know on 't,
  scurce,
Unless he scratches, goin' down, with them 'ere Gin'ral's spurs.
I 've ben a votin' Demmercrat, ez reg'lar as a clock,
But don't find goin' Taylor gives my narves no gret 'f a shock ;
Truth is, the cutest leadin' Wigs, ever sence fust they found
Wich side the bread gut buttered on, hev kep' a edgin' round ;
They kin' o' slipt the planks frum out th' ole platform, one by one,
An' made it gradooally noo, 'fore folks know'd wut wuz done,
Till, fur 'z I know, there aint an inch thet I could lay my han' on,
But I, or any Demmercrat, feels comf'table to stan' on,
An' ole Wig doctrines act'lly look, their occ'pants bein' gone,
Lonesome ez steddles on a mash without no hayricks on.

I spose it 's time now I should give my thoughts about the plan,
Thet chipped the shell at Buffalo, o' settin' up ole Van ;
I used to vote fer Martin, but, I swan, I 'm clean disgusted,—
He aint the man thet I can say is fittin' to be trusted ;
He aint half antislav'ry 'nough, nor I aint sure, ez some be,
He 'd go in fer abolishin' the deestrick o' Columby ;
An', now I come to recollec', it kin' o' makes me sick 'z
A horse, to think o' wut he wuz in eighteen thirty six.
An' then, another thing ;—I guess, though mebby I am wrong,
This Buff'lo plaster aint agoin' to dror almighty strong ;
Some folks, I know, hev gut th' idee thet No'thun dough 'll rise,
Though, 'fore I see it riz an' baked, I would n't trust my eyes ;
'T will take more emptins, a long chalk, than this noo party 's gut,
To give sech heavy cakes ez them a start, I tell ye wut.
But even ef they caird the day, there would n't be no endurin'
To stan' upon a platform with sech critters ez Van Buren ;—
An' his son John, tu, I can't think how thet 'ere chap should dare
To speak ez he doos ; wy, they say he used to cus an' swear !
I spose he never read the hymn thet tells how down the stairs
A feller with long legs wuz throwed thet would n't say his prayers.

This brings me to another pint : the leaders o' the party
Aint jest sech men ez I can act along with free an' hearty ;
They aint not quite respectable, an' wen a feller's morrils
Don't toe the straightest kin' o' mark, wy, him an' me jest quarrils.
I went to a free soil meetin' once, an' wut d' ye think I see ?
A feller wuz aspoutin' there thet act'lly come to me,
About two year ago last spring, ez nigh ez I can jedge,
An' axed me ef I didn't want to sign the Temprunce pledge !
He 's one o' them thet goes about an' sez you hed n't ough' ter
Drink nothin', mornin', noon, or night, stronger 'an Taunton water.
There 's one rule I 've ben guided by, in settlin' how to vote, ollers,—
I take the side thet *is n't* took by them consarned teetotallers.

Ez fer the niggers, I 've ben South, an' thet hez changed my min' ;
A lazier, more ongrateful set you could n't nowers fin'.
You know I mentioned in my last thet I should buy a nigger,

Ef I could make a purchase at a pooty mod'rate figger ;
So, ez there 's nothin' in the world I 'm fonder of 'an gunnin',
I closed a bargin finally to take a feller runnin'.
I shou'dered queen's-arm an' stumped out, an', wen I come t' th'
    swamp,
'T worn't very long afore I gut upon the nest o' Pomp ;
I come acrost a kin' o' hut, an', playin' round the door,
Some little woollyheaded cubs, ez many 'z six or more.
At fust I thought o' firin', but *think twice* is safest ollers ;
There aint, thinks I, not one on 'em but 's wuth his twenty dollars,
Or would be, ef I hed 'em back into a Christian land,—
How temptin' all on 'em would look upon an auctionstand !
(Not but wut *I* hate Slavery in th' abstract, stem to starn,—
I leave it ware our fathers did, a privit State consarn.)
Soon 'z they see me, they yelled an' run, but Pomp wuz out ahoein'
A leetle patch o' corn he hed, or else there aint no knowin'
He would n't ha' took a pop at me ; but I hed gut the start,
An' wen he looked, I vow he groaned ez though he 'd broke his heart ;
He done it like a wite man, tu, ez nat'ral ez a pictur,
The imp'dunt, pis'nous hypocrite ! wus 'an a boy constrictur.
"You can't gum *me*, I tell ye now, an' so you need n't try,
I 'xpect my eye-teeth every mail, so jest shet up," sez I.
"Don't go to actin' ugly now, or else I 'll let her strip,
You 'd best draw kindly, seein' 'z how I 've gut ye on the hip ;
Besides, you darned ole fool, it aint no gret of a disaster
To be benev'lently druv back to a contented master,
Ware you hed Christian priv'ledges you don't seem quite aware on,
Or you 'd ha' never run away from bein' well took care on ;
Ez fer kin' treatment, wy, he wuz so fond on ye, he said
He 'd give a fifty spot right out, to git ye, 'live or dead ;
Wite folks aint sot by half ez much ; 'member I run away,
Wen I wuz bound to Cap'n Jakes, to Mattysqumscot bay ;
Don' know him, likely ? Spose not ; wal, the mean ole codger went
An' offered—wut reward, think ? Wal, it worn't no *less* 'n a cent."

Wal, I jest gut 'em into line, an' druv 'em on afore me,
The pis'nous brutes, I 'd no idee o' the illwill they bore me ;

We walked till som'ers about noon, an' then it grew so hot
I thought it best to camp awile, so I chose out a spot
Jest under a magnoly tree, an' there right down I sot ;
Then I unstrapped my wooden leg, coz it begun to chafe,
An' laid it down 'long side o' me, supposin' all wuz safe ;
I made my darkies all set down around me in a ring,
An' sot an' kin' o' ciphered up how much the lot would bring ;
But, wile I drinked the peaceful cup of a pure heart an' min',
(Mixed with some wiskey, now an' then,) Pomp he snaked up
    behin',
An', creepin' grad'lly close tu, ez quiet ez a mink,
Jest grabbed my leg, an' then pulled foot, quicker 'an you could
    wink,
An', come to look, they each on 'em hed gut behin' a tree,
An' Pomp poked out the leg a piece, jest so ez I could see,
An' yelled to me to throw away my pistils an' my gun,
Or else thet they 'd cair off the leg an' fairly cut an' run.
I vow I did n't b'lieve there wuz a decent alligatur
Thet hed a heart so destitoot o' common human natur ;
However, ez there worn't no help, I finally give in
An' heft my arms away to git my leg safe back agin.
Pomp gethered all the weapins up, an' then he come an' grinned,
He showed his ivory some, I guess, an' sez, " You 're fairly pinned ;
Jest buckle on your leg again, an' git right up an' come,
'T wun't du fer fammerly men like me to be so long frum hum."
At fust I put my foot right down an' swore I would n't budge,
" Jest ez you choose," sez he, quite cool, " either be shot or trudge."
So this blackhearted monster took an' act'lly druv me back
Along the very feetmarks o' my happy mornin' track,
An' kep' me pris'ner 'bout six months, an' worked me, tu, like sin,
Till I hed gut his corn an' his Carliny taters in ;
He made me larn him readin', tu, (although the critter saw
How much it hut my morril sense to act agin the law,)
So 'st he could read a Bible he 'd gut ; an' axed ef I could pint
The North Star out ; but there I put his nose some out o' jint,
Fer I weeled roun' about sou'west, an', lookin' up a bit,
Picked out a middlin' shiny one an' tole him thet wuz it.

Fin'lly, he took me to the door, an', givin' me a kick,
Sez,—" Ef you know wut 's best fer ye, be off, now, double quick ;
The wintertime 's acomin' on, an', though I gut ye cheap,
You 're so darned lazy, I don't think you 're hardly wuth your keep ;
Besides, the childrin's growin' up, an' you aint jest the model
I 'd like to hev 'em immertate, an' so you 'd better toddle ! "

Now is there any thin' on airth 'll ever prove to me
Thet renegader slaves like him air fit fer bein' free ?
D' you think they 'll suck me in to jine the Buff'lo chaps, an' them
Rank infidels thet go agin the Scriptur'l cus o' Shem ?
Not by a jugfull ! sooner 'n thet, I 'd go thru fire an' water ;
Wen I hev once made up my mind, a meet'nhus aint sotter ;
No, not though all the crows thet flies to pick my bones wuz
                cawin',—
I guess we 're in a Christian land,—
                    Yourn,
                            BIRDOFREDUM SAWIN.

[Here, patient reader, we take leave of each other, I trust
with some mutual satisfaction. I say *patient*, for I love not that
kind which skims dippingly over the surface of the page, as
swallows over a pool before rain. By such no pearls shall be
gathered. But if no pearls there be (as, indeed, the world is not
without example of books wherefrom the longest-winded
diver shall bring up no more than his proper handful of mud),
yet let us hope that an oyster or two may reward adequate
perseverance. If neither pearls nor oysters, yet is patience itself
a gem worth diving deeply for.
    It may seem to some that too much space has been usurped
by my own private lucubrations, and some may be fain to bring
against me that old jest of him who preached all his hearers
out of the meeting-house save only the sexton, who, remaining
for yet a little space, from a sense of official duty, at last gave
out also, and, presenting the keys, humbly requested our
preacher to lock the doors, when he should have wholly relieved
himself of his testimony. I confess to a satisfaction in the self

act of preaching, nor do I esteem a discourse to be wholly thrown away even upon a sleeping or unintelligent auditory. I cannot easily believe that the Gospel of Saint John, which Jacques Cartier ordered to be read in the Latin tongue to the Canadian savages, upon his first meeting with them, fell altogether upon stony ground. For the earnestness of the preacher is a sermon appreciable by dullest intellects and most alien ears. In this wise did Episcopius convert many to his opinions, who yet understood not the language in which he discoursed. The chief thing is, that the messenger believe that he has an authentic message to deliver. For counterfeit messengers that mode of treatment which Father John de Plano Carpini relates to have prevailed among the Tartars would seem effectual, and, perhaps, deserved enough. For my own part, I may lay claim to so much of the spirit of martyrdom as would have led me to go into banishment with those clergymen whom Alphonso the Sixth of Portugal drave out of his kingdom for refusing to shorten their pulpit eloquence. It is possible, that, having been invited into my brother Biglow's desk, I may have been too little scrupulous in using it for the venting of my own peculiar doctrines to a congregation drawn together in the expectation and with the desire of hearing him.

I am not wholly unconscious of a peculiarity of mental organization which impels me, like the railroad-engine with its train of cars, to run backward for a short distance in order to obtain a fairer start. I may compare myself to one fishing from the rocks when the sea runs high, who, misinterpreting the suction of the undertow for the biting of some larger fish, jerks suddenly, and finds that he has *caught bottom*, hauling in upon the end of his line a trail of various *algæ*, among which, nevertheless, the naturalist may haply find somewhat to repay the disappointment of the angler. Yet have I conscientiously endeavoured to adapt myself to the impatient temper of the age, daily degenerating more and more from the high standard of our pristine New England. To the catalogue of lost arts I would mournfully add also that of listening to two-hour sermons. Surely we have been abridged into a race of

Birdofredom Sawin, with only one leg to stand upon.

George Cruickshank (1792–1878), one of the foremost English satiric illustrators, designed this frontispiece for the pirated Hotten edition of The Biglow Papers (London, 1859).

pigmies. For, truly, in those of the old discourses yet subsisting to us in print, the endless spinal column of divisions and subdivisions can be likened to nothing so exactly as to the vertebræ of the saurians, whence the theorist may conjecture a race of Anakim proportionate to the withstanding of these other monsters. I say Anakim rather than Nephelim, because there seem reasons for supposing that the race of those whose heads (though no giants) are constantly enveloped in clouds (which that name imports) will never become extinct. The attempt to vanquish the innumerable *heads* of one of those aforementioned discourses may supply us with a plausible interpretation of the second labor of Hercules, and his successful experiment with fire affords us a useful precedent.

But while I lament the degeneracy of the age in this regard, I cannot refuse to succumb to its influence. Looking out through my study-window, I see Mr. Biglow at a distance busy in gathering his Baldwins, of which, to judge by the number of barrels lying about under the trees, his crop is more abundant than my own,—by which sight I am admonished to turn to those orchards of the mind wherein my labors may be more prospered, and apply myself diligently to the preparation of my next Sabbath's discourse.—H.W.]

Glossary.

A.

Act'lly, *actually.*
Air, *are.*
Airth, *earth.*
Airy, *area.*
Aree, *area.*
Arter, *after.*
Ax, *ask.*

B.

Beller, *bellow.*
Bellowses, *lungs.*
Ben, *been.*
Bile, *boil.*
Bimeby, *by and by.*
Blurt out, *to speak bluntly.*
Bust, *burst.*
Buster, *a roistering blade;* used also as a general superlative.

C.

Caird, *carried.*
Cairn, *carrying.*
Caleb, *a turncoat.*
Cal'late, *calculate.*
Cass, *a person with two lives.*
Close, *clothes.*
Cockerel, *a young cock.*
Cocktail, *a kind of drink;* also, *an ornament peculiar to soldiers.*
Convention, *a place where people are imposed on ; a juggler's show.*

Coons, *a cant term for a now defunct party;* derived, perhaps, from the fact of their being commonly *up a tree.*
Cornwallis, *a sort of muster in masquerade;* supposed to have had its origin soon after the Revolution, and to commemorate the surrender of Lord Cornwallis. It took the place of the old Guy Fawkes procession.
Crooked stick, *a perverse, froward person.*
Cunnle, *a colonel.*
Cuss, *a curse;* also, *a pitiful fellow.*

D.

Darsn't, used indiscriminately, either in singular or plural number, for *dare not, dares not,* and *dared not.*
Deacon off, *to give the cue to;* derived from a custom, once universal, but now extinct, in our New England Congregational churches. An important part of the office of deacon was to read aloud the hymns *given out* by the minister, one line at a time, the congregation singing each line as soon as read.
Demmercrat, leadin', *one in favor of extending slavery; a free-trade lecturer maintained in the custom-house.*

Desput, *desperate*.
Dō', *don't*.
Doos, *does*.
Doughface, *a contented
lick-spittle;* a common variety
of Northern politician.
Dror, *draw*.
Du, *do*.
Dunno, dno, *do not* or *does not
know*.
Dut, *dirt*.

E.

Eend, *end*.
Ef, *if*.
Emptins, *yeast*.
Env'y, *envoy*.
Everlasting, an intensive, without
reference to duration.
Ev'y, *every*.
Ez, *as*.

F.

Fence, on the ; said of one who
halts between two opinions ; a
trimmer.
Fer, *for*.
Ferfle, ferful, *fearful;* also an
intensive.
Fin', *find*.
Fish-skin, used in New England to
clarify coffee.
Fix, *a difficulty, a nonplus*.
Foller, folly, *to follow*.
Forrerd, *forward*.
Frum, *from*.
Fur, *far*.
Furder, *farther*.
Furrer, *furrow*. Metaphorically, *to
draw a straight furrow* is to live
uprightly or decorously.

Fust, *first*.

G.

Gin, *gave*.
Git, *get*.
Gret, *great*.
Grit, *spirit, energy, pluck*.
Grout, *to sulk*.
Grouty, *crabbed, surly*.
Gum, *to impose on*.
Gump, *a foolish fellow, a dullard*.
Gut, *got*.

H.

Hed, *had*.
Heern, *heard*.
Hellum, *helm*.
Hendy, *handy*.
Het, *heated*.
Hev, *have*.
Hez, *has*.
Holl, *whole*.
Holt, *hold*.
Huf, *hoof*.
Hull, *whole*.
Hum, *home*.
Humbug, *General Taylor's
antislavery*.
Hut, *hurt*.

I.

Idno, *I do not know*.
In'my, *enemy*.
Insines, *ensigns;* used to designate
both the officer who carries the
standard, and the standard
itself.
Inter, intu, *into*.

GLOSSARY

J.

Jedge, *judge.*
Jest, *just.*
Jine, *join.*
Jint, *joint.*
Junk, *a fragment of any solid substance.*

K.

Keer, *care.*
Kep, *kept.*
Killock, *a small anchor.*
Kin', kin' o', kinder, *kind, kind of.*

L.

Lawth, *loath.*
Less, *let 's, let us.*
Let day-light into, *to shoot.*
Let on, *to hint, to confess, to own.*
Lick, *to beat, to overcome.*
Lights, *the bowels.*
Lily-pads, *leaves of the water-lily.*
Long-sweetening, *molasses.*

M.

Mash, *marsh.*
Mean, *stingy, ill-natured.*
Min', *mind.*

N.

Nimepunce, *ninepence, twelve and a half cents.*
Nowers, *nowhere.*

O.

Offen, *often.*
Ole, *old.*
Ollers, olluz, *always.*
On, *of ;* used before *it* or *them,* or at the end of a sentence, as, *on 't, on 'em, nut ez ever I heerd on.*
On'y, *only.*
Ossifer, *officer* (seldom heard).

P.

Peaked, *pointed.*
Peek, *to peep.*
Pickerel, *the pike, a fish.*
Pint, *point.*
Pocket full of rocks, *plenty of money.*
Pooty, *pretty.*
Pop'ler, *conceited, popular.*
Pus, *purse.*
Put out, *troubled, vexed.*

Q.

Quarter, *a quarter-dollar.*
Queen's arm, *a musket.*

R.

Resh, *rush.*
Revelee, *the réveille.*
Rile, *to trouble.*
Riled, *angry ; disturbed,* as the sediment in any liquid.
Riz, *risen.*
Row, a long row to hoe, *a difficult task.*
Rugged, *robust.*

S.

Sarse, *abuse, impertinence.*
Sartin, *certain.*
Saxon, *sacristan, sexton.*
Scaliest, *worst.*
Scringe, *cringe.*
Scrouge, *to crowd.*
Sech, *such.*
Set by, *valued.*
Shakes, great, *of considerable consequence.*
Shappoes, *chapeaux, cocked-hats.*
Sheer, *share.*
Shet, *shut.*
Shut, *shirt.*
Skeered, *scared.*
Skeeter, *mosquito.*
Skooting, *running,* or *moving swiftly.*
Slarterin', *slaughtering.*
Slim, *contemptible.*
Snaked, *crawled like a snake ;* but *to snake any one out* is to track him to his hiding-place ; *to snake a thing out* is to snatch it out.
Soffies, *sofas.*
Sogerin', *soldiering ;* a barbarous amusement common among men in the savage state.
Som'ers, *somewhere.*
So 'st, *so as that.*
Sot, *set, obstinate, resolute.*
Spiles, *spoils ; objects of political ambition.*
Spry, *active.*
Steddles, *stout stakes driven into the salt marshes,* on which the hay-ricks are set, and thus raised out of the reach of high tides.
Streaked, *uncomfortable, discomfited.*
Suckle, *circle.*
Sutthin', *something.*
Suttin, *certain.*

T.

Take on, *to sorrow.*
Talents, *talons.*
Taters, *potatoes.*
Tell, *till.*
Tetch, *touch.*
Tetch tu, *to be able ;* used always after a negative in this sense.
Tollable, *tolerable.*
Toot, used derisively for *playing on any wind instrument.*
Thru, *through.*
Thundering, a euphemism common in New England, for the profane English expression *devilish.* Perhaps derived from the belief, common formerly, that thunder was caused by the Prince of the Air, for some of whose accomplishments consult Cotton Mather.
Tu, *to, too ;* commonly has this sound when used emphatically, or at the end of a sentence. At other times it has the sound of *t* in *tough,* as, *Ware ye goin' tu ? Goin' ta Boston.*

U.

Ugly, *ill-tempered, intractable.*
Uncle Sam, *United States ;* the largest boaster of liberty and owner of slaves.
Unrizzest, applied to dough or bread ; *heavy, most unrisen,* or *most incapable of rising.*

V.

V spot, *a five-dollar bill.*
Vally, *value.*

W.

Wake snakes, *to get into trouble.*
Wal, *well;* spoken with great
  deliberation, and sometimes
  with the *a* very much flattened,
  sometimes (but more seldom)
  very much broadened.
Wannut, *walnut (hickory).*
Ware, *where.*
Ware, *were.*
Whopper, *an uncommonly large
  lie;* as, that General Taylor is in
  favor of the Wilmot Proviso.
Wig, *Whig;* a party now dissolved.
Wunt, *will not.*
Wus, *worse.*
Wut, *what.*
Wuth, *worth;* as, *Antislavery*
  perfessions 'fore 'lection aint
  wuth a Bungtown copper.
Wuz, *was,* sometimes *were.*

Y.

Yaller, *yellow.*
Yeller, *yellow.*
Yellers, *a disease of peach-trees.*

Z.

Zack, Ole, *a second Washington,
  an antislavery slaveholder, a
  humane buyer and seller of men
  and women, a Christian hero
  generally.*

Index

A.

A. B., information wanted concerning, 110.

Adam, eldest son of, respected, 55.

Æneas goes to hell, 128.

Æolus, a seller of money, as is supposed by some, 129.

Æschylus, a saying of, 89, *note*.

Alligator, a decent one conjectured to be, in some sort, humane, 140.

Alphonso the Sixth of Portugal, tyrannical act of, 142.

Ambrose, Saint, excellent (but rationalistic) sentiment of, 76.

"American Citizen," new compost so called, 131.

American Eagle, a source of inspiration, 84—hitherto wrongly classed, 89—long bill of, *ib.*

Amos, cited, 76.

Anakim, that they formerly existed, shown, 144.

Angels, providentially speak French, 64—conjectured to be skilled in all tongues, *ib.*

Anglo-Saxondom, its idea, what, 63.

Anglo-Saxon mask, 63.

Anglo-Saxon race, 61.

Anglo-Saxon verse, by whom carried to perfection, 57.

Antonius, a speech of, 81—by whom best reported, *ib.*

Apocalypse, beast in, magnetic to theologians, 116.

Apollo, confessed mortal by his own oracle, 116.

Apollyon, his tragedies popular, 107.

Appian, an Alexandrian, not equal to Shakspeare as an orator, 81.

Ararat, ignorance of foreign tongues is an, 90.

Arcadian background, 133.

Aristophanes, 75.

Arms, profession of, once esteemed especially that of gentlemen, 56.

Arnold, 82.

Ashland, 133.

Astor, Jacob, a rich man, 122.

Astræa, nineteenth century forsaken by, 130.

Athenians, ancient, an institution of, 82.

Atherton, Senator, envies the loon, 97.

Aye-Aye, the, an African animal, America supposed to be settled by, 66.

B.

Babel, probably the first Congress, 90—a gabble-mill, *ib.*

Baby, a low-priced one, 125.

Bagowind, Hon. Mr., whether to be damned, 99.

Baldwin apples, 144.

Baratarias, real or imaginary, which most pleasant, 129.

Barnum, a great natural curiosity recommended to, 87.

Monarch, a pagan, probably not favored in philosophical experiments, 57.

Money-trees desirable, 127—that they once existed shown to be variously probable, 128.

Montaigne, a communicative old Gascon, 109.

Monterey, battle of, its singular chromatic effect on a species of two-headed eagle, 88.

Moses held up vainly as an example, 102—construed by Joe Smith, *ib.*

Myths, how to interpret readily, 117.

N.

Naboths, Popish ones, how distinguished, 66.

Nation, rights of, proportionate to size, 63.

National pudding, its effect on the organs of speech, a curious physiological fact, 66.

Nephelim, not yet extinct, 144.

New England overpoweringly honored, 87—wants no more speakers, *ib.*—done brown by whom, *ib.*—her experience in beans beyond Cicero's, 117.

Newspaper, the, wonderful, 106— a strolling theatre, *ib.*—thoughts suggested by tearing wrapper of, 107—a vacant sheet, *ib.*—a sheet in which a vision was let down, 108—wrapper to a bar of soap, *ib.*—a cheap impromptu platter, *ib.*

New York, Letters from, commended, 111.

Next life, what, 101.

Niggers, 52—area of abusing, extended, 85—Mr. Sawin's opinions of, 138.

Ninepence a day low for murder, 59.

No, a monosyllable, 66—hard to utter, *ib.*

Noah, inclosed letter in bottle, probably, 110.

Nornas, Lapland, what, 129.

North, has no business, 95— bristling, crowded off roost, 114.

North Bend, geese inhumanly treated at, 115—mentioned, 133.

North star, a proposition to indict, 98.

O.

Off ox, 113.

Officers, miraculous transformation in character of, 63—Anglo-Saxon, come very near being anathematized, *ib.*

O'Phace, Increase D., Esq., speech of, 81.

Oracle of Fools, still respectfully consulted, 81.

Orion, becomes commonplace, 108.

Orrery, Lord, his letters (lord!), 111.

Ostracism, curious species of, 82.

P.

Palestine, 64.

Palfrey, Hon. J. G. (a worthy representative of Massachusetts), 82, 87, 88.

Pantagruel recommends a popular oracle, 81.

160

Panurge, his interview with
Goatsnose, 117.
Papists, female, slain by zealous
Protestant bomb-shell, 131.
Paralipomenon, a man suspected
of being, 116.
Paris, liberal principles safe as
far away as, 103.
Parliamentum Indoctorum
sitting in permanence, 81.
Past, the, a good nurse, 93.
Patience, sister, quoted, 61.
Paynims, their throats
propagandistically cut, 64.
Penelope, her wise choice, 74.
People, soft enough, 104—want
correct ideas, 125.
Pepin, King, 111.
Periwig, 114.
Persius, a pithy saying of, 86,
note.
Pescara, Marquis, saying of, 56.
Peter, Saint, a letter of
(*post-mortem*), 111.
Pharisees, opprobriously referred
to, 103.
Philippe, Louis, in pea-jacket, 106.
Phegyas quoted, 99.
Phrygian language, whether
Adam spoke it, 57.
Pilgrims, the, 84.
Pillows, constitutional, 56.
Pinto, Mr., some letters of his
commended, 111.
Pisgah, an impromptu one, 129.
Platform, party, a convenient one,
125.
Plato, supped with, 110—his man,
115.
Pleiades, the, not enough
esteemed, 108.
Pliny, his letters not admired, 111.
Plotinus, a story of, 93.

Plymouth Rock, Old, a Convention
wrecked on, 84.
Point Tribulation, Mr. Sawin
wrecked on, 127.
Poles, exile, whether crop of beans
depends on, 62, *note.*
Polk, President, synonymous with
our country, 72—censured,
84—in danger of being
crushed, 86.
Polka, Mexican, 65.
Pomp, a runaway slave, his nest,
139—hypocritically groans like
white man, *ib.*—blind to
Christian privileges, *ib.*—his
society valued at fifty dollars,
ib.—his treachery, 140—takes
Mr. Sawin prisoner, *ib.*—cruelly
makes him work, *ib.*—puts
himself illegally under his
tuition, *ib.*—dismisses him
with contumelious epithets, 141.
Pontifical bull, a tamed one, 64.
Pope, his verse excellent, 57.
Pork, refractory in boiling, 63.
Portugal, Alphonso the Sixth of,
a monster, 142.
Post, Boston, 74—shaken visibly,
76—bad guide-post, *ib.*—too
swift, *ib.*—edited by a colonel,
ib.—who is presumed officially
in Mexico, *ib.*—referred to, 89.
Pot-hooks, death in, 118.
Preacher, an ornamental symbol,
101—a breeder of dogmas, *ib.*—
earnestness of, important, 142.
Present, considered as an annalist,
102—not long wonderful, 108.
President, slaveholding natural
to, 105—must be a Southern
resident, 125—must own a
nigger, *ib.*
Principle, exposure spoils it, 83.

Trees, various kinds of extraordinary ones, 127, 128.
Trowbridge, William, mariner, adventure of, 65.
Truth and falsehood start from same point, 69—truth invulnerable to satire, *ib.*—compared to a river, 81—of fiction sometimes truer than fact, *ib.*—told plainly, *passim.*
Tuileries, exciting scene at, 88.
Tully, a saying of, 83, *note.*
Tweedledee, gospel according to, 103.
Tweedledum, great principles of, 103.

U.

Ulysses, husband of Penelope, 74 —borrows money, 129. (For full particulars of, see Homer and Dante.)
University, triennial catalogue of, 77.

V.

Van Buren fails of gaining Mr. Sawin's confidence, 138—his son John reproved, *ib.*
Van, Old, plan to set up, 138.
Venetians, invented something once, 129.
Vices, cardinal, sacred conclave of, 66.
Victoria, Queen, her natural terror, 88.
Virgin, the, letter of, to Magistrates of Messina, 111.
Vratz, Captain, a Pomeranian, singular views of, 56.

W.

Walpole, Horace, classed, 109— his letters praised, 111.
Waltham Plain, Cornwallis at, 59.
Walton, punctilious in his intercourse with fishes, 66.
War, abstract, horrid, 113—its hoppers, grist of, what, 123.
Warton, Thomas, a story of, 78.
Washington, charge brought against, 135.
Washington, city of, climatic influence of, on coats, 84— mentioned, 93—grand jury of, 98.
Washingtons, two hatched at a time by improved machine, 135.
Water, Taunton, proverbially weak, 138.
Water-trees, 128.
Webster, some sentiments of, commended by Mr. Sawin, 137.
Westcott, Mr., his horror, 97.
Whig party, has a large throat, 76 —but query as to swallowing spurs, 137.
White-house, 114.
Wife-trees, 128.
Wilbur, Rev. Homer, A. M., consulted, 49—his instructions to his flock, 58—a proposition of his for Protestant bombshells, 65—his elbow nudged, 68—his notions of satire, 69—some opinions of his quoted with apparent approval by Mr. Biglow, 72—geographical speculations of, 73—a justice of the peace, *ib.*—a letter of, 74— a Latin pun of, *ib.*—runs against a post without injury, 76—does not seek notoriety (whatever some malignants may affirm),

Wilbur, Rev. Homer, A.M., (cont'd.)
77—fits youths for college,
ib.—a chaplain during late war
with England, 79—a shrewd
observation of, 82—some
curious speculations of, 90–92
—his martello-tower, 90—
forgets he is not in pulpit, 98,
119–120—extracts from sermon
of, 101, 106—interested in John
Smith, 109—his views
concerning present state of
letters, 109–111—a stratagem
of, 115—ventures two hundred
and fourth interpretation of
Beast in Apocalypse, 116—
christens Hon. B. Sawin, then
an infant, 119—an addition to
our *sylva* proposed by, 127—
curious and instructive
adventure of, 129—his account
with an unnatural uncle, 131—
his uncomfortable imagination,
ib.—speculations concerning
Cincinnatus, 133—confesses
digressive tendency of mind,
141—goes to work on sermon

(not without fear that his
readers will dub him with a
reproachful epithet like that
with which Isaac Allerton, a
Mayflower man, revenges
himself on a delinquent debtor
of his, calling him in his will,
and thus holding him up to
posterity, as "John Peterson,
The Bore"), 144.
Wilbur, Mrs., an invariable rule of,
77—her profile, 78.
Wildbore, a vernacular one, how
to escape, 90.
Wind, the, a good Samaritan, 119.
Wooden leg, remarkable for
sobriety, 121—never eats
pudding, *ib.*
Wright, Colonel, providentially
rescued, 62.
Wrong, abstract, safe to oppose, 85.

Z.

Zack, Old, 136.

THE END.

Annotations

Annotations

Sir Leslie Stephen, convinced by the literary worth of *The Biglow
Papers*, thought it not unlikely that English students would encounter on examination papers such questions as "What was that
'darned proviso matter' about which a distinguished candidate
'never had a grain of doubt?' Who was 'Davis of Miss.?' and why
was he likely to place the perfection of bliss in 'skinning that same
old coon?' What was the plan which 'chipped the shell at Buffalo
of setting up old Van?' " With such young men Sir Leslie could
sympathize; he remembered when he had first read Lowell's book
twenty-five years before:

> Upon these and numberless other difficulties, some of which,
> it may be added, still remain buried for us in the profoundest
> night, we could only look in the spirit which causes a youthful
> candidate to twist his hair into knots, and vaguely interrogate
> universal space in hopes of an answer.[1]

Lowell was aware of the "difficulties" inherent to political satire,
and he knew his own work was not excepted. Writing in 1890 to
H. E. Scudder, the Houghton Mifflin editor helping him prepare the
"Riverside Edition" of his works, Lowell asked to see Frank Beverly
Williams, the man Scudder had suggested doing "illustrative notes"
for *The Biglow Papers* in the collected edition, and spoke specifically
about the nature of the annotations he thought necessary:

> I am not feeling very well this evening, or I would look over
> the Biglow Papers to get a notion of what I think is needed. Of
> course there needs nothing very elaborate, but there are allu-
> sions to utterly extinct speeches & the like, which I now can't
> understand myself. It is this kind of thing I should wish to have
> looked up & briefly elucidated.[2]

1. "Mr Lowell's Poems," *Cornhill Magazine* 31 (January 1875): 65.
2. 4 February 1890: A.L.s., Middlebury College Library, Middlebury,
Vermont. Quoted by permission.

The notes written by Williams for the "Riverside Edition"—brief explanations of the political and topical backgrounds of the papers —are of interest because of Lowell's approval; but the great number of errors and the unevenness of their worth as a literary aid suggest, not surprisingly when we remember his failing health, that Lowell gave his approval without having carefully examined the notes. The present editor has therefore decided to regard Williams's notes like any nonauthorial commentary on The Biglow Papers, to use them when helpful, but not to be restricted by their idiosyncrasies and point of view. They are available in most collected editions of Lowell's works.[3]

What Williams's notes did not do, and what Lowell did not ask to be done, were to translate the Latin and Greek and identify or explain literary and historical allusions, those eccentricities which for N. P. Willis, and perhaps the majority of readers since, smothered what was good in the book.[4] The inaccessibility of much of Parson Wilbur's wisdom and humor to a century increasingly ignorant of its past has undoubtedly been the greatest barrier to a wider acquaintance with the book in our times. But this need be no real problem.

The annotations that follow are admittedly more elaborate than Lowell would have thought desirable or necessary. They have been written, however, not to lead the reader away from the text, but rather to enable it to be read with increased understanding and enjoyment. Lowell's wide reading and scholarship were unusual even in the nineteenth century; they are hardly to be found today. While annotation is not provided for information readily available in standard desk dictionaries (I have consulted Funk & Wagnalls's Standard College Dictionary and The American Heritage Dictionary of the English Language), or for what seems to be common knowledge even in these times of extraordinary cultural transmutation, my aim otherwise has been completeness. If my zeal towards achiev-

3. When quoted below, the page reference is to the "Riverside Edition" of The Writings of James Russell Lowell in Ten Volumes (Boston and New York: Houghton, Mifflin and Co., 1890), vol. 8.

4. Hurry-Graphs; or, Sketches of Scenery, Celebrities and Society, Taken from Life (New York: Charles Scribner, 1851), p. 48.

ing this goal seems to some excessive, I can only hope that the position of the annotations separate from the text will to some degree assuage those readers' annoyance. I have been reluctant to explain Wilbur's jokes, and I have presumed some ingenuity on the readers' part in transcribing Hosea's dialect spelling into standard English orthography, should that be necessary.

Translations, unless otherwise noted, are by the editor. Editions of works cited are usually dated before 1848, though there are only a few instances where I can be certain that these were the ones Lowell read. It is perhaps unnecessary to point out that Lowell picked up many quotations and allusions at second hand: authorities quoted in footnotes of Pierre Bayle's *Dictionary*, "familiar quotations" of Latin authors printed in schoolbooks, and so forth. When I have known this to be the case, I have indicated it in the annotations. A useful, but unfortunately limited, source for identifying Lowell's quotations are two of his commonplace books in the Houghton Library, Harvard University. Quotations from these books in the annotations refer to

Commonplace Book I: "Index Rerum," entries dated 1836–1840, bMS Am 765 (954);
Commonplace Book II: Notebook dated by Lowell, 1 January 1848, bMS Am 765 (951).

George P. Clark's dissertation, "Classical Influences and Background in the Writings of James Russell Lowell" (Yale University, 1948); William James De Saegher's dissertation, "James Russell Lowell and the Bible" (University of California, Los Angeles, 1964); Arthur W. M. Voss's dissertation, "A Study of *The Biglow Papers* by James Russell Lowell" (Yale University, 1941), and his "Backgrounds of Lowell's Satire in 'The Biglow Papers,'" *New England Quarterly* 23 (March 1950): 47–64; as well as the notes by Frank Beverly Williams have been helpful both for their good sense and worthy scholarship. Professor Leo M. Kaiser kindly answered questions about several of the Latin quotations. The editor acknowledges especially Josiah Quincy Bennett and Anthony W. Shipps who were ever ready to help him when his knowledge and imagination failed.

4.1   Aristarchus, "whose looks . . . to a boy": Christopher
Marlowe, *Edward II* 5.4.55. Aristarchus of
Samothrace (c. 220–143 B.C.) was a celebrated
Greek grammarian, schoolmaster, and editor.

4.3   pancratic: "Fully disciplined or exercised in mind,
having a universal mastery of accomplishments"
(*Oxford English Dictionary;* hereafter cited *OED*).

4.3   pantechnic: "Comprehending all the arts" (*OED*).

4.7   Hameliners: Hameln, Germany, the location of
the legend of the Pied Piper, for a long time dated
its public documents from the event, believed to
have taken place in the thirteenth century.

4.17   *cymbula sutilis:* Cf. Virgil, *Aeneid* 6.413–14:
"gemuit sub pondere cymba / sutilis et multam
accepit rimosa paludem": (describing Aeneas
boarding Charon's boat) "the boat made of skins
stitched together groaned under the burden and
let in much water through its seams." Wilbur's
frequent use of "perverted quotations" (quotations
wrenched from their contexts for purposes of
humor) is generally not noted by the editor.

4.18–19   to carry . . . in her mouth: To make the water foam
at the cutwater; thus to make good speed.

5.20   Vallumbrozer: See Milton, *Paradise Lost* 1.302–3:
"Thick as Autumnal Leaves that strow the Brooks /
In *Vallombrosa.*" Vallombrosa is a summer resort
in Tuscany, Italy.

5.25   *Oldfogrumville:* See 24.31n.

6.21   *credite, posteri!:* "Believe me, posterity!" Horace,
Odes 2.19.2.

6.26   French "Revolution": The revolution of February
1848.

6.27   Bungtown coppers were "worthless copper coins" (Richard H. Thornton, *An American Glossary*, 2 vols., Philadelphia: J. B. Lippincott Co., 1912).

6.31–32   mace of Richard ... scymitar of Saladin: See 64.12n.

8.5–6   "highest heaven of invention": Cf. Shakespeare, *King Henry V* Prologue. 1–2: "O, for a Muse of fire, that would ascend / The brightest heaven of invention."

8.27   Caleb Cushing (1800–1879), Massachusetts lawyer and politician, left the Whig party early in the 1840s because of his opposition to Clay's control of that party. He became an ardent supporter of territorial expansion and President Polk's policy in the Mexican War. See 57.6n.

8.31   Speech is silver: silence is golden: This masterful parody of Thomas Carlyle begins with a quotation from Carlyle's Golden Gospel of Silence, *Sartor Resartus* bk. 3, chap. 3: "As the Swiss Inscription says: *Sprechen ist silbern, Schweigen ist golden* (Speech is silvern, Silence is golden); or as I might rather express it: Speech is of Time, Silence is of Eternity."

9.8   Thersites: A mythological Greek soldier noted for ugliness, cowardice, and hateful, ridiculing language.

9.17   Zingali: Or *zingari*, "gypsies" (Italian).

9.31   Melesigenes: A name given to the blind Greek poet Homer, who some ancients believed was born on the banks of the Meles River in Asia Minor.

9.32   caliginose: Or "caliginous," dim, obscure.

9.32   nephelegeretous: Apparently Lowell's coinage from the Greek noun νεφεληγερέτα, cloud-gatherer.

10.7   wingless (and even featherless) biped: See
             110.5n.

10.11   Nemean lion: In the first of Hercules' twelve labors
             he crushed to death the monstrous lion of Nemea.

10.15   Remus-spring: Romulus ordered Remus killed for
             having ridiculed the newly-built wall of Rome by
             jumping over it.

10.21   Xantippes: Xanthippe was the ill-humored wife of
             the ancient Greek philosopher Socrates; a proverbial
             scold.

11.7   Johann Christoph Gottsched (1700–1766),
             German critic, philologist, and dramatist whose
             insistence on neoclassical rules of composition
             made his name proverbial for pedantry.

13.3   crooknecks: Milledge B. Seigler suggests that
             "crooknecks," as referred to here, are not ordinary
             squashes, but gourd powder flasks commonly used
             during the revolutionary war, and that a queen's
             arm "was probably the regulation arm issued to the
             British infantry and known as 'Brown Bess'"
             (*Explicator*, vol. 8, November 1949, item 14).

14.15–17.31   The following translation of "Mr. Wilbur's Studies
             in Entomology," reprinted here with minor
             corrections by the editor, is by Vernon Purinton
             Squires and George St. John Perrott, and was first
             published in *Quarterly Journal of the University of
             North Dakota* 3 (October 1912): 51–56. Professors
             Squires and Perrott prefaced their translation with
             the admission: "It must be confessed that much
             of the fun vanishes when the odd Latin sentences
             are Englished, but enough remains to give us a
             peep at the merry mind and happy good humor of
             one of our greatest countrymen" (p. 52).

Quite a number having declared that they will
be purchasers of the book, George Nichols of
Cambridge will publish a work about an important
but hitherto neglected department of natural
history with the following title, namely:
    An Attempt at a Somewhat More Perfect
Account of the Buzzing Beetle, Commonly called
HUMBUG, by HOMER WILBUR, Master of Arts,
President of the Natural History Society of
Jaalam (also Secretary and Fellow—the only
one, alas!) and perchance a future Fellow of
many other learned (or unlearned) societies
both at home and abroad.

INTRODUCTION

TO THE GENTLE READER:

Before I had left college, having carefully
investigated the various entomological systems,
which have been very painstakingly worked out
by men most deeply versed in this science, I
could not help perceiving with regret that,
though otherwise most worthy of praise, they all
made an omission of great importance. Then
being led by some impulse from above or
captivated by the charm of the work, I (like
another Curtius[1]) solemnly devoted myself to
filling up the gap. Nor did I relinquish the task
thus imposed by Fate until I had completed a
little pamphlet somewhat inelegantly couched in
the vernacular. Then puffed up with boyish
enthusiasm and never having plumbed the
depths of the folly of booksellers (to say nothing
of the "Reading Public"), I thought I had
composed something which men would (so to
speak) swallow like hot cakes. But when I had
submitted my manuscript to one publisher after

another, and was returned to my study with
nothing more substantial than an emphatic *No,*
a great horror and pity for the Lambertian[2]
dullness implanted by the wrath of the gods in
the skulls of fellows of this stripe seized me.
Forthwith I determined to publish the book at my
own expense, having no doubt at all that the
"World of Science" (as the saying is) would
amply fill my purse. However, I reaped no crop
from my poor little field except the empty
satisfaction of deserving well of the Republic.
This precious bread of mine having thus been
cast on the turbid literary waters, befouled as it
were by the touch of the Harpies (namely those
rascally booksellers mentioned above) returned
home to me in a few days. And then when I could
not myself live on such food, it occurred to me
for the first time that the baker (that is to say, the
printer) would nevertheless have to be paid.
Yet I did not on this account lose heart; but, just
as little boys hold their little boats in hand by a
string (in order that when drifting from their
proper course they may draw them back to the
bank), with firm purpose I recalled from its
quest of the golden fleece my paper Argo trailing
in the waves, I myself rather having been the
one to be shorn and skinned. To change the
metaphor, I drew back my boomerang which was
going wide of its mark until, occasion serving,
I might hurl it with greater force. But while I was
brooding over these plans, and trusting, like
Saturn, the famous child-eater, to subsist on the
offspring of my brains, I was overtaken by a
pitiable though not unheard of misfortune. For
just as they say the Scythians, because of their
piety and parsimony devoured their dead
parents, so this, my first-born son, more cruel

than the Scythians, attempted to swallow me,
although alive and kicking. However, I did not on
this account disinherit my hungry child. Indeed
I rather regarded this hunger of his as a sign of
virility and strength, and sought food for
satisfying it, keeping, however, my own hide
whole. And as I perceived that money was the
only suitable thing for his gushing gastric juice
to digest, I looked around to see where I might
easiest raise a loan. Under these circumstances,
I got my uncle, John Doolittle, Esq., to supply the
necessary money so that there might be no need
of my leaving the university before taking the
bachelor's degree. Then wishing to protect the
interests of my generous benefactor, I assigned
to my aforesaid uncle all the copies of the first
edition of my work as yet unsold together with
the privilege of printing and publishing the same
for ever. From that day marked with a black
stone, insistent and ever increasing family cares
constantly assailed me to such an extent that I
never could free that precious pledge from the
brazen chains.

After the recent death of my uncle, when
among the other relatives I went to hear the
reading of the will, my eager ears were greeted by
these words: "Since I am convinced that my
beloved nephew Homer by long and intimate
acquaintance with poverty is a most suitable
person to guard riches and to use generously and
prudently what the gods have intrusted to him,
—therefore, moved by these ideas and because of
my great affection for him, I give and bequeath
to my dear nephew aforesaid these possessions of
mine, all and singular, not to be weighed or
counted, which follow, to-wit: five hundred books
which the said Homer pledged to me in the year

of grace 1792, with the privilege of publishing
and reprinting this scientific work of his (as they
call it) if he so choose. Nevertheless, dear God,
I pray thee to open the eyes of my nephew Homer
and move him so that he will hide away these
books of his in the library of one of his many
castles in Spain."

When I had heard these hardly credible words,
my heart leaped in my bosom. Then, since the
pamphlet written in English had disappointed
the hope of its author, and since on account of
the din of party strife the study of natural history
is at low ebb in our republic, I determined to put
out a Latin edition. I was also led to this decision
because I do not know what is the good of
academic training and two diplomas unless they
make us skilled in the dead languages (and
damned, too, as that rascal, William Cobbett,[3]
used to say).

But all of the first edition is in my hands still,
and I retain it as the rattle on which I used to cut
my eye teeth.

A SPECIMEN OF THE WORK

(*According to the example set by Johannes
Physiophilus in his specimen of Monkology.*)

HUMBUG No. 12. *Military*, WILBUR. *Butcher*,
JABLONSKY.[4] *Accursed*, DESFONT.[5]

[Fabricius[6] inappropriately calls this species
the cyclops which is distinguished by an eye
single to its own interest. Isaac Noman more
happily maintains that there is no distinction
between the military humbug and the devil bug
(see Fabricius, 152).]

It inhabits the southern states of America.

Gorgeous with gold stripes; very often,
however, dirty, as one wont to frequent butcher

shops, attracted by the smell of blood. He likes to
sun himself astride the fence, and cannot be
dislodged from his perch without great trouble.
His popular name is *Candidate*. His head displays
a crest as of plumes. For his food he cleverly
milks the public cow; his paunch is enormous;
his power of suction is hard to estimate. Lazy,
fatuous; fierce nevertheless and always ready to
fight. He creeps like a snake.

Although I have frequently dissected his
brains with the greatest care, I have never been
able to detect even that rudiment of a brain
common to almost all insects.

Concerning this military humbug, I have
noted one peculiar fact; namely, that this bug
uses slaves from Guinea (see Fabricius, 143)
and is therefore held by many in very great
respect as showing marks of almost human
intelligence.

HUMBUG No. 24. *Critical*, WILBUR. *Zoilean*,[7]
FABRICIUS. *Pigmean*, CARLSEN.

[Johannes Stryx very foolishly confuses this
species with the pointed bug (see Fabricius, nos.
64–109). But although I have submitted as
many specimens as possible to microscopic
examination, I have never found a single one
showing indications of any point whatever.]

Exceedingly fearful and when pursued hides
itself in the nearest anonymous chink frequently
crying out, *we, we*. Foolish, lazy.

He lives everywhere in the world where it is
dry; making his nest by tireless boring. As for his
food, he lives on books: selecting especially dry
ones, and by chance sinking

NOTES: 1. One Roman legend claims that
Curtius, fully armed and on horseback, leaped
into a wide gap which had opened in the Forum

and into which Rome was to throw her most prized possession. The self-sacrifice of this brave young citizen caused the chasm to close; 2. Daniel Lambert (1770–1809) was a famous English fat man whose name became proverbial for immensity; 3. William Cobbett (1763–1835) was an English writer and political radical who in his youth attacked democracy, but in later years attacked the idea of any government and urged radical reforms; 4. Karl Gustave Jablonski (1756–1787) was a Prussian entomologist who, like the names that follow, is represented as having also distinguished the species by giving it a name; 5. René Louiche Desfontaines (1750–1833) was a French botanist; 6. Johann Christian Fabricius (1745–1808) was a Danish entomologist; 7. Zoilus was a carping third century B.C. Greek critic.

21.1   *MELIBŒUS-HIPPONAX:* Meliboeus is a shepherd in Virgil's *Eclogues*. His name suggests not only the pastoral nature of Virgil's poems but also the fact of political oppression, since Meliboeus is introduced in the first eclogue as being driven from his farm by a tyrannical Roman government. Hipponax, the Greek poet (sixth century B.C.), was considered by the ancients a master of satirical verse and the inventor of parody. Of all the Greek satirists, he is reputed the most bitter and biting. Only fragments of his verse have survived. By coupling the two names, Wilbur announces both the pastoral and satiric qualities of his and his young parishioner's production.

21.14   Francis Quarles (1592–1644), the English poet, published the *Emblems* in 1635.

21.15   Margaritas, munde porcine . . . en, siliquas accipe:

"O, swinish world, you have trampled pearls; so, take the husks." *Jacobus Caroli Filius ad Publicum Legentem:* James (Russell Lowell) the son of Charles (Lowell) to the Reading Public. See Lowell's letter to Mrs. Horace Mann, quoted in "Introduction," p. xiv, above: "This much by way of apology (since you have expressed an interest in me) for my apparent deviation to preaching instead of singing, & for my seeming to prefer the husks of Hosea Biglow to more ambrosial diet. But I assure you that Mr Biglow has a thousand readers for my one...."

23.10–11   *S. Archæol. Dahom.... et Scient. Kamtschat.:* Englished, these fictitious societies are the Archeological Society of Dahomey and the Academy of Literature and Science of Kamchatka.

23.18   Socrates: The celebrated Greek philosopher was sentenced to drink hemlock after being found guilty of "impiety" and the corruption of youth by a jury of Athenian citizens.

23.22   John Locke's *An Essay Concerning Human Understanding* was first published in 1690. To the title page of the second edition (1694) was added: "Written by John Locke, Gent."

24.2   triennial catalogue: Wilbur's *alma mater* must have followed the practice initiated by President Leonard Hoar, Harvard College, in 1674, of issuing triennially a catalogue of the graduates of the college, printed in Latin with the names of publicly distinguished graduates in capital letters.

24.31   *Fogrum:* Or fogram, "an antiquated or old-fashioned person, a fogy" (*OED*).

25.5–11   TO ALL EDITORS OF ACADEMIC CATALOGUES THROUGHOUT THE WORLD. Not in the least asking

for a diploma from your famous academy, which
should be honored most zealously by men, but only
that you might know how much glory my name
will bring to your catalogue in the future (the
diploma perhaps having been granted), I add for
that reason all honorary titles, not so much hoped
for as probable.   *₊* *Distinguished by large letters
as President of the Jaalam Society of Natural
History.*

27.15   Samuels: Perhaps the association arises in
Wilbur's mind from the fact that Hannah, having
long desired a son before the Lord granted her
wish, dedicated her child Samuel to His service in
thanksgiving (see I Samuel 1.1–28). Or perhaps
Wilbur considers his sermons characterized by that
gift of prophecy granted to Samuel in a time when
few were called (see I Samuel 3.1).

28.12   Alexander Pope (1688–1744) and Oliver Goldsmith
(1728–1774) were eighteenth-century English
writers who respected the neoclassical rules of
poetic composition.

28.23   tire: Obsolete variant of "tier."

28.27   Daughter of Danaus: According to Greek
mythology, the daughters of Danaus, who at their
father's command had murdered their husbands,
were condemned to fetch water eternally in leaky,
sieve-like jars in the Underworld. The allusion
becomes a pun when it is noted that Lowell's two
schoolmistresses before attending the school kept
by William Wells were both named Dana: Miss
Mary Dana and Sophia Dana, later Mrs. George
Ripley. See Ethel Golann, "A Lowell Autobiography,"
New England Quarterly 7 (June 1934): 358.

30.5   the prophet's carpet: See Acts 10.11–12: Peter "saw

heaven opened, and a certain vessel descending
unto him, as it had been a great sheet knit at the
four corners, and let down to the earth: Wherein
were all manner of four-footed beasts of the earth,
and wild beasts, and creeping things, and fowls
of the air."

30.31   Argus: Not only Odysseus's faithful hound (see
The Odyssey 17.292), but the name of a
Newfoundland dog owned by Lowell in his youth.

31.6   Old Joe: In "Memories of a Hundred Years,"
Edward Everett Hale, a boyhood acquaintance of
Lowell, recalled his friend having cross-questioned
an old white-headed "negro who remembered Earl
Percy's march from Cambridge Bridge to
Lexington" (*Outlook* 72, 4 October 1902: 312).

31.6   Hugh Percy, Duke of Northumberland (1742–
1817), an officer of British forces in the American
colonies in 1775–1777, participated in the Battle of
Lexington and Concord on 19 April 1775 by
leading reinforcements to the aid of the retreating
British.

31.25   *Gratulatio:* Harvard dedicated to the English king
in honor of his accession a collection of Latin,
Greek, and English verses written by students and
graduates of the college, *Pietas et Gratulatio*
(Boston, 1761). In a copy of the 1867 "Large
Paper" edition of the first series of *The Biglow
Papers* presented to Thomas Bailey Aldrich (now
in the Houghton Library, Harvard University),
Lowell has here added a footnote: "Fact. 'Twas my
grandfather, & very bad verses they were!" The
verses by Judge John Lowell (1743–1802) are
printed in English on pages 20–24 of the Harvard
volume.

31.32	Willard's clocks: Simon Willard (1753–1848) was a well-known clockmaker in Roxbury, Massachusetts.
31.35	sweet-water: "A variety of white grape, of specially sweet flavour" (*OED*).
32.14	pagan: The Latin adjective *paganus* meant originally "of the country or village, rustic."
32.23–24	John Gay (1685–1732) and Matthew Prior (1664–1721) were English neoclassical poets, understandably favorites of Wilbur.
33.14	noonin': "A rest or repose at noon" (*OED*).
37.32	their harmless rigs: *"To run a* (or *the*) *rig, to run* (one's) *rigs*, to play pranks, to run riot" (*OED*).
38.28	*Obsta principiis:* "Resist the beginnings." Cf. Ovid, *The Cures for Love*, line 91.
39.10	Hagar, Sarah's Egyptian bondmaid, was the mother of Abraham's son Ishmael. After the birth of Isaac to Sarah and Abraham, Hagar and Ishmael were sent into the wilderness (see Genesis 16–21).
39.11–12	to found a democracy: Lowell in middle age would not agree with this popular nineteenth-century notion expressed by Wilbur. While noting in "New England Two Centuries Ago" (1865), that "Puritanism . . . laid, without knowing it, the egg of democracy," he is careful to emphasize that the early New Englanders' "idea was not to found a democracy . . . as gentlemen seem to think whose notions of history and human nature rise like an exhalation from the good things at a Pilgrim Society dinner" (*Writings*, 2:3, 12–13).
39.14	thirty-seventhly: Wilbur must be referring to the early New Englanders' patience to listen to the

reading of the names of "the Thirty," David's
Warriors, listed in II Samuel 23.24–39. The list
actually includes thirty-two names, but the total
given at the end is "thirty and seven in all."

39.19   *storge:* "Natural affection; usually, that of parents
for their offspring" (*OED*).

39.20   lotus: After eating the fruit of this plant in the land
of the Lotus-eaters, the comrades of Odysseus lost
all desire to return to their island home, Ithaca (see
The Odyssey 9.94–97).

39.23   burn their ship: By thus destroying the means of
retreat generals both in the Classical Age (e.g.,
Agathocles, the tyrant of Syracuse) and more
recent times (Cortes in Mexico) promoted and
strengthened the courage of their armies.

40.7   ποῦ στῶ : "Where I may stand" or the basis from
which to work. This phrase is attributed to the
Greek mathematician and physicist, Archimedes,
who said he could move the world given an adequate
fulcrum or leverage ground. See Pappus of
Alexandria, *Collection,* ed. F. Hultsch, 3 vols.
(Berlin, 1875–1878), bk. 8, proposition 11.

40.13   *Græculus esuriens:* Juvenal, *Satires* 3.78:
Græculus esuriens, in cœlum, jusseris, ibit: "Tell
a hungry Greek to go to heaven,—he will go."

40.15   Juan Fernandez: On an island of this group in the
Pacific Ocean, Alexander Selkirk was stranded
from 1704 to 1709, suggesting to Daniel Defoe the
story of *Robinson Crusoe* (London, 1719).

40.16–17   *In cœlum, jusseris, ibit:* See 40.13n.

40.22–23   Fulke Greville ... and Browne: Illustrious English
writers active during the century following the
coronation of Elizabeth I. Browne could be either

William (1591–1643) or, more probably, Sir Thomas (1605–1682).

40.25   Naseby, Marston Moor, Worcester: Locations of important battles of the English Civil War (1645, 1644, 1651); in each the royalist forces lost.

42.13–14   *"Quem recitas, meus . . . incipit esse tuus":* "That book you recite, Fidentinus, is mine; but your garbled recitation begins to make it your own." Martial, *Epigrams* 1.38.

42.33–43.11   "Neow is the . . . . uv a loot": *Richard III* 1.1.1–13.

43.19   Doyle: William M. S. Doyle (1769–1828), a Boston portrait painter and silhouettist.

43.32–33   Plotinus and Agesilaus: See Porphyry's *On the Life of Plotinus* 1.5–6, and Plutarch's life of the Spartan king, *Agesilaus* 2.2.

43.33–44.1   modern instances: Like the classical examples, these names are found in a note to the article on Scioppius in Pierre Bayle's *Dictionary* (see *The Dictionary Historical and Critical of Mr Peter Bayle*, ed. Des Maizeaux, 5 vols., London, 1734–1738, 5: 97–98). Bayle claims that unlike the others listed, "it is not true that [Scioppius] would not suffer his picture to be drawn." Scioppius, or Kaspar Schoppe (1576–1649), was a German classical scholar and Roman Catholic controversialist; Palaeottus, or Gabriele Paleotti (1524–1597), an Italian cardinal and writer; Pinellus, or Giovanni-Vincenzo Pinelli (1535–1601), an Italian patron of letters and book collector; Velserus, or Markus Welser (1558–1614), a German historian, statesman, and merchant; and Thomas Gataker (1574–1654), an English Puritan divine, classical and biblical scholar.

44.2   Cromwell: See 44.4n.

44.3   Cæsar: See Suetonius, *The Lives of the Cæsars*
            1.45.

44.4   Lord Protector: Oliver Cromwell (1599–1658),
            Lord Protector of Great Britain, is reported to have
            said to Sir Peter Lely while sitting for this English
            portrait painter: "I desire you would use all your
            skill to paint my picture truly like me, and not
            flatter me at all; but remark all these roughnesses,
            pimples, warts, and every thing as you see me,
            otherwise I never will pay a farthing for it" (Horace
            Walpole's *Anecdotes of Painting in England . . .
            Collected by the Late Mr. George Vertue*, ed. James
            Dallaway, 5 vols., London, 1826–1828, 3:31–32).

44.7   Recording Angel: The popular notion of a heavenly
            scribe who records both the good and evil deeds
            of men, perhaps less known today than a century
            ago, was derived in the Christian religion primarily
            from the apocryphal Book of Enoch. See 72.17.

44.13   Augustin Ruiz: See Samuel Purchas, *Hakluytus
            Posthumus or Purchas His Pilgrimes,* 5 vols.
            (London, 1625–1626), 4:1561 (bk. 8, chap. 3, sec.
            2). Lowell's reference is to *Hakluyt's Collection of
            the Early Voyages, Travels, and Discoveries, of the
            English Nation. A New Edition, with Additions,* 5
            vols. (London: R. H. Evans, 1809–1812).

45.14–15   *fuste potius quam argumento erudiendi:* "Must be
            taught by the cudgel rather than by an argument."
            Unidentified; it is possible that this and the
            several other unidentified Latin quotations below
            are, like that on the title page, Lowell's work. If this
            is the case, Lowell may have had in mind Cicero,
            "Quid nunc te, asine, litteras doceam? Non opus est
            verbis, sed fustibus": "What, you ass! am I to teach

you your letters? For that I shall not need words, but a cudgel" (*Oration against Lucius Calpurnius Piso* 73).

45.20–21   Bilham Comit. Salop.: Bilham Comitatus (i.e., in the county of) Shropshire; the county real (in western England), the village fictitious.

45.32   familists: Members of the sixteenth and seventeenth century religious sect called the Family of Love, originating in Holland, but active in England and to a lesser extent in America. They held "that absolute obedience was due to all established governments, however tyrannical" (*OED*).

46.6   Rev. Moody Pyram: This name, like the others mentioned in Wilbur's genealogical studies, appears to be fictitious. The work of William Hubbard (1621–1704), Colonial historian, Lowell probably has in mind is *A General History of New England, from the Discovery to MDCLXXX*, published by the Massachusetts Historical Society in 1815; corrected edition, 1848.

49.4   Joseph T. Buckingham (1779–1861), a prominent liberal journalist, edited the Boston *Courier* from 1824 to 1848.

49.10   cruetin Sarjunt: When Congress declared war against Mexico on 13 May 1846, it authorized President Polk to call for 50,000 volunteers and appropriated $10 million to meet the costs of the war. On 26 May, Massachusetts governor George N. Briggs honored Polk's request of one regiment from the state, notwithstanding the objections of many Whigs and abolitionists opposed to the war. While at the time it might have seemed to Hosea that "Massachusetts, God forgive her, She's akneelin' with the rest," in fairness to the Bay State it should be mentioned that of the 14 representatives who opposed the declaration of war (as against 174 who favored it), she could claim 5. In the Senate John Davis of Massachusetts was one of the two senators who voted against the bill.

49.23   Day and Martin, English manufacturers of boot polish, advertised their product in verse. John Camden Hotten, probably on the authority of Sydney Gay, claims that "'always on hand, like *Day and Martin*'s blacking,' is a common simile" in the United States (*The Biglow Papers*, London: Hotten, 1859, p. 164).

49.24   full chizzle: Full chisel: "Strenuously; at full tilt" (Thornton, *An American Glossary*).

49.32   *Aut insanit, aut versos facit:* "He's either crazy, or making verses." Horace, *Satires* 2.7.117.

50.2   Simplex Mundishes: *Simplex munditiis,* "simple elegance." Horace, *Odes* 1.5.5.

54.5–6   Haint they sold . . . env'ys wiz?: "South Carolina, Louisiana, and several other Southern States at an early date passed acts to prevent free persons of color from entering their jurisdictions. These acts bore with particular severity upon colored seamen, who were imprisoned, fined, or whipped, and often sold into slavery. On the petition of the Massachusetts Legislature, Governor Briggs, in 1844, appointed Mr. Samuel Hoar agent to Charleston, and Mr. [Henry] Hubbard to New Orleans, to act on behalf of oppressed colored citizens of the Bay State. Mr. Hoar was expelled from South Carolina by order of the Legislature of that State, and Mr. Hubbard was forced by threats of violence to leave Louisiana. The obnoxious

acts remained in force until after the Civil War"
(Williams, p. 399).

54.30   go to work an' part: Though "propositions to secede
were not uncommon in New England at this time"
(Williams, p. 399), Hosea's sentiments are not
necessarily those of Lowell. At a New England
Anti-Slavery Convention in May 1844, Lowell and
Maria White opposed a resolution for disunion
which carried 250 to 24 (H. E. Scudder, *James
Russell Lowell*, 2 vols., Boston and New York:
Houghton, Mifflin and Co., 1901, 1:176). Ferris
Greenslet correctly concludes: "He was never in the
extreme left wing of the abolitionists . . ." (*The
Lowells and Their Seven Worlds*, Boston:
Houghton Mifflin Co., 1946, p. 253).

55.1–2   Man hed ough' . . . has noways jined: Cf. Matthew
19.6: "What therefore God hath joined together,
let not man put asunder."

55.6   Book of Job: 1.7 and 2.2; "that individual" is Satan.

55.8   Hugh Latimer (1485?–1555) was himself bishop
of Worcester from 1535 to 1539; nevertheless, as a
leader of the Reformation in England, Latimer
was continually opposed by bishops of papist
sympathies, and in 1555 he was declared a heretic
and burnt at the stake. He asked his London
congregation in his famous "Sermon of the Plough,"
18 January 1548: "who is the most diligentest
bishop and prelate in all England, that passeth all
the rest in doing his office? . . . I will tell you: it is
the devil" (*Sermons by Hugh Latimer*, ed. George
Elwes Corrie, Cambridge, England, 1844, p. 70).

55.10   Cainites: "A sect of heretics in the second century
[which] professed reverence for Cain and other
wicked Scriptural characters" (*OED*).

56.1   Fernando Francesco Davalos, Marquis of Pescara
        (1489–1525), Italian *condottiere* of Spanish origin.
        Cf. Matthew 6.24: "No man can serve two
        masters. . . ."

56.3   κατ' ἐξοχήν: Preeminently.

56.8   Captain Vratz: John Evelyn wrote in his *Diary* on
        10 March 1682: "This day was executed Coll. Vrats,
        and some of his accomplices, for the execrable
        murder of Mr. Thynn, set on by the principal
        Koningsmark; he went to execution like an
        undaunted hero, as one that had done a friendly
        office for that base coward C. Koningsmark. . . .
        Vrats told a friend of mine who accompanied him
        to yᵉ gallows, and gave him some advice, that he did
        not value dying of a rush, and hop'd and believ'd
        God would deale with him like a gentleman. Never
        man went so unconcern'd for his sad fate"
        (*Memoirs of John Evelyn*, ed. William Bray, 5 vols.,
        London, 1827, 3:64).

56.14–15 *Exemplo plus quam ratione vivimus:* "We live more
          by example than by reason." Proverbial.

57.6   THE MASSACHUSETTS REGIMENT: Although
        Governor Briggs ordered the recruitment of a
        regiment in May 1846, it was only after great
        difficulty in meeting the quota that the regiment
        was mustered into service in January 1847. Caleb
        Cushing of Newburyport accepted the command
        of the regiment; second in command was Isaac
        Hull Wright of Roxbury. A public rally was held at
        Faneuil Hall on 23 January 1847 for the regiment,
        with John A. Bolles and Robert Rantoul among
        the speakers. The regiment left for New Orleans the
        next month and by mid-April was stationed at
        Matamoras in Mexico. The Massachusetts regiment
        did march to Mexico City, but it seems never to

have been involved in battle. See Voss, "Backgrounds of Lowell's Satire in 'The Biglow Papers,'" p. 49n.

57.23   Sir Thomas Browne (1605–1682), English writer and physician. See his *Pseudodoxia Epidemica* (London, 1646), bk. 5, chap. 23.

57.26   Psammeticus: This Egyptian king ordered two children reared apart from the hearing of any language, believing the language they thus naturally spoke would indicate the oldest nation on earth. See Herodotus, *History* 2.2.

57.30   James the Fourth (1473–1513), king of Scotland. Lowell might have read of the "recent investigations" in the sixteenth-century *Chronicles of Scotland* by Robert Lindsay of Pitscottie: "The king also caused tak ane dumb voman, and pat her in Inchkeith, and gave hir tuo bairnes with hir, and gart furnisch hir in all necessares thingis perteaning to thair nourischment, desiring heirby to knaw quhat languages they had when they cam to the aige of perfyte speach. Some sayes they spak guid Hebrew, but I knaw not by authoris rehearse, etc." (2 vols., Edinburgh, 1814, 1:249–50).

58.6   *pro aris et focis:* "For altars and hearths," or, proverbially, "for hearth and home." Cicero, *On the Nature of Gods* 3.40.

58.20   *pongshong:* "Penchant," whose English pronunciation in the nineteenth century was closer to the modern French pronunciation than to the modern Anglicized pronunciation.

58.20–21 soshiashun of idees: Association of Ideas, the Lockean notion, though described as early as Plato, of "the mental connexion between an object and ideas that have some relation to it" (*OED*).

58.33   Longinus: See *On the Sublime* 16.

58.36   *Odi profanum vulgus:* Horace, *Odes* 3.1.1.

59.1   October trainin': The annual fall drill of the state militia.

59.5   cry quarter: Surrender.

59.25   Caleb: It was widely rumored that General Cushing, when in Mexico, broke his leg in attempting a rendezvous with a pretty Mexican girl.

59.31   John Augustus Bolles (1809–1878), a Boston lawyer and former Massachusetts secretary of state. In 1839 the American Peace Society in Boston published his *Essay on a Congress of Nations, for the Pacific Adjustment of International Disputes.* He presented Lieutenant Colonel Wright with a sword at the Faneuil Hall rally.

61.2   Robert Rantoul (1805–1852), a prominent Boston lawyer and Massachusetts Democrat, was appointed in 1846 United States District Attorney for Massachusetts. A reformer, he was opposed not only to the extension of slavery but also to capital punishment. "Public attention had recently been called to his views [on the latter issue] by some letters to Governor Briggs on the subject, written in February, 1846" (Williams, p. 400).

61.6   Antonio Blitz (1810–1877), an immensely popular English magician and ventriloquist, came, in 1834, to America where he remained until his death. His success caused his name to be frequently assumed by imitators.

61.21   Saltillo (meaning "a little hop or leap") is the capital of Coahuila in Mexico. The battle of Buena Vista was fought nearby in February 1847.

61.23	bluenose tater: A purplish potato grown in southeastern Canada and New England.
62.7	*cimex lectularius:* Bed-bug.
62.22	queen o' Sheby: See I Kings 10.
62.36	Xisle Poles: About 100,000 Poles went into exile during the "Great Emigration" following the failure of the Polish Rising of 1830.
63.31	linkum vity: Lignum vitae, a tree whose unpleasant-tasting resin was thought to have medicinal power.
64.5–6	*Capita vix duabus Anticyris medenda:* "Heads scarcely curable by two Anticyras." Unidentified. There were two towns in ancient Greece called Anticyra, one in Phocis, the other in Thessaly near Mount Oeta. Both were famous for producing hellebore, the sovereign remedy for madness. The author of the Latin (perhaps Lowell) would probably wish us to have in mind Horace's famous line in *The Art of Poetry:* "tribus Anticyris caput insanabile" (line 300), the poet whose madness is not to be cured by three Anticyras.
64.9	Gomara: Francisco López de Gómara (1511?– 1565?), biographer of Cortés and first historian of the conquest of Mexico, published his *Historia de las Indias* in 1552. Lowell's more likely source is William H. Prescott's *History of the Conquest of Mexico,* 3 vols. (New York, 1843), 2:341. "More than one grave historian refers the preservation of the Spaniards to the watchful care of their patron Apostle, St. James, who, in these desperate conflicts, was beheld careering on his milk-white steed at the head of the Christian squadrons, with his sword flashing lightning, while a lady robed in white—supposed to be the Virgin—was distinctly

seen by his side, throwing dust in the eyes of the
infidel!" Lowell's probable use of Prescott—who
wrote "The two pillars, on which the story of the
Conquest mainly rests, are the Chronicles of
Gomara and of Bernal Diaz" (2:474)—could
account for his later alteration of Díaz to Gómara
(see Emendations).

64.12   Richard I, "Coeur de Lion" (1157–1199), king of
England, engaged in a crusade to the Holy Land,
1189–1192. He was principally opposed by Saladin
(1138–1193), sultan of Egypt and Syria. According
to the medieval English romance of *Richard Coeur
de Lion*, Richard ordered the execution of sixty
thousand Saracen captives at Acre in 1190 after
Saladin failed to bring him the holy cross:
> They were led into the place full even.
> There they heard angels of heaven;
> They said, "Seigneures, tuez, tuez!
> Spares hem nought, and beheadeth these!"
> King Richard heard the angels' voice,
> And thanked God, and the holy cross.

(Quoted in George Ellis, *Specimens of Early
English Metrical Romances*, rev. ed., J. O. Halliwell,
London, 1848, p. 318.)

64.35   *revocare gradum:* "To retrace one's steps." Virgil,
The Aeneid 6.128.

64.37   Echetlæus: Pausanias records the legend "that
there chanced to be present in the battle [at
Marathon] a man of rustic appearance and dress.
Having slaughtered many of the foreigners with a
plough he was seen no more after the engagement.
When the Athenians made enquiries at the oracle
the god merely ordered them to honour Echetlaeus
(*He of the Plough-tail*) as a hero" (*Description of
Greece* 1.32.5; trans. W. H. S. Jones).

65.1   *Dioscuri:* The sons of Jupiter, Castor and Pollux, were often reported by the ancients to have appeared mounted on white horses to lead armies into battle.

65.12   victory gained on the Sabbath: The Battle of Cerro Gordo, 18 April 1847.

65.13   Josephus: It is Pliny (*Natural History* 31.18) who says the Sabbatical River dries up every Sabbath. Josephus (*The Jewish War* 7.96–99) writes that it flows only on the seventh day.

65.17   William Trowbridge: See Cotton Mather, *Magnalia Christi Americana* (London, 1702), bk. 6, chap. 1, p. 9, from which Wilbur quotes.

65.29   Chief Magistrate: President Polk's wife banned both dancing and the serving of alcoholic beverages in the White House.

65.34–35 *pro propagandâ fide:* "For the propagating of the faith"; from the name of the Roman Catholic committee of Cardinals in charge of foreign missions: Congregatio de Propaganda Fide.

65.36   Cambridge Platform: The statement of church discipline and organization which organized the Congregational Church in America in 1648.

65.36–37 Thirty-nine Articles: The statement of doctrinal formulae of the Church of England.

66.7   Izaak Walton (1593–1683), English writer, whose most famous book is *The Compleat Angler, or the Contemplative Man's Recreation* (London, 1653), a leisurely treatise on the arts of fishing and companionship.

66.13   *fishers* of men: See Matthew 4.19: Christ said to Simon Peter and Andrew, "Follow me, and I will make you fishers of men."

66.15   Naboth, the Jezreelite, was stoned to death for refusing to sell his vineyard to King Ahab who coveted it. See I Kings 21.

66.27   herpetic: As used here, a nonce word meaning "crawling, reptilian" (*OED*).

66.29   *e corde cordium:* From the heart of hearts.

66.31   Tag, Rag, and Bobtail: "The common herd, the rabble" (*OED*).

66.36   Solon: "Thus public evil descends on the house of every man." Solon, the great Athenian lawgiver and poet (c. 640–c. 558 B.C.), is quoted in Demosthenes, *On the Embassy* 255.

68.8   "Our country, right or wrong": Stephen Decatur's answer to a toast at a dinner in Norfolk, Virginia, April 1816: "Our country! In her intercourse with foreign nations, may she always be in the right; but our country, right or wrong." Quoted by Alexander S. Mackenzie, *Life of Stephen Decatur* (Boston, 1846), p. 295.

68.10   Fencibles: Soldiers "liable only for defensive service at home" (*OED*).

69.2   WHAT MR. ROBINSON THINKS: George Nixon Briggs (1796–1861), Whig governor of Massachusetts from 1844 to 1851, was enthusiastically renominated by his party in 1847. Briggs was strongly opposed to the war, arguing that it was unjust and entered upon only for the purpose of extending slavery. His Democratic opponent, Caleb Cushing, at the time a leading general in Mexico, chose not to return to campaign in Massachusetts. Late in the contest, John P. Robinson, a lawyer in Lowell, Massachusetts, and a prominent Whig, made known his intention to vote for Cushing. In a public letter dated 21 October 1847, Robinson wrote: "I have been no advocate of the war itself. I think it an exceedingly unfortunate one. But, as the country is involved in the war, it is the duty of every good citizen to stand by his country" (quoted in Claude M. Fuess, *The Life of Caleb Cushing*, 2 vols., New York: Harcourt, Brace and Co., 1923, 2:68). Cushing was defeated by about 14,000 votes.

69.12–13   *tenues in auras:* "Dissolved in the air." Virgil, *The Aeneid* 2.791 and elsewhere.

69.13–14   *Longum iter per . . . efficace per exempla:* "The way is long of teaching by precepts, short and helpful by examples." Seneca, *Letters* 6.5. Had Wilbur referred to the text he would have corrected *efficace* to *efficax.*

70.6–7   *aliquid sufflaminandus erat:* "He needed to be somewhat repressed." Cf. Ben Jonson's well-known remarks about Shakespeare: "Hee was (indeed) honest, and of an open, and free nature: had an excellent *Phantsie;* brave notions, and gentle expressions: wherein hee flow'd with that facility, that sometime it was necessary he should be stop'd: *Sufflaminandus erat;* as *Augustus* said of *Haterius"* (*Timber: or, Discoveries,* London, 1641, in *Ben Jonson,* ed. C. H. Herford, Percy and Evelyn Simpson, 11 vols., Oxford: Clarendon Press, 1925–1952, 8:584). The Latin reference is to Seneca the Rhetorician, *Disputations* 4.Preface.7.

70.8   *aqua fortis:* "Strong water," i.e., nitric acid.

70.12–13   *Est ars etiam maledicendi:* "There is even an art to slandering." Joseph Justus Scaliger (1540–1609), the Renaissance scholar, is noted in *Commonplace Book I* as author.

70.15–18   Dr. Fuller, that ". . . are not lions": Thomas Fuller, *The Holy State* (Cambridge, England, 1642), p. 122.

72.18   *per contry: Per contra,* on the other hand.

73.9   that pernicious sentiment: See 68.8n.

73.19   Caleb Strong: Massachusetts lawyer and Federalist statesman (1745–1819) was governor of the state 1800–1807, 1812–1816. One of his more noted acts as governor was his refusal to order into federal service the state militia at the beginning of the War of 1812.

73.20   *Patriæ fumus igne alieno luculentior:* "The smoke in one's country is brighter than a foreign fire." The Latin is Erasmus's translation (*Adages* 1.2.16) of Lucian, *My Native Land* 11.

73.21   *Ubi libertas, ibi patria:* "Where liberty dwells, there is my country." Latin proverb.

73.33   *"Our country, however bounded!":* Robert C. Winthrop (1809–1894), a leading Massachusetts Whig, in his toast at a Fourth of July dinner, 1845, said in support of the Union: "OUR COUNTRY,— Whether bounded by the St. John's and the Sabine, or however otherwise bounded or described, and be the measurements more or less,—still our country, to be cherished in all our hearts, to be defended by all our hands!" This sentiment, known as "Mr. Winthrop's however-bounded toast," was widely and effectively used by those who supported the federal government on the issue of the Mexican War (see Robert C. Winthrop, Jr., *A Memoir of Robert C. Winthrop,* Boston: Little, Brown, and Co., 1897, p. 45). The St. John and the Sabine rivers were northeastern and southwestern boundaries of the United States.

74.4   *quasi noverca:* As if a stepmother.

74.7   Penelope: After giving his daughter Penelope in marriage to Odysseus, Icarius tried to persuade

Odysseus to remain in Lacedaemon. Failing in this, he followed the departing couple and begged his daughter to remain. Annoyed, Odysseus asked Penelope whether she wished to go with him or her father. Penelope made no reply, but covering her face with her veil indicated to Icarius her desire to go with her lawful husband to her new home in Ithaca. See Pausanias, *Description of Greece* 3.20.10–11.

74.18   Boston Morning Post: The paragraph Wilbur refers to reads: "James Russell Lowell, the abolition poet, has written a doggerel, which is published in the Courier. One line of this elegant production runs thus: —'*We kind o' thought Christ went agin war and pillage.*' Certainly the whigs have all the talent, 'all the learning and all the *decency.*'" The *Post* was a leading Democratic newspaper. Wilbur's reply was printed in the *Boston Courier,* 6 November 1847.

74.32   'Sic vos non vobis': "Thus you work, but not for yourself." When a rival claimed authorship for lines written by Virgil honoring Augustus, the Roman poet wrote on the palace door: "Hos ego versiculos feci, tulit alter honores" ("I wrote these lines, another took the credit") and underneath four incomplete lines, each beginning "Sic vos, non vobis." The rival was challenged to complete the lines, but failed. Virgil completed the poem, thus winning undisputed credit for the stolen lines. See Aelius Donatus, *Life of Virgil* 17.

75.3   *digito monstrari,* &c.: *Digito monstrari, et dicier: Hic est!:* "To be pointed at and have it said: There he is!" Persius, *Satires* 1.28.

75.4   *merces:* wages, pay.

75.6   *fidus Achates:* "Trusty Achates." Virgil, *The Aeneid*

ANNOTATIONS

	1.188. Achates' fidelity to Aeneas made these words proverbial.
75.12–13	Aristophanes: Wilbur probably has in mind this Athenian's masterpiece both of comic drama and of literary criticism, *The Frogs*, in which the grand, romantic manner of Aeschylus is humorously opposed to the realistic, colloquial style of Euripides.
75.17–18	*apage Sathanas!:* Begone, Satan!
75.25	Dean Swift: See Jonathan Swift, *Travels . . . by Lemuel Gulliver* (London, 1726), part 2, "A Voyage to Brobdignag," chap. 7. Swift's satire is directed against those who take cities by elections, i.e., politicians.
75.29	Winfield Scott (1786–1866) rose to military prominence in the War of 1812, and in 1841 became general-in-chief of the United States Army. His performance during the Mexican War brought him back into public notice and his name was mentioned in 1847 as a possible Whig candidate for the presidency. In 1852 he unsuccessfully ran as Whig opponent to Franklin Pierce.
76.1	Amos ix.1: "I saw the Lord standing upon the altar: and he said, Smite the lintel of the door, that the posts may shake."
76.1	editor of that paper: Charles Gordon Greene (1804–1886), who founded the *Boston Post* in 1831.
76.13	'The Green Man': A common public-house sign in England (*OED*).
76.19–21	Saint Ambrose . . . *a spiritu sancto est:* "Truth, by whomever spoken, is from the Holy Ghost." Wilbur asks parenthetically: "why not, then, howsoever?" Cf. Commentary on I Corinthians 12.3 in the

Ambrosiaster, a book of anonymous commentaries on the epistles of St. Paul, traditionally, though incorrectly, ascribed to St. Ambrose. *Commonplace Book I* indicates Lowell copied the quotation from Sir Walter Raleigh, *The Historie of the World* (London, 1634), bk. 1, chap. 1, sec. 2.

76.22–23   'The plainest words . . . the weightiest matters': Richard Baxter (1615–1691), "Preface to the Reader," *A Treatise of Conversion* (1657) in *The Practical Works*, 23 vols. (London, 1830), 7:ix.

76.32   sound doctrines of protective policy: A chief feature of the Whig platform was a high tariff that protected American industries, which in the 1840s were chiefly in New England.

76.36–77.1   *horresco referens:* "I shudder as I speak." Virgil, *The Aeneid* 2.204.

77.2   "*The Liberator* was William Lloyd Garrison's anti-slavery paper, published from 1831 to 1865. The 'heresies' of which Mr. Wilbur speaks were Garrison's advocacy of secession, his well-known and eccentric views on 'no government,' woman suffrage," (Williams, p. 402), anti-sabbatarianism, etc.

77.10–11   *væ mihi si non evangelizavero:* "Woe to me should I not preach!" *Ambrosiaster*, Commentary on I Corinthians 9.16.

77.32–33   *Ingenuas didicisse,* &c.: *Ingenuas didicisse fideliter artes emollit mores nec sinit esse feros:* "A faithful study of the liberal arts humanizes character and does not permit it to be cruel." Ovid, *Letters from the Black Sea* 2.9.47–48.

78.29   decencies of apparel: Scott was nicknamed "Old Fuss and Feathers" because of his meticulousness in dress and behavior.

ANNOTATIONS

78.34–35   Thomas Warton (1728–1790) was elected
            professor of poetry at Oxford in 1757 and created
            poet laureate in 1785. Richard Mant recorded in his
            biographical sketch that Warton "was fond of
            drinking his ale and smoking his pipe with persons
            of mean rank and education: . . . [and] he delighted
            in popular spectacles, especially when enlivened
            by the music of a drum" (Thomas Warton, *The
            Poetical Works*, ed. Richard Mant, 2 vols., Oxford,
            1802, 1:ciii).

79.5–6   *Nescio quâ dulcedine . . . cunctos ducit:* Cf.
            Nescioqua natale solum dulcedine cunctos ducit:
            "I know not by what unique charm the native land
            draws men together" (Ovid, *Letters from the Black
            Sea* 1.3.35–36); and *hinc nescio qua dulcedine
            laetae progeniem nidosque fovent:* "hence it is that,
            glad with some strange joy, they cherish home
            and family" (Virgil, *Georgics* 4.55–56).

79.13–14   *Semel insanivimus omnes:* "We have all been mad
            some time or other." Baptista Mantuanus
            (1448–1516), *Eclogues* 1.118.

79.20   Turell's life: See Ebenezer Turell, *The Life and
            Character of the Reverend Benjamin Colman, D.D.*
            (Boston, 1749), p. 6. Colman (1673–1747) was a
            prominent New England minister and the first
            pastor of the Brattle Street Church in Boston.

79.29   Jortin: John Jortin (1698–1770), English
            theologian and ecclesiastical historian. Lowell
            probably has in mind the earlier sections of Jortin's
            Remarks on Ecclesiastical History, 5 vols. (London,
            1751–1773).

81.3   D. O'PHACE: Wilbur's gloss of "doughface" should
            be supplemented by Mitford M. Mathews, ed., *A
            Dictionary of Americanisms* (Chicago: University

of Chicago Press, 1951): "A northern congressman who did not oppose slavery in the South and its extension; [later] a northerner who favored the South during the Civil War period." This politician's name can also be read: "increase de (the) office."

81.4   EXTRUMPERY: Literally, *out of the trumpery,* "a humorous perversion of 'extempore' " (*OED*).

81.4   STATE STREET: The business and financial center of Boston.

81.7   *totidem verbis:* In just so many words.

81.19   Antonius: It has been suggested that Shakespeare's portrayal of Antony in *Julius Caesar* is indebted to Appian of Alexandria (second century A.D.), *The Civil Wars,* translated into English in 1578. Antony's funeral oration is in bk. 2, chap. 20 of Appian; in Shakespeare—"Friends, Romans, Countrymen, lend me your ears"—act 3, sc. 2.

81.30   *Parliamentum Indoctorum:* "The sixth parliament of Henry IV [1404] was called the *parliamentum indoctorum* [the unlearned parliament], because there were no lawyers in it. Held at Coventry." Lowell, *Commonplace Book II.*

81.32   Oracle of Fools: Pantagruel's praise of the good counsel of fools is in bk. 3, chap. 37 of *The Histories of Gargantua and Pantagruel* by François Rabelais.

82.1   ambassador: Valentine Dale (d. 1589). See James Howell, *Familiar Letters,* 3d ed. (London, 1655), vol. 4, letter 2.

82.16   *ostracism:* By popular vote, using for a ballot ὄστραχον, a potsherd, the Greeks could temporarily banish from the country any person whose presence endangered the people's liberty. Lowell's pun arises from the fact that ὄστραχα is also the Greek word for the shell of an oyster, and ὄστρεον means oyster.

82.24   John Gorham Palfrey (1796–1881), a Unitarian clergyman, theologian, and a historian of New England, was a "Conscience" Whig member of Congress from Massachusetts, 1847–1849. Early in December 1847, the Whig representatives nominated Robert C. Winthrop, also of Massachusetts, as their candidate for speaker of the House. Palfrey decided not to vote for Winthrop after learning that Winthrop was not inclined to use the influence of the speaker to appoint committees to encourage a quick settlement of the Mexican War and to discourage the extension of slavery. Palfrey's refusal to vote for his party's candidate caused him to be bitterly denounced and his resignation demanded by the "Cotton" Whigs of Massachusetts.

82.35   Benedict Arnold (1741–1801), American revolutionary patriot, general, and traitor.

83.21   Some flossifers: Probably a reference to the followers of Fourier (see 90.3n). Emerson wrote in "Montaigne; or, The Skeptic" (first delivered as a lecture in 1846): "Charles Fourier announced that 'the attractions of man are proportioned to his destinies;' in other words, that every desire predicts its own satisfaction" (Representative Men: Seven Lectures, Boston, 1850, p. 182).

83.28–29   Nec vero habere ... aliquam, nisi utare: "Nor is it sufficient to possess this virtue [of patriotism] as if it were some kind of art, unless we put it in practice." Cicero, On the Republic 1.2. The passage continues: "An art, indeed, though not exercised, may still be retained in knowledge; but virtue

consists wholly in its proper use and action" (trans.
C. D. Yonge). The treatise was discovered in 1820.

83.29–33   John Milton, *Areopagitica* (London, 1644). The
italics are Wilbur's.

83.35–36   *Pereant qui ante nos nostra dixerint:* "Let the
plague take those who have said our good things
before us!" Aelius Donatus, a fourth-century Latin
grammarian and teacher of rhetoric, quoted by
his student, St. Jerome, in his *Commentary on
Ecclesiastes* (1.9–10).

84.9   Springfield Convention: The Whig state convention
was held at Springfield, Massachusetts, on 29
September 1847. A list of resolutions adopted is
printed in *Niles' National Register* 73 (9 October
1847): 84, and, while somewhat more formally
stated, does not differ substantially from the
remarks of Increase D. O'Phace.

85.9   soft sodder: Soft-sawder, or flattery.

85.31   Horners: "Little Jack Horner / Sat in the corner, /
Eating a Christmas pie; / He put in his thumb, /
And pulled out a plum, / And said, What a good boy
am I!" Traditional nursery rhyme.

86.3   Washinton's mantelpiece fell upon Polk: See
I Kings 19.19 where Elijah's prophetic powers are
transferred to Elisha by the former casting his
mantle upon the latter.

86.9   ass: As Balaam travelled to Moab, an angel thrice
blocked his way, though visible only to the ass
Balaam rode. When the ass refused to proceed
Balaam struck the animal. Finally, the ass rebuked
Balaam: "What have I done unto thee, that thou
hast smitten me these three times?" See Numbers
22.21–35.

86.13   old viper: Cf. Aesop's fable, "The Viper and the
File": "A Viper entering into a smith's shop began
looking about for something to eat. At length,
seeing a File, he went up to it and commenced
biting at it; but the File bade him leave him alone,
saying 'You are likely to get little from me, whose
business it is to bite others'" (trans. Thomas
James, *Aesop's Fables*, London, 1848).

86.35   *Magister artis, ingeniique largitor venter: Quis*
expedivit psittaco suum chaere, picamque docuit
verba nostra conari? magister artis, ingenique
largitor venter: "Who made it easy for the parrot to
say 'good day'? Who taught the magpie to attempt
to use our words? It was the master of arts, the
granter of genius, the Belly." Persius, *Satires*
Prologue.8–11.

87.24   Gennle Tom Thumb: Charles Sherwood Stratton
(1838–1883), a Connecticut midget, during the
1840s captured the curiosity of the American and
European publics and a fortune for himself and for
his manager, P. T. Barnum, "the greatest American
showman."

87.29   primy fashy: *Prima facie*, at first sight, on first
view.

87.30   paronomashy: Paronomasia.

87.31   *loosus naytury: Lusus naturae*, a freak of nature.

88.20   black eagle: The imperial Russian black eagle was
depicted with two heads facing in opposite
directions.

88.21   Monteery: At Monterrey a four-day battle was
fought in September 1846 between the forces under
General Taylor and the Mexicans who held the
town. With the capitulation of the city on 24

September, the campaign on the Rio Grande was ended.

88.22   Victory: Victoria (1819–1901), Queen of the United Kingdom of Great Britain and Ireland.

88.23   Cherry Buster: At the village of Churubusco, near Mexico City, the forces of Santa Anna were defeated by the advance American forces of General Scott on 20 August 1847.

88.24   Philip Lewis: Louis Philippe (1773–1850), king of the French (1830–1848), lived in exile in the United States from 1796 to 1800. A popular belief about the residence of the young duc d'Orleans in America is recorded in one of Hotten's glosses: "Louis Philippe, who, in early life, kept a small school in the State of Louisiana. His name is yet shown scratched on the wall" (*The Biglow Papers*, London, 1859, p. 78). The Tuileries was the royal residence in Paris until its destruction in 1870. See 106.30n.

88.33   "Dat veniam corvis, vexat censura columbas": "The dove is censured, while the raven is spared." Juvenal, *Satires* 2.63.

88.34   Jortin: Lowell copied the following quotation from John Jortin's *Remarks on Ecclesiastical History*, 2:1, in *Commonplace Book I:* "It seems to be rashness for us, who know so little of the powers of intellectual and spiritual agents, and of the scheme of divine Providence, to affirm that (the miracles of the Old and New Testament excepted) God never wrought any, or never suffered any to be wrought by spirits good or evil."

89.14   Post: See 74.18n.

89.26   Hammon: Egyptian god, whose oracle existed for some centuries at Oasis Siwa in Libya. It was here

	Alexander came to be acknowledged the son of the god.
89.28–29	"Rapida fortuna ac . . . eripuit, exsilio dedit" : "Swift and fickle fortune has cast me headlong from royalty and given me up to exile" (lines 219–220).
89.33	Aeschylus : "Everyone is severe who has just come to power." *Prometheus Bound*, line 35.
90.3	Foorier : François Marie Charles Fourier (1772–1837) was a French philosopher and social reformer whose radical socialist doctrines were introduced in the United States by Albert Brisbane, Horace Greeley, George Ripley, among others, in the 1840s. The famous Brook Farm experiment became largely a demonstration of Fourier's teachings.
90.28	Ararats : It was "upon the mountains of Ararat" that Noah's ark rested at the end of the flood. See Genesis 8.4.
90.33	Shakers : Or the United Society of Believers in Christ's Second Appearing, a communal American religious sect, which prohibited the use of buttons on clothing.
91.3–4	Second Advent delusion : William Miller (1782–1849), a New England-born Baptist, prophesied that the Second Coming of Christ would occur on 2 March 1843. When the event failed to occur, the date was several times postponed. Some of Miller's followers afterward formed the sect of Seventh-Day Adventists.
91.5	gift of tongues : Or glossolalia, is the ability to speak so that all hearers, no matter their native language, can understand. See Acts 2.4–13.
91.15–16	*ex nihilo nihil fit:* "Nothing can come from nothing." Marcus Aurelius, *Meditations* 4.4.

91.17–18   *vivâ voce:* By the living voice.

91.19   Copres: Lowell copied in *Commonplace Book I* under the heading "Zeal" this passage from Jortin's *Remarks on Ecclesiastical History,* 2:116: "Copres, a Monk of the fourth century, is said to have stood half an hour in the midst of a great fire, unhurt, to confute a poor Manichæan Doctor who could not perform the same exploit. Rufinus *Vit. Patrum.*"

91.29   Serbonian bog: Milton's name for Lake Serbonis in ancient Egypt: "A gulf profound as that *Serbonian* Bog/Betwixt *Damiata* and Mount *Casius* old,/ Where Armies whole have sunk" (*Paradise Lost* 2.592–94).

91.30   Tesephone: Source of story unidentified.

92.1   emblematic fish: Hanging above the rail of the visitor's gallery opposite the speaker's desk in the Massachusetts House of Representatives' chamber in the State House is a carved wooden effigy of a codfish, the well-known Sacred Cod. "The codfish was chosen as an emblem of the Commonwealth because it symbolizes the source of its original wealth, since a cargo of fish was the first product of American industry to be exported from Massachusetts. It is the evidence of courage and fortitude of the original colonists, and a reminder of the struggles and privations of Pilgrim and Puritan alike and their relief from want and famine" (*The Massachusetts State House,* compiled by the State Library, Boston: State Library, 1961, pp. 45–46).

92.3   Pythagoreans: Lowell noted in *Commonplace Book I* the following passage from Charles Blount's annotated translation of *The Two First Books of Philostratus* (London, 1680), p. 53: "They [the disciples of Pythagoras] had the greatest respect for Fish, by reason of their silence, says *Athenaeus*, 20."

92.7   Faneuil Hall was a Boston market building and public hall, called from the time of the American Revolution the "cradle of liberty" because of the important patriotic meetings held there.

93.2   THE DEBATE IN THE SENNIT: In April 1848, Daniel Drayton and Captain Edward Sayres attempted to transport seventy-six slaves from Washington, D.C., to the North and freedom. Sayres's schooner, the *Pearl*, was quickly overtaken, the slaves recaptured, and the white men arrested. During the excitement that followed the capture and arrests, the office of the *National Era*, an abolitionist newspaper published in Washington, D.C., was threatened by a mob which believed the paper's editor, Gamaliel Bailey, was involved in planning the attempted escape. The abolitionists in Congress decided to make an issue of the incident, and on 20 April Senator John P. Hale of New Hampshire introduced a bill providing "that any property destroyed by any riotous or tumultuous assemblage shall be paid for by any town or county in the District where it occurs" (*Congressional Globe*, 21 April 1848, p. 656). The bill's implication of sympathy for the opponents of slavery brought forth a heated attack by southern senators. "Hale stood almost alone with his resolution, which was soon arrested by an adjournment. A similar resolution [read by John G. Palfrey] failed in the House. Drayton and Sayres were convicted by the District Court and sentenced to long terms of imprisonment. In 1852 Senator Sumner secured for them an unconditional pardon from President Fillmore" (Williams, p. 404). The debate is printed

in full in the *Appendix to the Congressional Globe,
for the First Session, Thirtieth Congress*
(Washington, D.C., 1848), pp. 500–510. Lowell
could have read it in the *National Anti-Slavery
Standard* (27 April 1848), which copied the debate
from Houston's official report.

93.12 Philip Barton Key (1818–1859), son of Francis
Scott Key, the author of "The Star-Spangled
Banner."

93.16 *Ahenea clavis:* Lowell's translation permits him to
pun on both words: *ahenea clavis* is a key made of
brass, and District Attorney Key is brazen, that is,
in English jargon, "shameless" or "impudent."
While *ahenea* was used frequently in Latin verse as
an epithet for *clavis,* the deftness of the pun makes
a Latin literary allusion here seem unlikely. In
the sentence immediately preceding there is a
verbal allusion to Shakespeare, *Richard II*
3.2.54–55: "Not all the waters in the rough rude
sea / Can wash the balm off from an annointed
king."

93.18 John C. Calhoun (1782–1850), a leading southern
statesman and politician, was senator from South
Carolina, 1832–1843, 1845–1850. While, as
Arthur Voss points out, "the speeches of some of
the other senators provided better targets for satire
than those of Calhoun" ("Backgrounds of Lowell's
Satire in 'The Biglow Papers,'" p. 53), Lowell
chose the South Carolina senator to be the principal
speaker because, in Calhoun's own words during
the debate, he was "considered almost the exclusive
defender of this great institution of the South
[i.e., slavery], upon which not only its prosperity
but its very existence depends" (*Appendix to the
Congressional Globe,* p. 501). The other senators in

the "debate" are Henry S. Foote of Mississippi,
W. P. Mangum of North Carolina, Lewis Cass of
Michigan, Jefferson Davis of Mississippi, Edward A.
Hannegan of Indiana, Spencer Jarnagin of
Tennessee, Charles G. Atherton of New Hampshire,
W. T. Colquitt of Georgia, Reverdy Johnson of
Maryland, James D. Westcott of Florida, and Dixon
H. Lewis of Alabama. Senators Cass, Atherton,
Colquitt, and Lewis did not, in fact, participate in
the congressional debate, and Jarnagin was no
longer a senator.

93.27   Plotinus: This story is told about the neo-Platonic
philosopher (A.D. 204–270) by his student
Porphyry in *On the Life of Plotinus* 3.

94.14   Sir Kay: The legendary King Arthur's cynical,
boastful foster-brother and seneschal.

95.24   by the gret horn spoon!: "A ludicrous oath"
(Thornton, *An American Glossary*).

96.16   skinnin' thet same old coon: Wilbur's gloss should
be supplemented by Thornton, *An American
Glossary:* "From the slyness of [the raccoon], the
word came to be used as a nick-name, and was
specially applied in 1840 to the adherents of
'Tippecanoe and Tyler too.' Any defeat of the
'Whigs' was termed by the Democrats 'skinning
the coon.'"

97.12   raisin' permiscoous Ned: *"To raise (promiscuous,
merry) Ned*, to stir up trouble, to 'raise Cain'"
(Mathews, *A Dictionary of Americanisms*).

97.27   hallylugers: Hallelujahs.

98.18   Jonah: When this Hebrew prophet attempted to
flee God's word, a great storm was directed against
the ship in which he traveled. The others on board,

fearing the threat Jonah's presence made to their safety, cast him into the sea where he was swallowed by a great fish (see Jonah 1.1–17).

98.31   Ham: One of the three sons of Noah (Genesis 10.1) and in folk tradition the father of the black race (the word "ham" means black, dark-colored). See 141.10n.

99.16–17   the goats and the sheep: See Matthew's account of Jesus' parable of the Last Judgment (25.31–46).

99.20–21   *Quid sum miser . . . patronum rogaturus?*: "What shall I, a wretched man, then plead? Whom can I ask to be my protector?" From the "Dies Irae," a medieval hymn about the Day of Judgment sung at the Requiem Mass.

99.34   *Discite justitiam . . . non temnere divos:* "Learn to heed justice and do not scorn God." Virgil, *The Aeneid* 6.620. As noted in the Index (160.28a), this line is spoken by Phlegyas, condemned to Tartarus, that part of the underworld where the wickedest suffer punishment, for having sinned against Apollo.

101.2   THE PIOUS EDITOR'S CREED: Arthur Voss suggests that although this paper "may be taken as a general indictment of those Northern newspaper editors who supported the Mexican War and slavery, it is likely that Lowell was satirizing in particular the editor of the *Boston Morning Post* [see 76.1n.]" ("Backgrounds of Lowell's Satire in 'The Biglow Papers,'" p. 54).

101.5   Ezekiel xxxiv.2: The passage continues: "prophesy, and say unto them, Thus saith the Lord God unto the shepherds; Woe be to the shepherds of Israel that do feed themselves! should not the shepherds feed the flocks?"

101.28   Leonard Chappelow (1683–1768), an English orientalist, published in 1752 *A Commentary on the Book of Job* which argued that the Hebrew poem had been translated from an Arabic original.

101.33   *staboy!:* An exclamation of encouragement, most generally addressed to dogs (Thornton, *An American Glossary*).

101.33–102.1 "to bark and bite as 't is their nature to": Cf. the popular children's hymn by Isaac Watts, "Against Quarreling and Fighting" (*Divine Songs*, London, 1715):
> Let dogs delight to bark and bite,
>   For God hath made them so;
> Let bears and lions growl and fight,
>   For 'tis their nature too.

102.2   *odium theologicum:* "Theological hatred," the animosity caused by differences of opinion on theological doctrines.

102.12   ποιμὴν λαῶν : "Shepherd of the host." This phrase is used repeatedly in Homer to describe leaders and heroes. For instance, *The Iliad*, 2.243.

102.18   Numbers xxxiii.12: "And they took their journey out of the wilderness of Sin, and encamped in Dophkah"; from the description of the route from Egypt to Canaan of the Israelites.

102.23   Joseph Smith (1805–1844), the Mormon prophet, founded the Church of Jesus Christ of Latter-Day Saints in 1830 and was its flamboyant leader until his martyrdom in 1844.

102.26   *Immemor, O, fidei, pecorumque oblite tuorum!:* "Oh, unmindful of the faith, and forgetful of your flocks." John Milton, "In Quintum Novembris," line 93.

103.5   Payris: Paris and the Revolution of February 1848.

103.29   furrin missions: Lowell is undoubtedly referring to
               Caleb Cushing, who in 1843 was appointed head
               of the Chinese Mission with a stipend of $9,000 a
               year and numerous *attachés*. The extravagance and
               display of the mission was criticized at the time
               but later defended by Cushing's biographer: "It is
               probable that a more modest equipment would have
               been less graciously received by the Chinese"
               (Claude M. Fuess, *The Life of Caleb Cushing*, 2
               vols., New York: Harcourt, Brace and Co., 1923,
               2:417).

104.5–6   The bread comes . . . tu, fer sartin: Cf. Ecclesiastes
               11.1: "Cast thy bread upon the waters: for thou
               shalt find it after many days."

104.27–32   I du believe . . . bear his souperscription: Cf.
               Matthew 22.20–21: Holding up a coin, Christ said
               to the Pharisees and the Herodians, "Whose is this
               image and superscription? They say unto him,
               Caesar's. Then saith he unto them, Render
               therefore unto Caesar the things which are
               Caesar's; and unto God the things that are God's";
               and Acts 17.28: "For in Him we live, and move,
               and have our being."

105.18   Go into it baldheaded: "'To go it bald-headed'; in
               great haste, as where one rushes out without his
               hat" (*The Biglow Papers, Second Series*, Boston,
               1867, p. lvii).

105.19–20   holdin' slaves . . . Presidunt: A reference to General
               Zachary Taylor, Whig candidate, who would be
               elected by popular vote president of the United
               States on 7 November 1848.

106.7–10   This heth my . . . hev fed me: Cf. Psalms 22 and 23.

106.30   Louis Philippe, king of France, escaped Paris during
          the February Revolution of 1848 with his wife in
          disguise and by a back door of the Tuileries palace,
          traveling to England as a Mr. and Mrs. Smith. It
          was rumored at the time that they crossed the
          channel in a fishing boat, but the passage was
          actually made in a steamer. See G. W.
          Featherstonhaugh's letter to Lord Palmerston,
          Havre, 3 March 1848, in *The Letters of Queen
          Victoria*, ed. A. C. Benson and Viscount Esher, 3
          vols. (London: John Murray, 1907), 2:184–87.

106.31–32 That other . . . Napoleon Bonaparte Smith: This
          must refer to Charles Louis Napoleon Bonaparte,
          known as Louis Napoleon. While appearing to favor
          the republican government established after the
          February Revolution, he was all the time plotting to
          regain the absolute power once held by his uncle,
          the great Napoleon. Elected a member of the new
          National Assembly, Louis Napoleon was made
          president of the Second French Republic in
          December 1848. Four years later he was proclaimed
          emperor, Napoleon III.

107.10   lever: See 40.7n.

107.30   this great Globe Theatre: The Globe was the
          London theater in which Shakespeare was
          associated both financially and professionally.

107.32   Apollyon: "The angel of the bottomless pit," or the
          destroyer. See Revelation 9.11.

108.15   Dimitry Bruisgins: Unidentified.

108.19   Acts x. 11, 12: See 30.5n.

109.2–3   A LETTER FROM A CANDIDATE: "In the campaign of
          1848 the Whigs determined to have substantially no
          platform or programme at all, in order to retain

the Southern element in their party. Accordingly a colorless candidate was selected in the person of General Zachary Taylor, who, it was said, had never voted or made any political confession of faith. He was nominated as the 'people's candidate,' and men of all parties were invited to support him. He refused to pledge himself to any policy or enter into any details, unless on some such obsolete issue as that of a National Bank. After it became apparent that his followers were chiefly Whigs, he declared himself a Whig also" (Williams, p. 406). In a letter to Captain J. S. Allison, 22 April 1848, Taylor wrote: "I AM A WHIG, *but not an ultra Whig*" (*Niles' National Register,* 74, 5 July 1848, p. 8). In an editorial on "Presidential Candidates," *National Anti-Slavery Standard,* 11 May 1848, part of which is used in Wilbur's afterwords to this paper, Lowell ridiculed the foolish practice of presidential candidates' writing letters to anyone who wanted to know their political positions. In the same editorial Lowell summed up Taylor's claims to the presidency: "He is a general, a slaveholder, and nobody knows what his opinions are" (*The Anti-Slavery Papers of James Russell Lowell,* 2 vols., Boston and New York: Houghton, Mifflin and Co., 1902, 1:62).

109.6   Sydney Howard Gay (1814–1888), Lowell's friend, was editor of the *National Anti-Slavery Standard* between 1843 and 1857.

109.14–15   *Nihil humanum a me alienum puto:* "Nothing human is foreign to me." Cf. Terence, *The Self-Tormentor* 1.1.25.

109.15–16   John Smith: Perhaps the English captain and American colonist, but more likely a common name for a common fellow.

109.22   Empedocles was a fifth century B.C. philosopher,
            scientist, and poet of Agrigentum in Sicily, whose
            curiosity, it is said, led him to the flames of the
            volcano of Etna and thus to his death.

109.23   Rhinothism: The practice of being nosy. Lowell's
            coinage from the Greek.

109.29–30   Michel Eyquem de Montaigne (1533–1592), whose
            Essays appeared between 1580 and 1595; Horace
            Walpole (1717–1797), famous for his voluminous
            Correspondence.

110.5   two-legged fowls without feathers: See Plato,
            Timaeus 91: "the race of birds was created out of
            innocent light-minded men who, although their
            minds were directed toward heaven, imagined, in
            their simplicity, that the clearest demonstration of
            the things above was to be obtained by sight; these
            were remodeled and transformed into birds, and
            they grew feathers instead of hair" (trans.
            B. Jowett). In Diogenes Laertius's *Lives of Eminent
            Philosophers* one reads: "Plato had defined Man
            as a two-footed featherless animal, and was much
            praised. Diogenes the Cynic plucked a fowl and
            brought it into his school, and said: 'Here is Plato's
            man'" (6.40).

110.9   *Omnibus hoc vitium est:* "This is a fault of all."
            Horace, *Satires* 1.3.1. The passage reads: "This is a
            fault of all singers, that when among their friends
            they are never inclined to sing, however much
            asked; unasked, they never cease."

110.14–15   the mote in their neighbour's eye: See Matthew 7.3:
            "And why beholdest thou the mote that is in thy
            brother's eye, but considerest not the beam that is in
            thine own eye?"

110.17   Jonah: See 98.18n.

111.2   Pliny the Younger (A.D. 62–113), a Roman writer and administrator, prepared a collection of his own letters.

111.3   Cato: A series of letters written by the British Whig pamphleteers John Trenchard (1662–1723) and Thomas Gordon (d. 1750) were published under the pseudonym "Cato" in the *London Journal* and the *British Journal* (1720–1723). They were collected in four volumes, *Cato's Letters: or, Essays on Liberty, Civil and Religious, And other Important Subjects* (London, 1723–1724), and frequently reprinted.

111.3   Mentor: In Greek legend, Mentor was the faithful adviser to Telemachus, the son of Odysseus. Lowell may have known and had in mind a series of letters printed in the *Kingston* (Canada) *Herald*, 1839–1844, signed "Mentor" and written by George Okill Stuart (1776–1864), a prominent Canadian clergyman (graduate of Harvard, 1801).

111.3   George, First Baron Lyttelton (1709–1773), English statesman and literary patron, whose prose works include *Letters from a Persian in England, to His Friend at Ispahan* (1735) and *Observations on the Conversion and Apostleship of St. Paul* (1747), both in the form of letters.

111.3–4   Philip Dormer Stanhope, Fourth Earl of Chesterfield (1694–1773), is famous for his *Letters* (1774) to his son.

111.4   Charles Boyle, Fourth Earl of Orrery (1676–1731), was the editor of the spurious *Epistles of Phalaris* (1695). His son John, Fifth Earl of Orrery (1707–1762), wrote *Remarks on the Life and Writings of Dr. Jonathan Swift* (1751) as a series of letters to his son.

111.4   Jacob Behmen: Or Jakob Böhme (1575–1624), German mystic, whose *Epistles* were translated into English in 1649, and frequently reprinted thereafter.

111.4   Seneca, a first century Roman philosopher, is included in St. Jerome's catalogue of saints by virtue of his correspondence with St. Paul (see *De Viris Illustribus* 12). The letters are believed to be spurious.

111.8–9   Thomas Gray (1716–1771), William Cowper (1731–1800), Horace Walpole (1717–1797), James Howell—sometimes spelled Howel— (1594?–1666), and Charles Lamb (1775–1834) are acknowledged epistolary masters in English. "D.Y." are the pseudonymous initials of Edmund Quincy (1808–1877), Lowell's friend and fellow abolitionist. As a contributing editor to the *National Anti-Slavery Standard,* his "Letters from Boston" were printed in that journal every fortnight.

111.10   Letters from New York: Two series of *Letters from New-York* (New York and Boston, 1843 and 1845) were written by Lowell's friend and fellow abolitionist, Lydia Maria Child (1802–1880).

111.13   Pinto: Lowell's friend, Charles F. Briggs (1804–1877), printed in the New York *Evening Mirror* a series of letters signed "Ferdinand Mendez Pinto."

111.20   Abgarus: The tradition of a correspondence between Christ and Abgar, king of Edessa, was recorded by Eusebius in his *Ecclesiastical History* (1.13) early in the fourth century.

111.21   King Pepin: In 755, St. Peter, in the person of Pope Stephen III, wrote a letter to Pepin the Short, King of the Franks, offering him and his troops eternal life in heaven if they came to the aid of Rome, then besieged by Aistulf, king of the Lombards, but threatening damnation of their souls should they disregard the plea. Pepin was sufficiently impressed by the forgery to come to the relief of the pope.

111.22   Messina: There was preserved in the Cathedral of Messina, Sicily, until its destruction in 1908, a celebrated letter attributed to the Blessed Virgin Mary which, so it was claimed, was written by her to the Messinians when she heard of their conversion by Saint Paul in A.D. 42.

111.23   Annas and Caiaphas: These two high priests are mentioned several times in the New Testament (see Luke 3.2). Lowell's source for the legend of a letter from the Sanhedrim (or Sanhedrin) of Toledo is unidentified.

111.23–24   Galeazzo Sforza: This fifteenth-century duke of Milan was assassinated in 1476. His brother Lodovico il Moro (1451–1508) became duke in 1494 after the mysterious death of his nephew Gian Galeazzo, the son of Galeazzo. The story of a letter is unidentified.

111.24–25   St. Gregory Thaumaturgus: "Gregory, called Thaumaturgus, a disciple of Origen, is said to have wrought many miracles; but . . . some of them are of a very suspicious kind, as his writing Laconic Epistles to Satan, and laying commands upon him, which were punctually obeyed." Jortin, *Remarks on Ecclesiastical History*, 2:246.

111.26   a nun of Girgenti: Suor Maria Crocifissa who in the seventeenth century is reported to have received a letter from the devil. See Girolamo Turano, *Vita e Virtù della Venerabile Serva di Dio, Suor Maria Crocifissa della Concezzione* (Venice, 1709).

Girgenti is the former name of Agrigento in Sicily. (I wish to thank Professore Santi Correnti, L'Università di Catania, for this information.)

111.29   *sat prata biberunt:* "The meadows have drunk enough." Virgil, *Eclogues* 3.111. Thus Palaemon ends the singing contest between two shepherds, Menalcas and Damoetas. He means, "Stop singing, my ears have had enough."

113.13   Proviso: In August 1846, Congressman David Wilmot, a Democrat from Pennsylvania, introduced into a bill appropriating two million dollars to enable President Polk to negotiate peace with Mexico the following amendment: "That, as an express and fundamental condition to the acquisition of any territory from the Republic of Mexico by the United States, by virtue of any treaty which may be negotiated between them, and to the use by the Executive of the moneys herein appropriated, neither slavery nor involuntary servitude shall ever exist in any part of said territory" (*Congressional Globe,* 12 August 1846, p. 1217). This amendment, known as the Wilmot Proviso, failed ever to pass both the House and the Senate, but the principle manifested in the amendment and the controversy it gave rise to were important factors in the later creation of the Republican party.

113.22   off ox: "An unmanageable, cross-grained fellow" (*The Biglow Papers, Second Series,* Boston, 1867, p. lviii).

114.1   breachy: "Apt to break through fences" (Thornton, *An American Glossary*).

114.27   Your head with ile I 'll kin' o' 'nint: Cf. Psalms 23.5: "thou anointest my head with oil. . . ."

114.30   brustlin': "Raising of the feathers; vapouring,
          blustering" (*OED*).

115.14   *Litera scripta manet:* "The written letter remains."
          Proverbial.

115.16   General Harrison: President William Henry
          Harrison's home was in North Bend, Ohio.

115.17   *cordon sanitaire:* "Sanitary line," or the guard
          placed around an infected area.

115.18   Spielberg: A castle on this hill in Czechoslovakia
          was used during the nineteenth century as a prison
          for political prisoners of the Hapsburg regime.

115.24   Plato's original man: See 110.5n.

115.25   *Parva componere magnis:* "To compare small
          things with great." Virgil, *Georgics* 4.176 and
          Eclogues 1.23.

115.31   Complete Letter-Writer: The common name for
          handbooks supplying model letters for all occasions.

116.1   Sabellianism: The heretical doctrine of the
          followers of Sabellius (third century) who regarded
          God the Father and God the Son as one person
          rather than as separate persons, thus denying the
          Son a personality distinct from the Father.

116.2   Paralipomenon: The name in the Vulgate and
          vernacular Roman Catholic Bibles for the Old
          Testament books known to English Protestants as
          I and II Chronicles.

116.4   the letter killeth: II Corinthians 3.6: God "also hath
          made us able ministers of the new testament; not
          of the letter, but of the spirit: for the letter killeth,
          but the spirit giveth life."

116.10   *Omne ignotum pro mirifico:* "The unknown is ever

magnified." Cf. Tacitus, *Agricola* 30: *omne ignotum pro magnifico.*

116.12   Hammon: See 89.26n.

116.14   wherein Apollo confessed that he was mortal: Eusebius claims that shortly after the birth of Christ the emperor Augustus visited Delphi and inquired who Apollo's successor would be. When the Pythia did not answer, Augustus asked an explanation. Apollo answered through his priestess: "A Hebrew boy, the divine king, commands me to depart from this temple and go to Hades. Leave our altar now, and speak not of this in the future." Eusebius's story is quoted in Georgius Cedrenus, *Compendium of History* (ed. Immanuel Bekker, 2 vols., Bonn, 1838, 1:320).

116.15   Didymus (63 B.C.–A.D. 10) was an indefatigable Greek grammarian whose prodigious number of books (over 3,500) earned him the surname Chalcenterus, "bowels of brass."

116.20   Beast in the Apocalypse: See Revelation 13.1. Found among Wilbur's posthumous papers were his "latest conclusions concerning the Tenth Horn of the Beast in its special application to recent events" (*The Biglow Papers, Second Series*, Boston, 1867, p. 171).

116.22   lethiferal: "Causing death, fatal" (*OED*).

116.22–23   *Non nostrum est tantas componere lites:* "It is not for us to settle such disputes." Virgil, *Eclogues* 3.108.

117.8–9   Pythagoras to his disciples . . . used as ballots: "According to Aristotle in his work *On the Pythagoreans*, Pythagoras counselled abstinence from beans either because they are like the genitals,

or because they are like the gates of Hades . . . as
being alone unjointed, or because they are
injurious, or because they are like the form of the
universe, or because they belong to oligarchy, since
they are used in election by lot" (Diogenes Laertius,
Lives of Eminent Philosophers 8.34, trans., R. D.
Hicks).

117.10   *quod videlicet . . . obtundi existimaret:* "Because he
thought indeed that human feelings are blunted by
that kind of food." Lowell copied in *Commonplace
Book I* one of Jacob Le Duchat's annotations to
his and Bernard de La Monnoye's edition of the
Oeuvres de Maitre François Rabelais (Amsterdam,
1711): "Jean de La Bruyère, livre VII, chapitre II
de son *De re cibaria:* 'Pythagoram illum primum
philosophum à fabarum esu omninò abstinuisse,
multorum monumentis traditur: quòd videlicet
sensus obtundi eo cibo existimaret, et somno sopitis
tumultuosa somnia excitari et mentem quoque
variè perturbari'" (*Oeuvres de Rabelais,* Édition
Variorum, ed. Esmangart et Éloi Johanneau, 9 vols.,
Paris, 1823, 4:353).

117.11   *pugnis et calcibus:* "With fists and feet," or with
one's greatest effort. Cf. Cicero, *Tusculan
Disputations* 5.27.77.

117.22–23   *Vos exemplaria Græca . . . manu, versate diurna:*
"Model yourselves on Greek examples by night and
by day." Horace, *The Art of Poetry,* lines 268–269.
Horace's examples are poetic meter.

117.31   Panurge and Goatsnose: See Rabelais, *The
Histories of Gargantua and Pantagruel,* bk. 3,
chap. 20.

117.33–34   Egyptian darkness: Intense darkness; the ninth
plague of Egypt. See Exodus 10.21.

118.2–3   Dighton rock hieroglyphic: Near Dighton,
           Massachusetts, was found the famous "Dighton
           Rock," with its inscriptions thought once to have
           been made by Norse explorers, but now believed
           the work of American Indians.

118.10   that famous brevity of Cæsar's: *Veni-Vidi-Vici:* "I
           came, I saw, I conquered." Suetonius, *The Lives of
           the Caesars* 1.37.

119.2   A SECOND LETTER: Sawin's "enumeration of his
           qualifications [for public office] clearly suggests
           Taylor" (Arthus Voss, "Backgrounds of Lowell's
           Satire in 'The Biglow Papers,'" p. 56).

119.5   *miles emeritus:* Veteran soldier.

119.5   *Quantum mutatus!:* "How changed!" Virgil, *The
           Aeneid* 2.274.

120.24–25 *In aliis mansuetus . . . Christum, non ita:* "In all
           other things I shall be mild, but in blasphemies
           against Christ I shall not be so." Unidentified.

122.13   John Jacob Astor (1763–1848) amassed a great
           fortune in the fur trade and other enterprises and
           was at the time of his death the richest man in
           America.

122.35   shakin' fever: Fever and ague (Mathews, *A
           Dictionary of Americanisms*).

123.5   shiver-de-freeze: Cf. *chevaux-de-frise.*

124.24   Santy Anny's pin: General Santa Anna lost one leg
           in defending Vera Cruz against the French in
           1838. The casualty enabled him to regain his
           popularity with the people which he had previously
           lost.

125.1   "Timbertoes": The letters of a humorist who signed
           himself "Enoch Timbertoes" appeared in the *New*

York Constellation. Allen Walker Read has suggested that the author of the letters was the paper's editor, Dr. Asa Greene ("The World of Joe Strickland," *Journal of American Folklore* 76, 1963:307). See also Walter Blair, *Native American Humor* (San Francisco: Chandler Publishing Co., 1960), pp. 42, 47.

127.3b Faneuil Hall: See 57.6n.

127.25–26 *Quærenda pecunia primum, virtus post nummos:* The rule of the bankers, "Seek money first; virtue after coins." Horace, *Epistles* 1.1.53–54.

127.27–28 *Quid non mortalia . . . auri sacra fames?:* "Whither do you not drive man's heart, cursed greed of gold?" Virgil, *The Aeneid* 3.56–57.

127.32–33 bread-trees: Or bread-fruit trees (*Artocarpus Incisa*) of the South Sea islands (*OED*).

127.33 butter: Bog-butter is "a fatty hydrocarbon found in the peat-bogs of Ireland" (*OED*).

127.34 Milk-trees: The *Brosimum Galactodendron* or cow-tree.

127.34–128.1 Sir John Hawkins (1532–1595), a British naval commander, whose voyage in 1564 to the Canary Islands is reported in the third volume of Hakluyt's *The Principal Navigations* (London, 1600). There one reads that on the island Hierro Hawkins found "a certaine tree that raineth continually, by the dropping whereof the inhabitants and cattell are satisfied with water, for other water have they none in all the Iland" (p. 502). Noted in *Commonplace Book II*.

128.2 Lynn: A city in Massachusetts well-known for its manufacture of shoes and leather.

128.7   Louis XI (1423–1483), king of the French. Pierre
               Matthieu, *Histoire de Louys XI* (Paris, 1610),
               quotes Claude de Seyssel: "que l'on voyoit autour
               des lieux où il se tenoit grand nombre de gens
               pendus aux arbres" (p. 499): "that there were seen
               about the places where [Louis XI] stayed large
               number of people hanging from the trees."

128.11   Diogenes (412?–?323 B.C.), the Cynic philosopher
               of Sinope, remarked on seeing some women hanged
               from an olive tree, "Would that every tree bore
               such fruit" (Diogenes Laertius, *Lives of Eminent
               Philosophers* 6.52).

128.18–19   *venerabile donum fatalis virgæ:* "Venerable, fateful
               wand," or the Golden Bough. Virgil, *The Aeneid*
               6.408–9.

128.29   garden of the Hesperides: Where grew golden
               apples.

128.30   that tree in the Sixth Æneid: See 128.18–19n.

129.5   Æolus: This keeper of the winds confined in a bag
               and gave to Ulysses all the unfavorable winds he
               could blow against Ulysses' vessel. The comrades
               of Ulysses thought the bag contained gold and
               silver and opened it, nearly bringing destruction on
               themselves and their ship. See Homer, *The Odyssey*
               10.1–75.

129.6   Ericus: In *Commonplace Book I* Lowell made a
               fuller notation: "Ericus, King of Swedeland, had a
               cap, & as he turned it, the wind he wished for
               would blow on that side."

129.8   Lapland Nornas: In Scandinavian mythology the
               nornas or norns are the dispensers of fate.

129.17   *hæc negotia penitus mecum revolvens:* "Turning
               these things over in my mind." Unidentified.

Perhaps this is Lowell's own slightly ironic parody of Latin expressions found in Sallust, Tacitus, Virgil, Seneca, and others, and which have the common meaning *"to turn over* or *revolve* in the mind; *to ponder, meditate,* or *reflect upon, consider."* Examples of these expressions can be found listed under *volvo* (II.B) in Lewis and Short, *Harpers' Latin Dictionary* (New York, 1879).

129.26   Pisgah: It was from the highest peak (Mount Nebo) of this mountain ridge northeast of the Dead Sea that Moses saw the Promised Land (Deuteronomy 34.1).

129.27   Alnaschar: In "The Barber's Tale of His Fifth Brother," *The Arabian Nights,* Alnaschar invested his small inheritance in glassware and, while musing on the great profits and delights its sale would bring, accidentally kicked over the tray of glass, losing both capital and profit.

129.36   Barataria is the island city in Cervantes's *Don Quixote,* over which Sancho Panza, the Don's squire, is made governor. Sancho, a gourmand, is quickly disenchanted with the rewards of government when at his lavish inauguration banquet each dish is taken away before he can taste it.

130.2   Spanish castles: Proverbial for imaginary castles in foreign lands. Its earliest appearance in English literature is in Chaucer's *The Romaunt of the Rose:* "Thou shalt make castels thanne in Spayne, / And dreme of joye, all but in vayne" (lines 2573–2574).

131.7   work on two different Sabbaths: The Battle of Cerro Gordo was fought on Sunday, 18 April 1847, and the fortress of Chapultepec was bombarded on

Sunday, 12 September 1847. The fortress fell the next day, though gallantly defended by "Los Niños," the hundred young cadets of the military college on the hill.

133.5 Selemnus: A river in Achaia in whose waters one could bathe and forget his passionate loves. See Pausanias, *Description of Greece* 7.23.1–3.

133.9 Cincinnatus: The celebrated Roman patrician who reluctantly left his plow in the furrow twice to serve as military dictator of the Republic when it faced danger. Both times his term was less than a month long.

133.22-23 Ashland . . . Bâton Rouge: "Ashland" was the home of Henry Clay in Lexington, Kentucky; North Bend, Ohio, of William Henry Harrison; Marshfield, Massachusetts, of Daniel Webster; Kinderhook, New York, of Martin Van Buren; and Baton Rouge, Louisiana, of Zachary Taylor.

134.5 General Court: The legal title of the state legislature of Massachusetts and New Hampshire.

134.17 *vox et præterea nihil:* "A voice and nothing more." A Latin proverb sometimes attributed to Seneca. See Plutarch's *Moralia,* "Sayings of the Spartans" 233: "A man plucked a nightingale and finding so little meat, said, 'You're all voice and nothing more.'"

134.21 *lactucas non esse dandas, dum cardui sufficiant:* "Lettuce is not to be given out when thistles are sufficient." Author unidentified; perhaps this is Lowell's version of the proverb cited by Erasmus: *Similes habent labra lactucas (Adages* 1.10.71). See also St. Jerome: *Similem habent labra lactucam asino cardus comedente:* "Lips have lettuce like themselves when an ass eats thistles" (*Letters* 7.5).

John Ray's explanation elucidates Wilbur's intent:
"Like lips like lettuce. . . . *Similes habent labra
lactucas.* A thistle is a sallet fit for an ass's mouth.
We use when we would signify that, things happen
to people which are suitable to them, or which they
deserve: as when a dull scholar happens to a
stupid or ignorant master . . ." (*A Collection of
English Proverbs,* Cambridge, England, 1670,
p. 114).

134.29   like sixty: "With great force or vigour; at a great
          rate" (*OED*).

136.1   To jest up killock: "To up killock" is to weigh
          anchor. In the Riverside Edition of *The Biglow
          Papers* an alternate spelling of this word appears:
          "killick." I have followed the spelling of copy-text
          (C1), believing that the change was made not for
          dialectal reasons, but simply because "killick" was
          the commoner spelling. The spelling was not
          altered in the Glossary.

136.3   Ole Zack: General Zachary Taylor won the Whig
          nomination for presidency over Henry Clay and
          Gen. Winfield Scott at the party's national
          convention in Philadelphia, June 1848. Millard
          Fillmore was the vice-presidential candidate. The
          Whig platform consisted of little more than a
          celebration of Taylor's military exploits, especially
          his defeat of Santa Anna at the Battle of Buena
          Vista.

136.9   Rough an' Ready: A Taylor sobriquet.

136.17   Lewis Cass (1782–1866) of Michigan was the
          presidential candidate of the Democratic party.

136.33   Wig, but without bein' ultry: See 109.2–3n.

137.1   *scratch:* A scratch-periwig or scratch-wig is "a
          small, short wig" (*OED*).

137.11   Mashfiel' speech: On 1 September 1848, in a speech
          at Marshfield, Massachusetts, Daniel Webster,
          while admitting that Taylor's nomination was "not
          fit to be made," said he would nevertheless vote
          for Taylor and hoped others would do likewise.
          "That sagacious, wise, far-seeing doctrine of
          availability lies at the bottom of the whole matter."
          The speech is printed in *The Works of Daniel
          Webster*, 6 vols. (Boston, 1851), 2:425–46.

137.14   bullethead: "An obstinate person" (Mathews, *A
          Dictionary of Americanisms*).

137.16   Rufus Choate (1799–1859) was a prominent
          Massachusetts lawyer and politician. According to
          his biographer, after Webster's unenthusiastic
          endorsement of Taylor at Marshfield (see
          137.11n.), "the Whigs turned to Choate, who
          helped them out by speaking before large mass
          meetings in Worcester and Salem" (Claude M.
          Fuess, *Rufus Choate: The Wizard of the Law*, New
          York: Minton, Balch & Co., 1928, p. 191).

138.2   chipped the shell: "To crack or break the shell of a
          nut" (*OED*).

138.2   Buffalo: "On August 9, 1848, the convention
          containing the consolidated elements of
          constitutional opposition to the extension of
          slavery met at Buffalo." Calling itself the Free Soil
          party, it declared in its platform: no more slave
          states and no more slave territory. "Martin Van
          Buren and Charles Francis Adams were the
          candidates selected. Van Buren was chosen because
          it was thought he might attract Democratic votes.
          His opposition to the extension of slavery was not
          very energetic. In his letter accepting the
          nomination he commended the convention for
          having taken no decisive stand against slavery in
          the District of Columbia" (Williams, p. 408).

138.8   eighteen thirty six: Sawin remembers that it was on the Democratic ticket that Van Buren won the presidential election of that year.

138.17   son John: President Van Buren's son John (1810–1866), after a somewhat riotous student life at Yale, entered New York politics. It was largely through his influence that the "Barnburners," a faction of the New York Democratic party, left the national convention in 1848 and joined in the Free Soil movement.

138.19   hymn: Cf. the traditional nursery rhyme:
> Goosey, goosey gander,
>   Whither shall I wander?
> Upstairs and downstairs
>   And in my lady's chamber.
> There I met an old man
>   Who would not say his prayers.
> I took him by the left leg
>   And threw him down the stairs.

138.30   Taunton water: Though it is today polluted, "the Great Taunton River, navigable and teeming with fish," the largest river in southeastern Massachusetts, was noted in Lowell's time for its clarity. (My thanks to Ms. Frances Gilchrist, Taunton Public Library, for this suggestion as to the meaning of Lowell's allusion.)

140.33   act agin the law: Legislation severely restricting and even denying education to black people had been in effect in the South since the colonial period.

141.10   the Scriptur'l cus o' Shem: One of the principal biblical arguments used by apologists for slavery. See Genesis 9.25–27: "Cursed be Canaan; a servant of servants shall he be unto his brethren. And he said, Blessed be the Lord God of Shem; and Canaan shall be his servant. God shall enlarge Japheth, and he shall dwell in the tents of Shem; and Canaan shall be his servant." Canaan was the son of Ham; see 98.31n.

142.4   Jacques Cartier: See Hakluyt, *The Principal Navigations*, 3 vols. (London, 1598–1600), 3:221: The second voyage of Jacques Cartier by the Grand bay up the river of Canada to Hochelaga, Anno 1535, chap. 8.

142.8   Simon Episcopius (1583–1643), the controversial leader of the Arminian Remonstrants in the Netherlands early in the seventeenth century, was noted for the sharpness and zeal of his writing and preaching.

142.12–13   Father John de Plano Carpini: Giovanni da Pian del Carpine was an early thirteenth-century Franciscan whose *History of the Mongols* was the first detailed European account of those people. Lowell copied the quotation, actually from William de Rubruquis's narrative of his journey to the East, also made in the thirteenth century, in *Commonplace Book II*, noting: "reference lost." The two narratives appear next to one another in Hakluyt's *The Principal Navigations*, 3 vols. (London, 1598–1600). De Rubruquis writes: "Also counterfeit messengers, because they feine themselves to be messengers, when as indeed they are none at all, they punish with death" (1:100).

142.17   Alphonso the Sixth: Samuel Pepys, Lowell's probable source, wrote of this profligate king of Portugal (1643–1675): "He had . . . little respect for Religion. . . . Since he was not able absolutely to forbear hearing of Sermons, he ordered the Preachers that they should shorten their Sermons; and some of them were Banished, because they did not obey this Order; and others forbore to Preach at all" (*The Portugal History*, London, 1677, p. 142).

144.5   Anakim: The sons of Anak, a tribe of giants in the Old Testament (see Numbers 13.33). Nephelim, the term designating the giants in several modern translations of the Bible, is derived from the Greek νεφέλη, cloud or mass of clouds.

144.12   Hercules: The second of Hercules' twelve labors was the destruction of the nine-headed Hydra. In the struggle as each head was cut off by Hercules, two would spring up. Only with the aid of his friend Iolaus, who burnt the stumps of each head with a hot iron, was Hercules able to defeat the monster.

148.21b   Cotton Mather: See *Magnalia Christi Americana,* bk. 6, chap. 3, *"Ceraunius. Relating Remarkables done by THUNDER,"* p. 14: *"Satan, let loose by God, can do wonders in the Air: He can raise Storms, he can discharge the* Great Ordinance of Heaven, *Thunder and Lightning; and by his Art can make them more* Terrible *and* Dreadful *than they are in their own nature.* 'Tis no Heresie or Blasphemy to think that the *Prince of the Power of the Air* hath as good Skill in *Chymistry* as goes to the making of *Aurum Fulminans"* (London, 1702).

153.42b   suspended *naso adunco:* Cf. Horace, *Satires* 1.6.5: *naso suspendis adunco:* "with turned up nose."

154.12b   Paul Pry: An impudent, inquisitive character in John Poole's farce, *Paul Pry* (1825).

156.1–2b   Stilling's Pneumatology: Johann Heinrich Stilling, pseudonym of Johann Heinrich Jung (1740–1817), German writer, whose *Theorie der Geister-Kunde* (Nurnberg, 1808), was translated into English as *Theory of Pneumatology, in Reply to the Question*

What Ought To Be Believed or Disbelieved concerning Presentiments, Visions, and Apparitions, According to Nature, Reason, and Scripture (London, 1834).

158.22a — Henry Fuseli (1741–1825), English painter and art critic.

158.19b — *nefandum!:* Abominable!

162.38–40b — Henry St. John, Viscount Bolingbroke (1678–1751), English statesman and writer, wrote to Jonathan Swift, 1 January 1721/2: "You churchmen have cried [Seneca] up for a great saint; and as if you imagined, that to have it believed that he had a month's mind to be a Christian, would reflect some honour on Christianity, you employed one of those pious frauds, so frequently practised in the days of primitive simplicity, to impose on the world a pretended correspondence between him and the great apostle of the Gentiles" (*The Correspondence of Jonathan Swift, D.D.*, ed. F. E. Ball, 6 vols., London: G. Bell and Sons, 1910–1914, 3:110). See 111.4n.

165.4b — Isaac Allerton (c. 1586–1658/9), Pilgrim father and last survivor of the *Mayflower* passengers. His will is printed in *The Mayflower Descendant*, 2 (1900): 155–57.

Textual Apparatus

Textual Commentary

In June 1846 Lowell wrote to Sydney Howard Gay, editor of the *National Anti-Slavery Standard:* "You will find a squib of mine in this week's 'Courier.' I wish it to continue anonymous, for I wish Slavery to think it has as many enemies as possible." Twenty-nine months later he announced to the same friend the publication of *The Biglow Papers* [First Series].[1] During those two years, Lowell had discovered in the newspaper verses of Hosea Biglow a book not in mind at the beginning; or as Wilbur wrote in the Introduction:

> When, more than three years ago, my talented young parishioner, Mr. Biglow, came to me and submitted to my animadversions the first of his poems which he intended to commit to the more hazardous trial of a city newspaper, it never so much as entered my imagination to conceive that his productions would ever be gathered into a fair volume, and ushered into the august presence of the reading public by myself. So little are we short-sighted mortals able to predict the event!

This fact presents the book's editor with bibliographical problems different from those of a more conventional work which has much of its existence in its author's mind before many of its words are before the public's eyes. In addition, such ordinary editorial issues as copy-text, substantive and accidental variants are complicated because parts of *The Biglow Papers* are written in dialect. Fortunately, the growth of *The Biglow Papers* is adequately documented —by manuscripts, by Lowell's correspondence, and by the texts— and editorial decisions have the courage given by recoverable and relevant facts.

Gay saved the manuscripts Lowell sent him for the *Standard*, and in 1951 his descendants presented them to the Houghton Library, Harvard University. These included fair-copy manuscripts of

1. The "squib" was Hosea's first poem: "Thrash away, you 'll *hev* to rattle." *Letters of James Russell Lowell,* ed. Charles Eliot Norton, 3 vols. (Boston and New York: Houghton, Mifflin and Co., 1904), 1:161, 195.

four of Hosea's verses, Wilbur's "Leaving the Matter Open," and a "Letter from Rev. Mr. Wilbur" (see Appendix to this volume). Though written over a period of several months (printed in the *Standard* between May and September 1848), the six manuscripts are of the same paper stock—ruled, gray wove paper measuring approximately 12¼ × 15¼ inches—and are written in black ink. These large sheets are either folded width-wise into folios of four pages or cut in half. "The Pious Editor's Creed" (MS2) is written on both sides of one half-sheet and is signed "H. B." "Letter from a Candidate for the Presidency in answer to suttin questions proposed by Hosea Biglow" (MS3) is likewise written on both sides of a half-sheet. "Letter from Birdofredum Sawin" (MS4: No. VIII) is written on both sides of one folded full sheet (4 pages) and on both sides of a half-sheet. Written in a hand probably not Lowell's in the upper left-hand corner of the first page is the note, "Don't cut." "Another letter from B. Sawin Esqʳ" (MS5) is likewise written on both sides of one folded full sheet and one half-sheet (6 pages). At the top of the half-sheet (page 5) is written in pencil, not by Lowell, "Robt. J. Johnson 300 W—— St.," and at the bottom of page 6, again in pencil, "Robert J. Johnson." "Leaving the Matter Open" (MS1) is written on 6 pages like MSS 4 and 5, addressed "For / Sydney H. Gay, / Nᵒ 142 Nassau St, / New York." and postmarked Cambridge, 22 July. While one can be certain that the *National Anti-Slavery Standard* printings of the verses were set from these manuscripts, there is no reason to suppose that they were returned to Lowell when he was preparing copy for *The Biglow Papers*.

In addition to the fair-copy manuscripts, there are working-drafts of several "Biglow" verses in Lowell's writing-books in the Houghton Library. The longest of these is Hosea's description of his early schooldays: "Propt on the marsh, a dwelling now, I see" (28.21– 30.36 in the present edition). It is included in a poem titled "Indian Summer," an early version of "An Indian-Summer Reverie." In the same writing-book is a later draft of this poem, much reworked, shortened, and considerably more like the published text of the poem in form and language. The "Biglow" verses do not appear in the revised draft. Lowell was using this writing-book as late as September 1847, since on its first leaf are his notations of the dates in that month when he received, read, or returned proof of *Poems, Second Series* (Cambridge and Boston, 1848). "Indian Summer" would have been written some time before, since its later version, "An Indian-Summer Reverie," was first published in *Poems, Second Series*. Typically, Lowell salvaged lines that seemed inappropriate to that poem and gave them to Hosea. These verses, written in pencil, appear on leaves 6, 7, and 10 (on the last is an 18-line insert, 29.1–18 in the present edition). The writing-book, of off-white wove paper, measuring $6\frac{1}{2} \times 8$ inches (Houghton Library number bMS Am 765:958; hereafter cited as *Writing-Book I*), also contains a draft of the verse "Old Joe is gone, who saw hot Percy goad" (31.6–19), written in pencil on leaves 9 and 10.

A draft of "The Two Gunners" is in a writing-book which Charles Eliot Norton, Lowell's literary executor, has labelled "J.R.L. / 184–?—185– / Notes and Rough-drafts." Bound in marbled boards with leather spine and corners, the leaves of light blue wove paper measure $6\frac{7}{8} \times 8$ inches (bMS Am 765:959; hereafter cited as *Writing-Book II*). "The Two Gunners" is written on the verso of leaf 11 and the recto of leaf 12 of signature 6. It is preceded by a draft of "The Burial of Theobald" (*The Liberty Bell*, Boston, 1849) and is followed by "A preliminary note to the second edition" of *A Fable for Critics* (published in January 1849). This suggests that the verses were written during the late fall or early winter of 1848, though they were not published until nine years later when Lowell added them to the Introduction of *The Biglow Papers* in the "Blue and Gold Edition" of his *Poetical Works* (Boston, 1858).

In another writing-book is a draft of the first 36 lines of "Leaving the Matter Open." Bound in green marbled boards with leather spine and corners, and of gray laid paper measuring $7\frac{5}{16} \times 8\frac{15}{16}$ inches, the writing-book is signed and dated by "J. R. Lowell—September 22. 1840— / PRIVATE Journal" (bMS Am 765:955). The 33 lines of verse, written in pencil on both sides of leaf 29, agree often in phrases and sometimes completely with the corresponding lines of the poem as printed in *The Biglow Papers*, but they were extensively reworked and rearranged before they became the opening of Wilbur's poem.

On the rectos of leaves 34 and 35 of this same writing-book are notes for Hosea's first verses printed in Buckingham's *Courier* (17 June 1846). Several of the lines composed at this time would be used in later, though still unanticipated, "Biglow" verses. Centered at the top of the first of these two pages is the single line: "Wal, fellers, here they be agin." Below that, towards the left: " 'T'will suit All them that go agin / A body with a soul in't, / That feel on-easy in a skin/Without a bagnet hole in't" (cf. 123.20–21 in the present edition). On the remainder of the page are the lines (cancellations are enclosed in angle brackets; undeciphered words are indicated by a question mark enclosed in square brackets following the questioned word):

> Wal, I declare my eyes are sot
> To see them darned recruiters
> A 'ticin fellers to be shot
> With them ere music-tooters!
> ⟨A struttin round our village lanes⟩
> It looks as though they took some pains
> To make themselves conspickus
> As chaps that blow out folks's brains—
> But that ain't goin to trick us.
>
> ⟨For all they look so dreadful smart⟩ Ef you should dress me jest
>   as smart
> You couldn't make callous [?]
> I vow I can't help thinkin
> ⟨About a feller in a cart⟩ I'd feel a kind o' in a cart
> Agoin to the gallows;

On the verso of leaf 34 is a draft of a poem beginning "Away, unfruitful love of books / For whose vain idiom we reject / The soul's original dialect. . . ." It continues on the recto of leaf 35 below these lines:

> Wal, as sure as I live, my eyes are sot
> To see them recruetin fellers acomin'
> Expectin' to tice folks out to be shot
> For ninepence a day & a little drummin
> ⟨A musket's⟩ ⟨gun⟩ Powder's a very good thing in its way

And so be balls when you aint the receiver
And a uniform's pooty but what ⟨good⟩ be they
Agin an attack o'the yaller fever?
⟨You may⟩ Feel dreadful big, that ⟨s all proper &⟩ ain't nothin but
    right,
⟨And may⟩ Stick as much feathers & lace as you please on
They'll skeer poor Amhoody [?] but how'll ⟨will⟩ you fight
Such a downright chap as the Rainy Season?

The point of this consideration of a few lines immensely revised
and improved before publication is to recognize that Lowell worked
at authorship like other professionals; first attempts were often
considerably unlike final versions. The opinion that he did otherwise, still commonly accepted in critical discussions, had its origins
in Lowell's ability to entertain an audience of friends with extempore verse, his ability to work quickly and for long periods without
interruption, and his own statements that any number of poems
were written "at one sitting," "at a white heat," and so forth. If such
statements were true in part, they also served to conceal, perhaps
most from the poet himself, flaws in the romantic theory of inspired composition. The fault with much of Lowell's poetry is that
he did not work on it long or hard enough to achieve that sustained
artistry and imaginative force characteristic of poetry of the first
order. Perhaps he couldn't; more likely he just didn't care enough.
While often quoting the words, Lowell rarely followed the spirit of
Horace's advice—*nonumque prematur in annum* (let it be kept
concealed till the ninth year)—and what man of letters as a man
of business, to use Howells's phrase, can afford that luxury? But the
verses of *The Biglow Papers* form something of an exception, like
his better poems in other genres. The evidence of his writing-books
and the collation of subsequent publications of many poems reveal
a Lowell less guilty of artistic negligence than he has been thought
in the past.[2] They also show something of the human cost of writing poetry.

2. G. Thomas Tanselle recently studied Lowell's revisions in *The Cathedral* after its first publication (1869), illustrating "the care with which
[Lowell] could work when he chose" ("The Craftsmanship of Lowell:

A fourth writing-book is undoubtedly the one Lowell used while putting together *The Biglow Papers* during the late summer and fall of 1848. Unfortunately it tells little about Lowell's method of work, since only four leaves of one signature and a tipped flyleaf remain complete. The wove paper is light blue, ruled, and measures 6¾ × 8 inches (bMS Am 765.963). Besides the five leaves there are stubs of the leaves of five signatures on which sometimes enough writing remains to enable one to identify what was written on the original leaf. These stubs show that the Latin advertisement for Wilbur's book (14.15–17.31 in the present edition) was written in this notebook. On some are words or word fragments in dialect verse, and there remain traces of many pages of Wilbur's prose. In one instance two complete lines remain, having been written parallel to the inner fold of the signature and inserted into the verse: "Ef you should multiply be ten the portion of the bravest one / You wouldn't have more'n half enough to speak of on a grave" (cf. 123.16–17 in the present text). Most interesting are notes (discussed in the Introduction, p. xxiii) for *The Biglow Papers* written on the recto of the first extant leaf:

> *largest* picture in yᵉ world & *greatest*.
> His grandfather a painter of the grandiose or Michael
> Angelo & Fuseli school. He never painted anything smaller than
> a house. The episode of his uncle's gallery of family portraits
> His father's prejudice against vowels.
> His life at college—Father's letter—Professor's lectures.
> Man supporting the sky.
> Man planting trees with the roots up.
> April fools & perennial ones.
> An army stopped by a tollgate-keeper who threatens to set
> his dog upon them.

Revisions in *The Cathedral*," *Bulletin of the New York Public Library* 70, January 1966: 50–63). Two other important studies of Lowell's "craftsmanship," both published in *The Papers of the Bibliographical Society of America*, are Hamilton Vaughan Bail, "James Russell Lowell's Ode," 37 (1943): 169–202, and James C. Armstrong and Kenneth E. Carpenter, "James Russell Lowell *On Democracy*," 59 (1965): 385–99.

P.W. "thought some" of having his effigies prefixed to the
work as likely to make it sell better

Perly the amateur pig—metempsychosis—Manco Capac.

On the other extant leaves of this notebook are jotted down ideas,
quotations, and allusions pertaining to *The Biglow Papers*, as well
as notes relating to other literary projects on Lowell's desk or in his
mind at this time.

The circumstances and the progress of publication of the first-
book edition of *The Biglow Papers* are well documented in Lowell's
Letters selected by Norton for his edition: from that of 13 November 1847 to Briggs, announcing Hosea's intention of "publishing a
volume of his own before long"; through the letters of September
and October 1848, reporting difficulties and delays in the preparation of copy and the stereotyping of the volume; to the letter of 10
November 1848 written to Gay on the day of the book's publication.[3]
It took an unusually long time to stereotype the plates. On 22 August 1848, Lowell told Briggs, ". . . I am to begin printing Hosea
forthwith."[4] Stereotyping must have begun soon after, because by
the end of September Lowell had "one hundred pages of Biglow
stereotyped & expect to get it out by the 15th pro° at farthest. It is
hard work. I have now to go to work & prepare some copy."[5] But
nearly a month later, on 27 October, he was "Still not out of the
mill! Stereotyping is such a slow process that I am not quit of the
printers yet, & I have proof to correct as soon as I have folded this."[6]
A week later, however, "Hosea is done with and will soon be out. It
made fifty pages more than I expected and so took longer."[7] In a
letter to Mrs. Horace Mann, 10 September 1848, Lowell had written
most fully about the special problems of printing *The Biglow Papers:*

3. *Letters*, 1:167, 189–95.
4. A.L.s., Houghton Library, Harvard University.
5. Lowell to Gay [30 September 1848]: A.L.s., Houghton Library, Harvard University.
6. A.L.s., Houghton Library, Harvard University. Gay has noted the
month and day on this letter which Lowell simply dated "Friday."
7. *Letters*, 1:195.

I have been so very busy now for some time. . . . My friend M^r
Hosea Biglow is printing a volume of his various contributions
toward a national literature, & I have undertaken to carry it
through the press for him. The peculiar spelling of my esteemed friend, & the necessity of adapting it to some uniform
rule, which shall at the same time fulfil the office of a guide to
the true provincial pronunciation, render this a very laborious
& harassing task. If you could see one of the proofsheets, you
would at once understand how great a demand they make both
upon my judgment & my eyesight. The notes subjoined to the
original poems by the Revd Mr Wilbur of Jaalam, in whom the
necessity of producing two discourses a week for nearly fifty
years, has not tended to foster a habit of compression, increase
the difficulties of the task. It is important that the volume
should appear as early as the 1st of October, & this, with other
necessary avocations, has employed my time to the exclusion
of everything else.[8]

The extraordinary amount of variation in accidentals which collation reveals to have been made between the newspaper printings
of the verses and the book publication supports Lowell's lament to
Mary Mann about his heavy revision on proof-sheets, and makes the
choice of copy-text for those sections of the text not extant in fair-
copy manuscripts but published first in newspapers more complicated than is usual.[9] Lowell's close supervision of the stereotyping

8. A.L.s., Massachusetts Historical Society, Boston. Quoted by permission. For mention in the printed *Letters* of Lowell's difficulty with proof,
see 1:189, 192, 193.

9. Since the theory and practice of editing literary texts have during
the past decade attracted the attention and the talents of many scholars
and critics of American literature, a review of terminology and proce-
dure seems increasingly unnecessary when they do not differ from the
currently recognized and accepted definitions and standards. My editorial principles and procedures are fundamentally those established and
recommended by the Center for Editions of American Authors, Modern
Language Association, in its manual, *Statement of Editorial Principles:
A Working Manual for Editing Nineteenth-Century American Texts*, Revised Edition (New York: Modern Language Association, 1972).

of the plates of the first-book edition gives the accidentals of that edition an authority greater than that of the newspaper texts. Collation of the newspaper printings against the fair-copy manuscripts prepared by Lowell for publication in Gay's New York weekly shows that the newspaper compositors were extremely careless in their work: words were misread, Lowell's spelling was not always followed, punctuation was altered. When manuscript is not extant from which the newspaper text was set, it is impossible to know the instances when the newspaper compositor did not follow Lowell's copy. It is difficult to imagine that the *Boston Courier* was much better than the *National Anti-Slavery Standard* in its typesetting. On 12 January 1846, Lowell asked Gay to print a list of errata, arguing: "My own particular martyrdoms in this kind are so numerous that I am become quite casehardened, but as you have lately copied three pieces of mine each more or less disguised, I resolved that *you* at least & your readers should be disenchanted" (A.L.s., Houghton Library). Undoubtedly Lowell did not restore to the original every change we can presume the *Courier* typesetters made, but these unauthorized changes must remain. Since neither the printer's copy Lowell prepared for book publication nor proof of the book has survived, any unauthorized changes that may have been made by the book compositor and not caught by Lowell likewise cannot be known. Every change in accidentals made between the *Boston Courier* texts and the first-book text must be accepted as Lowell's; the exception would be errors introduced into the first-book edition that were not present in the newspaper printings: but these do not occur.

For these reasons, copy-text for the parts of the present edition that do not exist in fair-copy manuscript is the text of the first-book edition and not the texts of the newspaper printings. To choose for copy-text the newspaper printings would necessitate recording in the list of emendations the many hundreds of changes in spelling and punctuation made between the earlier texts and the first-book edition. The present text would not be changed in any way. My decision has been against fruitless pedantry. The substantive variants between these newspaper texts which precede copy-text and the present text are recorded in the list of Pre-copy-text Substantive Variants immediately following this commentary. Also listed there are the substantive variants between the present text and the drafts in Lowell's writing-books of "Propt on the marsh, a dwelling now, I see," "Old Joe is gone, who saw hot Percy goad," and "The Two Gunners." The substantive differences between the incomplete draft of "Leaving the Matter Open" and the fair-copy-manuscript version of the poem are so considerable that a listing of variants would not only be unwieldly but of no purpose towards the establishment of a critical text. Nor does it merit reprinting as an appendix.[10]

When a fair-copy manuscript exists it has been chosen as copytext. A fair-copy manuscript has an authority that is never equalled by any other form of the text. Lowell did not have these manuscripts in hand, however, when he prepared copy for the book edition, but used instead copies of the newspaper printings. Where the newspaper text was in error, Lowell could not refer to the manuscript to see what the original reading had been; quite often he restored the earlier reading, but he also not infrequently introduced new readings; some of these unauthorized changes, however, went unnoticed by Lowell, remaining in *The Biglow Papers* until now. If the new reading introduced by Lowell into the text of the first-book edition because of an error in the newspaper text is not clearly inferior to the manuscript or copy-text reading, then I have let Lowell's emendation stand; he may have remembered the earlier reading, but preferred the new. In a few instances, however, Lowell introduced a reading that seems to the present editor decidedly inferior to the reading in manuscript. These superior readings of copy-text have been retained in the present edition; since the rejected readings are accidentals, they are not recorded in any of the lists which follow this commentary. The alterations in accidentals Lowell did not change either back to the manuscript reading or to a new preferred reading have been rejected as nonauthorial; if they are a correction of a mistake in the manuscript, they are retained in the present edition, but on the authority of the first-book edition rather than the

10. It should be mentioned that Lowell cannibalized several of his *Anti-Slavery Standard* editorials when preparing copy for Parson Wilbur. Cf. 93.32–94.36 in the present edition with *The Anti-Slavery Papers of James Russell Lowell* (Boston and New York: Houghton, Mifflin and Co., 1902), 1.149–50; 115.16–25 with 1:60–61. Less similar is 99.4–14 and 1:15.

newspaper text. Most of these unauthorized changes are of a nature that would not have attracted Lowell's notice; they are not wrong, but neither are they his. The use of manuscript as copy-text for these sections does not produce a text very different from that which would have resulted in using the text of the first-book edition as copy-text throughout; but there is a difference, and that difference is towards what the evidence shows to have been Lowell's intention.[11]

The Biglow Papers was published by George Nichols, a Cambridge bookseller and publisher, and also one of the proprietors of Metcalf and Company, the stereotypers of the book. Lowell's contract with Nichols has not survived. Probably it was not dissimilar to the agreement he had made with Nichols the preceding year for publication of Poems, Second Series. A copy of the "Memorandum of an agreement," dated 22 November 1847,[12] requires that the work "be stereotyped at [Lowell's] own sole expense . . . the copyright of said volume & the title to the stereotype plates thereof remaining with said Lowell." Nichols "agrees that he will print, bind & publish . . . at his own sole expense, the said editions of said volume, . . . & that he, the said Nichols, by advertising or otherwise will do all in his power to promote the sales of said volume." In the case of The Biglow Papers, however, John Bartlett, another Cambridge bookseller and compiler of quotations, was the distributor of the volume rather than Nichols.

There were two printings of The Biglow Papers in 1848: the first of 1,500 copies in early November which Lowell reported "gone in a week," and a second issued sometime before 20 December.[13] In an account statement from Bartlett, dated 13 March 1849, the total

11. The evidence that Lowell in preparing copy for the first-book edition used the newspaper printings and not manuscript copies of the verses is circumstantial, but convincing beyond any reasonable doubt. In addition to the changes just discussed, one substantive misreading by the newspaped compositor—"cut the" for "cut an'" (140.17)—was not corrected by Lowell in the first-book edition.

12. But in another place it is dated 23 November 1847. Perhaps this error was the reason for the copy's not being signed by either party. With the other business papers quoted in this Commentary, the memorandum is in the Houghton Library, Harvard University.

13. Lowell to Gay, 20 December 1848: Letters, 1:198.

number of copies of the two printings is said to be 1,750, from which Lowell received 30 author-copies and $223.70. Out of this Lowell had to pay Metcalf and Company $222.06 for stereotyping the volume. This resulted in a profit of $1.64, much below the $50 he thought he might make when he wrote Gay, 20 December 1848: "If the relative positions of author and publisher were established on a proper footing, I ought to have cleared at least $400 by these two editions [of The Biglow Papers]. As it is, I shall make $250, from which something like $200 will be deducted to pay for my stereotype plates."[14] Lowell would never be greatly successful in marketing his writings. In 1848, however, the financial results bordered on the absurd.

Bookmen have long argued about the priority of the three separate imprints of the first printing of The Biglow Papers. Lowell had asked Briggs to investigate the possibility that a New York publisher could distribute in that city copies of the book, and on 28 October Briggs wrote to Lowell: "Putnam says that you may put his name into 100 copies for his London agency and 500 for New York, if you would like for him to attend to the sale and distribution here."[15] Examination on the Hinman Collating Machine of copies of each of the three imprints presents no evidence, either of type change or type wear, that solves the issue of priority. Undoubtedly the sheets

14. Letters, 1:198. The cost of the stereotype plates for both The Biglow Papers and A Vision of Sir Launfal was $245.30 (BP: $222.06 + VSL: $23.24). Lowell's royalty from Bartlett for the first two printings of both volumes was $259.72 (BP: $223.70 + VSL: $36.02). The first two printings of A Vision of Sir Launfal totalled 1,000 copies.

15. Jacob Chester Chamberlain and Luther S. Livingston, A Bibliography of the First Editions in Book Form of the Writings of James Russell Lowell (New York: Privately Printed, 1914), p. 34. The date of this letter is conjectured upon evidence in Lowell's letter to Gay, 27 October 1848, Houghton Library, Harvard University. I have not located the original manuscript. The three imprints read: 1) CAMBRIDGE: / PUBLISHED BY GEORGE NICHOLS. / 1848. 2) CAMBRIDGE: / PUBLISHED BY GEORGE NICHOLS. / NEW YORK: / GEORGE P. PUTNAM, 155 BROADWAY. / 1848. 3) CAMBRIDGE: / PUBLISHED BY GEORGE NICHOLS. / LONDON: / PUTNAM'S AMERICAN LITERARY AGENCY, / J. CHAPMAN, 142 STRAND. / 1848.

of all three were printed at one press run, the only alteration being that made on the plate of the title page.[16] Collation does distinguish between two printings with the single Cambridge imprint, what Lowell referred to as two "editions," both dated 1848. The earlier impression is without necessary periods at xiii.8, following "dunce," and 82.5, following "scenes" (28.32 and 107.17 in the present edition), as are copies dated 1848 with the Cambridge-New York and Cambridge-London imprints. The missing punctuation is supplied in the second impression and continues to appear in later printings.[17]

16. There are likewise three binding states: 1) Brown paper boards, paper label on spine: THE / BIGLOW / PAPERS. / [rule] / 1848. / [enclosed within frame rule]; 2) Yellow glazed boards with paper label on spine as above; 3) Cloth (purple, red, brown, tan, black), covers stamped blind, spine stamped in gold capitals: BIGLOW / PAPERS. Only the single Cambridge imprint appears in the first two bindings; all three appear in cloth. Presentation copies of the first printing which I have seen have the single Cambridge imprint and are in paper or glazed boards. Lowell's undated inscriptions are written in the character and "handwriting" of Homer Wilbur, A.M.

17. The two printings can also be distinguished by type wear: the second "i" is not dotted in the page number "vii" ("Note to Title-Page" section), nor is it dotted in "climatic" at 162.22a in copies of the second printing (because these points are of use only in distinguishing printings of the first-book edition, corresponding page and line numbers in the present text are not given); the period following "130" at 161.40b is missing in the second printing; and the "A" in "Aint" at 9.1, the "r" of "fer" at 25.1, the "f" of "of" at 80.20, and the "C" of "Chalk" at 152.9a are slightly damaged in the later printing.

Much written about the first edition of *The Biglow Papers* is erroneous or of little textual import. Chamberlain and Livingston were the first to doubt George Willis Cooke's statement that copies of the 1848 edition were issued without "Notices of an Independent Press" (*A Bibliography of James Russell Lowell,* Boston and New York: Houghton, Mifflin and Co., 1906, pp. 93–94). The collector and his bibliographer argue that "this is undoubtedly an error, as the half-title and title are leaves 7 and 8 of the first signature 'a', followed by signature 'b', eight leaves, and 'c', six leaves. The text itself begins with a new series of signatures . . ." (pp. 33–34). None of the fifty libraries in America and Europe who reported their Lowell collections to me listed a copy of the 1848 edition without

In 1849 Lowell followed Longfellow's advice and became one of the growing number of New England writers who would during the next decade make the imprint of Ticknor and Fields the most prestigious in the country. As Lowell wrote his friend William Wetmore Story: "By this means I shall profit by what I write more than hitherto, which is certainly a desideratum."[18] Ticknor announced a "new edition" of *The Biglow Papers* early in 1851, but it was not until March 1853 that 500 copies of the book were printed, called on the title page "Third Edition." Five hundred more copies, also "Third Edition," were printed the following year.[19] These "editions" were only new printings from Lowell's 1848 stereotype plates, plates which would be used until 1881 when a "Twelfth Edition" appeared, the type by then so battered that the printed text is often illegible.[20] Except for the two periods supplied between the first two

---

these preliminary leaves. Lowell had completed these notices at least a month before the volume was published. He wrote to Briggs, 6 October 1848: "I have affixed some preliminary 'Notices of an Independent Press' to to [sic] Hosea which will make you laugh." (A.L.s., Houghton Library, Harvard University.)

18. 25 September 1849: Henry James, *William Wetmore Story and His Friends*, 2 vols. (Edinburgh and London: W. Blackwood and Sons, 1903), 1:181. Longfellow: W. S. Tryon, *Parnassus Corner: A Life of James T. Fields* (Boston: Houghton Mifflin Co., 1963), p. 132.

19. *The Cost Books of Ticknor and Fields and Their Predecessors: 1832–1858*, ed. W. S. Tryon and William Charvat (New York: Bibliographical Society of America, 1949), pp. 240, 282; the original of these papers, together with those of the successors of Ticknor and Fields— James R. Osgood and Company, Houghton, Mifflin and Co., etc.—are deposited in the Houghton Library, Harvard University.

20. The dates and publisher imprints of subsequent printings (called "editions") issued from these plates after 1848 are as follows: "Third Edition" (Boston: Ticknor, Reed, and Fields), 1853 and 1854; "Fourth Edition" (Boston: Ticknor and Fields), 1858 and 1860; "Fifth Edition" (Boston: Ticknor and Fields), 1862; "Sixth Edition" (Boston: Ticknor and Fields), 1866; "Seventh Edition" (Boston: Ticknor and Fields), 1867; "Eighth Edition" (Boston: Ticknor and Fields), 1868; "Ninth Edition" (Boston: James R. Osgood and Co.), 1872; "Tenth Edition" (Bos-

printings of the book, there is no change, other than type wear, in the plates. Standing errors remained uncorrected—the lack of a comma following "Scioppius" (44.1 in the present edition), a common misspelling of Faneuil Hall (92.7), and the newspaper misprint, "an' fairly cut the run" for "an' fairly cut an' run" (140.17) —and Lowell's revisions after 1848 were not incorporated.

When Lowell prepared copy for the "Blue and Gold Edition" of his *Poetical Works* in 1857 he made some revisions in the text of *The Biglow Papers*.[21] Besides adding "The Two Gunners" and "Leaving the Matter Open" to the Introduction, he made Wilbur's commentaries on the verses still more erudite and rendered Hosea's

ton: James R. Osgood and Co.), 1876; "Twelfth Edition" (Boston: Houghton, Mifflin and Co.), 1881. I have neither seen nor located an "Eleventh Edition." A "Large Paper" edition of twelve copies of the First Series was printed from these plates in 1867 and bound uniformly with a "Large Paper" edition of *The Biglow Papers, Second Series*. At the Beinecke Library, Yale University, is a copy of *The Biglow Papers* [First Series] consisting of the sheets of the first 1848 printing cut and rebound, a new title page preceding "Notices of an Independent Press" with the imprint: CAMBRIDGE, U.S. / PUBLISHED BY GEORGE NICHOLS. / LONDON: JOHN CHAPMAN, 142, STRAND. / 1849. The verso of the title page is blank. An equally curious copy of the First Series is a volume made from sheets of the second 1848 printing, uncut and bound in unlettered paper wrappers (Berg Collection, New York Public Library). Richard Curle, who purchased the book in London, is undoubtedly correct in supposing that it was sent to England "with the idea of finding a publisher or getting a review" (*Collecting American First Editions: Its Pitfalls and Pleasures*, Indianapolis: Bobbs-Merrill Co., 1930, p. 193).

21. On 15 September 1857 Lowell wrote to H. O. Houghton, printer of the "Blue and Gold Edition," that he had received proof—"I think that there is quite enough on a page & that the volume will look very well"— and asks if Houghton has received new copy. The following Monday (21 September 1857) he asked Houghton "to have the Biglow Papers lead off in Vol 2nd." This request was not followed, and in the second volume of the two-volume edition *The Biglow Papers* comes after *A Fable for Critics*. A.LL.s., Columbia University Library, New York City; Berg Collection, New York Public Library. Quoted by permission.

dialect more accurately in places.[22] In 1869 this edition was supplanted by the one-volume "Diamond Edition" of Lowell's *Poetical Works*, announced as the first complete edition, and called "Diamond" because of the painfully small type.[23] Lowell prepared copy and read proof of this edition, as he did again seven years later when the "Household Edition" of his poems was issued by James R. Osgood and Company, successor to Ticknor and Fields.[24]

The plates of the "Household Edition" continued to be used until after Lowell's death in 1891, though changes were made in the format, enlarging the volume as the canon of Lowell's poems increased. When Lowell revised the texts of many poems, including *The Biglow Papers*, for the multivolume "Riverside Edition" of his *Writings* published in 1890, some of the revisions, but not all, were introduced into the plates of the popular "Household Edition."[25] The

22. I have accepted as authorial changes in the spelling of dialect words when those changes (recorded in the list of Emendations below) reflect a "perfecting" of the dialect and when there is evidence that Lowell either prepared copy or read proof of the new edition with the variant spelling. The transcription of dialect in literary works cannot, and aesthetically should not, be phonetically perfect; its success finally depends on the illusion of accuracy it creates for the reader. My understanding of the New England dialect Lowell heard and recorded is founded primarily on James W. Downer's fine study of "Features of New England Rustic Pronunciation in James Russell Lowell's *Biglow Papers*" (dissertation, University of Michigan, 1958).

23. The plates of the "Blue and Gold Edition" continued to be used after 1869, but the page size of these later printings is larger and the binding changed.

24. Lowell to H. W. Longfellow, 3 May 1876: A.L.s., Houghton Library, Harvard University.

25. There was also a volume issued probably in the nineties (the title page is not dated, but the latest copyright date is 1890), printed from plates of the "Household Edition" which have been cut and rearranged making the two columns on each page longer, thereby shortening the volume almost one hundred pages. Titled *The Poetical Works of James Russell Lowell* (Boston and New York, n.d.), it is technically a new edition, but I have regarded it as a printing of the "Household Edition" in order to avoid unnecessary textual complexity. Lowell's publishers were

"Riverside Edition," reprinted many times and variously called the "Standard Library Edition," the "University Edition," the "Fireside Edition," remains the best collected edition of Lowell's works.[26] In 1904 Charles Eliot Norton edited in sixteen volumes the "Elmwood Edition" of Lowell's writings; it differed from the earlier edition "in the retention of the original titles of the various volumes of prose essays."[27] The two series of *The Biglow Papers*, printed in one volume of the "Riverside Edition," were separated. Several years earlier H. E. Scudder had edited in one volume the "Cambridge Edition" of *The Complete Poetical Works of James Russell Lowell* (Boston and New York: Houghton, Mifflin and Co., 1896), unattractively printed in double columns, but still in print.

In the summer of 1885 Lowell's publishers, by now known as Houghton, Mifflin and Company, published in their popular Riverside Aldine Series both series of *The Biglow Papers* in two volumes. A careless reprint of the 1848 edition, the "Aldine Edition" of the First Series repeats the first edition's errors listed above, introduces new errors (see list of Rejected Substantives below), and incorporates none of the revisions and additions Lowell had made since the first edition. In addition to this internal evidence, the facts of Lowell's life during the time when proof of the "Aldine Edition" would have had to be read—his wife's death in February 1885 and his return from England the following June—argue against his having had part in the preparation of this edition. The plates of the "Aldine

---

imaginative in marketing their publications and issued sheets printed from plates of the "Household Edition" in a variety of formats—from the elaborately bound, illustrated gift-book volumes, to the undecorated, cheaply priced readers' editions, and, later, schoolbook editions. In this commentary I have only attempted to suggest the complexity of the publishing history of *The Biglow Papers* when it was included in Lowell's "Poetical Works."

26. It was reprinted mostly during the 1890s; the latest printing from these plates I have examined is dated 1910. In England the "Riverside Edition" was issued under the London imprint of Macmillan and Company.

27. "Publishers' Note," *The Complete Writings of James Russell Lowell* (Boston and New York: Houghton, Mifflin and Co., 1904), 1:v.

Edition" were altered after the publication of the "Riverside Edition" in order to present Lowell's final text of *The Biglow Papers*. These corrections were based certainly on the text of the "Riverside Edition" and not on an independent preparation of copy by Lowell.[28]

The Biglow Papers enjoyed considerable popularity during the nineteenth century, and it was inevitable, in that time before effective international copyright agreements, that the book would be pirated by English publishers. The one hundred copies of the first printing of *The Biglow Papers* sent to Putnam's literary agency in London caused little stir; but after John Bright's mention of Hosea in a parliamentary debate (see Hansard's Parliamentary Debates, 9 June 1859), two English publishers hurried to issue editions: one "authorized," the other pirated.

In the spring of 1859 Lowell received a letter from the English writer, Thomas Hughes, author of the popular *Tom Brown's Schooldays,* proposing on behalf of Trübner and Company, London, that an authorized edition of *The Biglow Papers* be published in England and edited by Hughes. Lowell consented and announced happily to Norton, "I am to have a 'royalty' on every copy sold."[29] Hughes wrote a preface to the book, extravagantly praising the American poet and his work, added a few words and allusions to the Glossary, and afterwards became Lowell's lifelong friend.[30] The book, published

28. While admitting the textual worthlessness of the "Aldine Edition," I have nevertheless included it in the schedule of collation for two reasons: it was issued by Lowell's publishers during his lifetime, and it has recently been made available in an AMS Press reprint.

29. 26 May 1859: A.L.s., Houghton Library, Harvard University.

30. Hughes was assisted by John M. Ludlow. See *Dictionary of National Biography, Supplement,* 22:881. About the additions to the Glossary, Hughes wrote Lowell, 17 October 1859 (A.L.s., Houghton Library, Harvard University): "There are yet a few words & allusions which I have not mastered satisfactorily—e g 'aint they made your envy's wiz?' What is this? what above all is *wiz*? You will see a most audacious suggestion of mine in the glossary, but I fear the British scholiast is at fault —'raisin promiscoous Ned' I have not ventured to try my hand at; there are bounds to every mans audacity. (An American has called on Nutt [Trübner's publishing partner] & has solved or pretended to solve the

in the fall of 1859, was prefaced by a letter from Lowell, dated at Cambridge, 14 September 1859, sanctioning the Trübner edition.[31] But Lowell neither prepared copy nor read proof. Lowell wrote his letter of authorization for the Hughes edition after learning from Sebastian Evans, the manager of the ornamental department of a Birmingham glassworks, that John Camden Hotten intended to publish *The Biglow Papers* and had asked Evans "to undertake the supervision of an edition for him."[32] Lowell must have discouraged Evans, who had confessed in his letter to Lowell that he disapproved of literary piracy, and the English publisher turned elsewhere for help. Ironically he found it in Lowell's friend, Sydney Gay, then in England on a business holiday. Gay wrote to Lowell after the book's publication:

> I looked over all his notes, added, corrected, curtailed, & supplied him with the historical facts for his preface. . . . He frankly told me it was a piracy, but I did not like he should pillory as well as pirate your book. For my aid (daily for a fortnight) he gave me one copy very unwillingly. . . . For your share he voluntarily sends another copy to you.[33]

In spite of Gay's help and a clever illustration by the popular George Cruikshank, Hotten's edition is greatly inferior to Trübner's. Hotten added bracketed footnotes to those of Hosea and Wilbur, clumsily and often incorrectly explaining allusions he thought might stump

---

riddle with what success you will see in the Glossary)." These additions are "Loon, *the northern diver*"; "Ned, a slang phrase, going it like Ned, equivalent to our 'going like old Harry' " (see the annotation for 97.12 in the present edition); "Row-de-dow, *troublesome talk*"; "Shine, *a fancy or liking*, also written *shindy*"; "Swan, *to swear*"; "Wiz, *to whiz; go off* (like a rocket)."

31. The book was reprinted by Trübner several times. One printing was announced over the date 1861 as the "Third English Edition." In 1880 it was issued bound with Trübner's "authorized edition" of the Second Series.

32. Evans to Lowell, August 1859: A.L.s., Houghton Library, Harvard University.

33. 8 December 1859: A.L.s., Houghton Library, Harvard University.

English readers. The Glossary is almost doubled in entries. Hotten cancels Wilbur's humorous definition of "Doughface" and substitutes: "Doughfaces, *a contemptuous nickname applied to the Northern favorers and abettors of negro slavery, pliable politicians that can be bought or sold.*" In other places he out-Wilburs Wilbur: "Mink, *a small quadruped of the genus* MUSTELA, *quiet in its movements.*"[34] The book was reissued during the 1860s, and by 1865 new plates had been made. Before his death in 1873, Hotten claimed he had sold fifty thousand copies of the book; but the British pirate was known to exaggerate.[35]

Neither of these English editions has been used in preparing the text of the present edition; nor have the other pirated English editions of the book which followed soon after,[36] the Canadian edition pirated by R. Worthington (Montreal, 1866), and the score of editions, printing *The Biglow Papers* either separately or together with other of Lowell's poems, that appeared both in America and England when at the beginning of this century the poet's early work entered the public domain. Though interesting in what they tell of Lowell's reputation, these unauthorized editions are of no value in the preparation of a critical text.[37]

34. Lowell wrote Gay about Hotten's editorial additions: "what foretaste of immortality like being edited with philological notes? It makes me feel as if the grass were growing over me" (21 December 1859, *Letters,* 2:44).

35. I have seen no copy of the book printed from the new plates dated before 1865; see Nils Erik Enkvist, "The Biglow Papers in Nineteenth-Century England," *New England Quarterly* 26 (1953): 222.

36. Arthur Voss lists these editions in "*The Biglow Papers* in England," *American Literature* 21 (November 1949): 340–42. A case might be made for including the Hughes edition in the schedule of collation because of Lowell's authorization; but Lowell's mere sanctioning of this edition makes its text no more authorial than that of the Hotten edition. Both volumes were reprints of a later printing (1858: called the "Fourth Edition" on the title page) of the first-book edition and not of the revised "Blue and Gold Edition" (1858).

37. Nor have I included the contemporaneous newspaper reprintings of the verses after they first appeared in the *Boston Courier* and the *National Anti-Slavery Standard,* and the reprintings of Biglow verses in

The present edition is based, therefore, on editions of *The Biglow Papers* discussed above: those in whose preparation Lowell's participation was likely. The "Elmwood Edition" of *The Biglow Papers* is also included in the schedule of collation because of its widespread use.[38] As argued above, the fair-copy manuscripts serve as

nineteenth-century anthologies of humorous and dialect writings. The verses of the first number were reprinted in *The American Anti-Slavery Almanac, for 1847* (New York, n.d.), pp. 46–47, with Lowell's permission. Several important anthologies that reprinted Biglow verses soon after their publication were *Traits of American Humour*, ed. Thomas Chandler Haliburton (London, 1852); *The Humorous Poetry of the English Language*, ed. James Parton (New York, 1856); and *The Cyclopaedia of Wit and Humor*, ed. William E. Burton (New York, 1858).

38. The following printed materials and manuscripts were used in preparing this edition (location in parentheses; TW indicates the item is in editor's collection):

Printed items collated: copies of the *Boston Courier* and the *National Anti-Slavery Standard* (Boston Public Library); three copies of the first 1848 printing of *The Biglow Papers* with the single Cambridge imprint (TW); two copies of the first 1848 printing with the Cambridge-New York imprint (TW); one copy of the first 1848 printing with the Cambridge-London imprint (TW); one copy of the second 1848 printing of *The Biglow Papers* (TW); two copies of *The Biglow Papers* printed from the 1848 plates, one dated on title page 1868: "Eighth Edition," the other 1876: "Tenth Edition" (TW); two copies of the "Blue and Gold Edition" of *The Poetical Works of James R. Lowell* dated on title page 1858 (TW); one copy of the "Blue and Gold Edition" dated on title page 1869 (TW); two copies of the "Diamond Edition" of *The Poetical Works of James Russell Lowell,* one dated on title page 1869 (Harvard College Library: AL2395.191), the other 1873 (the Library of the University of California at Los Angeles: PS2305.A1 1873); three copies of the "Household Edition" of *The Poetical Works of James Russell Lowell,* two dated on title page, 1876 and 1877, the third with latest copyright date 1890 (TW); two copies of the "Aldine Edition" of *The Biglow Papers,* one dated on title page 1885 and noted on spine "First Edition" (TW), the second dated on title page 1892 and noted on the verso of title page "Sixth Edition" (James H. Maguire, Boise, Idaho); three copies of the "Riverside Edition" of *The Biglow Papers,* one dated on title page 1890 (TW), the others, 1892 (UCLA, PS 2300.E90 v.9) and 1896 (TW); one copy of copy-text for the verses of the last four papers and Wilbur's poem, "Leaving the Matter Open" (34.23–38.34), and the text of the first-book edition is copy-text for the remainder of the 1848 text. Except for "Leaving the Matter Open," fair-copy manuscript is not extant for the other major additions Lowell made nine years after the first-book edition:

1. The last six stanzas of "The Courtin' " (13.23–14.14 in the present edition),[39]

---

the "Standard Library Edition" of *The Biglow Papers* (printed from the plates of the "Riverside Edition") with latest copyright date 1890 (Edwin H. Cady, Hillsboro, North Carolina); two copies of the "Elmwood Edition" of *The Biglow Papers*, both dated on title page 1904 (TW).

Manuscripts collated: two of Lowell's notebooks containing drafts of "Propt on the marsh, a dwelling now, I see," "Old Joe is gone, who saw hot Percy goad," and "The Two Gunners" (Houghton Library, Harvard University); "The Pious Editor's Creed," "Letter from a Candidate . . . ," "Letter from Birdofredum Sawin," "Another letter from B. Sawin Esq:," and "Leaving the Matter Open" (Houghton Library, Harvard University).

39. This poem was doubled in length when Lowell printed it following the Introduction to *The Biglow Papers, Second Series* (Boston, 1867), pp. lxxvii–lxxx. Arthur Voss has printed a transcription of a copy (Houghton Library, Harvard University) of the final version together with an account of the poem's composition that Lowell sent to his friend Judge E. R. Hoar, 22 September 1864 ("The Evolution of Lowell's 'The Courtin,' " *American Literature* 15, 1943: 42–50). This Harvard copy made for Charles Eliot Norton in 1892 differs both in accidentals and substantives from the text of the original manuscript sent to Hoar, a photostat of which was given to the Boston Athenaeum by M. A. DeWolfe Howe in 1933. I have not located the original. Lowell made a fair copy of the final version of the poem for the Baltimore Sanitary and Christian Commissions' Fair in 1864, and this was printed in facsimile in *Autograph Leaves of Our Country's Authors*, comp. John Pendleton Kennedy and Alexander Bliss (Baltimore, 1864), pp. 107–12. The original of this fair copy is in the University of Texas Library at Austin, and Lowell's letter sent to Kennedy with the manuscript, dated at Elmwood, 25 February 1864, is in the Peabody Institute, Baltimore. Lowell told Kennedy: "I should have chosen something else, but M: Bliss wrote asking me to copy the little pastoral I send. So I obey orders. I have tried to freshen

2. The last fifty lines of Hosea's poem, "Propt on the marsh, a dwelling now, I see" (29.23–30.36),

3. "The Two Gunners," together with the paragraph of prose preceding and the paragraph of prose following (32.14–34.22).

Copy-text for these sections is the text of the "Blue and Gold Edition" of Lowell's *Poetical Works* (Boston: Ticknor and Fields, 1858).

No editor, who also fancies himself a critic of literature, gladly accepts every revision an author makes in a text; whereas some seem for the better, others are decidedly inferior. Lowell believed, however, that this is finally not the editor's responsibility. Himself an experienced editor and critic, Lowell wrote in 1880 to Professor William Knight of the University of St. Andrews, then editing Wordsworth's poems:

> The question you propose is rather hard to answer, but I am inclined to think that the answer is to be sought rather on the moral than the aesthetic side. No doubt some of Wordsworth's changes of text seem clearly for the worse, but we can no longer call on him to give his reasons, & I think that surely *he* is the person who alone had the right to make them, as he alone is also responsible for them with posterity. Perhaps, too, the form in which we first read a poem & to which we have been accustomed has more weight with our judgment than we are conscious of. On the whole, though with great doubt, I incline to

it with a few new verses that I might more fully show my interest in your Fair. I have spoiled it perhaps" (quoted by permission). An original draft in pencil of "The Courtin' " (though of which version it is unclear) which Lowell gave to Richard Stoddard has apparently disappeared (see Richard Henry Stoddard, *Recollections: Personal and Literary*, ed. Ripley Hitchcock, New York: A. S. Barnes and Co., 1903, p. 103). The poem in its final form was twice issued as an illustrated gift book by Lowell's publishers: first in 1873, title page date 1874 (Boston: James R. Osgood and Co.), illustrated in silhouette by Winslow Homer; and in 1909, "set to pictures by Arthur I. Keller" (Boston and New York: Houghton Mifflin Co.).

think that your text should be Wordsworth's final one with the *variae lectiones* in the notes.[40]

The present text is not "definitive"; other editors might have proceeded differently, and their results would undoubtedly differ in particulars from mine. Modern man, taught by experience not to expect finality in the things of this world, should not look for it in the text of the book he reads. He must be satisfied with a "critical" text, responsibly and thoroughly performed. Such has been my intent.

40. 2 September 1880: A.L.s., Pierpont Morgan Library, New York City. Quoted by permission.

Pre-Copy-Text
Substantive Variants

The following list records substantive variants between texts preceding that chosen as copy-text and the text of the present edition. The reading of the present edition appears to the left of the bracket; the authority for that reading followed by a semicolon, the variant reading, and the source of that reading appear to the right of the bracket. *Not present* indicates that the reading of the present text does not appear in the text preceding copy-text and cited to the right of the semicolon. An asterisk preceding page and line numbers indicates that the reading is discussed in the Textual Notes. Since the whole of *The Biglow Papers* does not exist in texts preceding copy-text, only those sections indicated (parenthetically by page and line numbers) in the list of texts that follows are covered by this table. The following texts are referred to:

WB1 *Writing-Book I:* Notebook containing drafts of "Propt on the marsh, a dwelling now, I see" (28.21–30.36) and "Old Joe is gone, who saw hot Percy goad" (31.6–19).

WB2 *Writing-Book II:* Notebook containing draft of "The Two Gunners" (32.27–34.19).

NP1 "[For the Courier.]" *Boston Courier,* 17 June 1846, p. 2, col. 4 (49.8–55.4).

NP2 "Letter from a Volunteer in Saltillo," *Boston Courier,* 18 August 1847, p. 1, col. 6 (58.13–63.37).

NP3 "What Mr. Robinson Thinks," *Boston Courier,* 2 November 1847, p. 2, col. 2 (70.19–73.7).

NP4 "Letter from the Rev. Mr. Wilbur," *Boston Courier,* 6 November 1847, p. 1, cols. 5–6 (74.14–78.14).

NP5 "Remarks of Increase D'O. Phace, Esq.," *Boston Courier,* 28 December 1847, p. 1, col. 7 (82.27–90.7).

NP6   "The Debate in the Sennit," *Boston Courier*, 3 May 1848, p. 1, col. 6 (95.1–98.8).

c1   *The Biglow Papers*, Cambridge: George Nichols, 1848.

BG   *The Poetical Works of James R. Lowell*, 2 vols., Boston: Ticknor and Fields, 1858 ("Blue and Gold Edition").

HE   *The Poetical Works of James Russell Lowell*, Boston: James R. Osgood and Co., 1876 ("Household Edition").

RE   *The Writings of James Russell Lowell in Ten Volumes*, Boston and New York: Houghton, Mifflin and Co., 1890 ("Riverside Edition"), vol. 8.

3.1–28.20	*No text preceding copy-text*
28.21	now] c1; turned WB1
*28.27	who] BG; she WB1
28.29	She] BG; Who WB1
28.31	divine] BG; detect WB1
29.5	was called] c1; pronounced WB1
29.5	various] c1; different WB1
29.8	or] c1; & WB1
29.10	guttural] c1; hoarsest WB1
29.10	resounding] c1; smoothflowing WB1
29.15	name] c1; word WB1
29.20	long-eared] c1; classic WB1
29.23	too] BG; thence WB1
29.25	on] BG; with WB1
29.28	that] RE; which WB1
29.32	your] BG; the WB1
30.2	That still a space] BG; Room still above WB1
30.4	flagroot] BG; flagroots WB1
30.5	Nay] RE; And WB1
30.8	some] HE; the WB1
30.15	While] BG; And WB1
30.17	warned] BG; bade WB1
30.18	beast] BG; steed WB1
30.19	What a fine] BG; How fine a WB1

30.21	did] BG; rose WB1
30.21	well-thumbed] BG; weekday WB1
30.21	ardor rapt] BG; studied ease WB1
30.22	curve decorous] HE; scale proportioned WB1
30.22	each rank adapt] HE; all rank's degrees WB1
30.23–24	How did it . . . of social differences,] BG; *not present* WB1
30.25	so gave] BG; giving WB1
30.35	absence] BG; exile WB1
31.1–5	*No text preceding copy-text*
31.8	which] c1; that WB1
31.8	wonder] c1; horror WB1
31.10	faded and grown] c1; in the service WB1
31.13	on] c1; on the WB1
31.14	lengthening] c1; increasing WB1
31.16	fight] c1; fray WB1
31.17	squared more nearly . . . sense of right] BG; ended in a more propitious way WB1
31.19	hammered stone for life] c1; lingered out his days WB1
31.20–32.26	*No text preceding copy-text*
33.2	skeercely] BG; hardly WB2
33.4	he up] BG; jest laughed WB2
33.13	wuz] BG; ware WB2
33.22	Peleg's] BG; Josh's WB2
34.18–19	But Isrel kind . . . well on't.] BG; *not present* WB2
34.20–49.7	*No text preceding copy-text*
*49.32	*Aut insanit, aut versos facit.*—H.W.] c1; *not present* NP1
50.4	year] c1; years NP1
50.5	be.] c1; be. ¢ (but Hosea ses he's willin' to make his after david that he sed so.) NP1
51.22	go] c1; should NP1
51.32	This ere] c1; To be NP1
51.32	folks's] c1; folk's NP1
52.24	'em] c1; ye NP1
52.32	'S jest] c1; Is NP1

53.19	lot] BG; set NP1
53.20	guess they 'll] RE; they will NP1
55.5–58.12	*No text preceding copy-text*
58.24	oughter] c1; oughter to NP2
59.2	A] c1; Where a NP2
59.2	from there] c1; *not present* NP2
59.3	An' th' Cunnles, tu, could] c1; Where the Cunnles used to NP2
59.4	to] c1; off to NP2
59.8	along o'] BG; ahavin' NP2
*59.16	gallus.] c1; gallows. / [thatere's wot i cal natteral paythos, its tetchin'. H.B.] NP2
61.23	tater;] c1; tater; / [i *hed* insutted hear an S.A. on the coulter of the tater, but parson W. advised agin leavin on it In. i wood jist remark that taters air lookin' well hour way. H.B.] NP2
61.25	kind] c1; kinds NP2
61.30	thare 's] c1; thare is NP2
62.1	Is] c1; If NP2
62.15	I dars n't] c1; I'm 'fraid to NP2
63.4	Bein' they haint no] c1; Not havin' any NP2
63.14–18	An' there 's . . . out on 't.] c1; *not present* NP2
63.24	afore they] c1; before we NP2
63.25	Then] c1; When NP2
64.1–70.18	*No text preceding copy-text*
70.19	GUVENER B.] c1; ☞ Our friend, HOSEA BIGELOW, has sent the following squib, which we presume he wrote to ridicule the fashion, now getting to be quite prevalent, of asking Tom, Dick, and Harry, how they are going to vote, and then parading the letters they write in answer, as if they settled the right or wrong of the question at issue between the parties. We know of no one more likely to laugh at the thing than J. P. R. himself : — / WHAT MR. ROBINSON THINKS. / George N. Briggs NP3
70.28	Guess] c1; I guess NP3

SUBSTANTIVE VARIANTS

70.33	C. is] c1; Cushing's NP3
72.1	C.] c1; Cushing NP3
72.1	in] c1; *not present* NP3
72.9	good old] c1; old fashioned NP3
72.17	thet] c1; who NP3
72.30	out] c1; up NP3
73.3	God] c1; That God NP3
73.4	start] BG; drive NP3
73.7	Gee!] c1; Gee!/H.B. NP3
73.8–74.13	*No text preceding copy-text*
75.13–14	As regards their . . . plainness of speech,] c1; *not present* NP4
75.22	though] c1; but NP4
75.24	has] c1; exercises NP4
76.7	selected for animadversion, namely] c1; selected, viz NP4
76.14	should] RE; would NP4
76.19–23	Saint Ambrose affirms . . . . the weightiest matters.'] c1; *not present* NP4
77.19	journal.] c1; journal.* [footnote:] * Such a contribution to our columns would certainly be acceptable to our readers, and not unwelcome to ourself; but we should prefer that our reverend correspondent should send us a copy of the sermon he intends to prepare for Thanksgiving Day, now less than three weeks *ahead.* If he should comply with this suggestion, and permit us to publish it simultaneously with its delivery from the pulpit, we will make no charge for advertising the Circular—afterwards referred to —but return to him the proceeds of the sales of the Sermon,—deducting *reasonable* cost and commissions. ED. *of the Courier.* NP4
78.15–82.26	*No text preceding copy-text*
84.14	chat fer a spell] c1; cosily chat NP5
84.15	squabble] c1; fight for NP5
84.19	war is] BG; war's NP5

84.25	C] c1; G NP5
84.26	G] c1; F NP5
85.6	afore] c1; before NP5
86.11	substract] c1; take up NP5
86.11	off] c1; of NP5
88.15	fat] c1; blest NP5
89.6	she 'd] RE; she NP5
90.8–94.36	*No text preceding copy-text*
95.2	MR.] c1; ☞ We are happy to hear again from our friend Hosea Biglow. As it seemed to us that his phonographic orthography might possibly occasion some obscurity in the meaning, we have taken the liberty to make a few corrections. / mr. NP6
95.8	BIGLOW] c1; BIGLOW. / THE DEBATE IN THE SENNIT—SOT TO A NUSSRY RHYME NP6
95.25	Freedom's] c1; Our NP6
97.19	aristoxy 's a tumblin'] HE; aristoxy is tumbled NP6
97.27	ery] c1; cry NP6
98.9-*end*	*No text preceding copy-text*

Emendations

The following list records substantive and accidental changes introduced into copy-text. The reading of the present edition appears to the left of the bracket; the authority for that reading, followed by a semicolon, the copy-text reading, and the copy-text symbol appear to the right of the bracket. The curved dash ∼ indicates the same word that appears before the bracket and is used in recording punctuation variants. *Not Present* indicates that the reading of the present text does not appear in copy-text. An asterisk preceding page and line numbers (rules and illustration captions are not counted as lines) indicates that the reading is discussed in the Textual Notes. While no emendation is made solely on the authority of the editor, it is unlikely that Lowell was directly responsible for every change in accidentals appearing in texts after copy-text which the editor has introduced because of either its punctuative necessity or its dialectal superiority (see note 22, page 256).

The following texts are referred to:

MS1   Holograph manuscript, "Leaving the Matter Open."

MS2   Holograph manuscript, "The Pious Editor's Creed."

MS3   Holograph manuscript, "Letter from a Candidate . . . ."

MS4   Holograph manuscript, "Letter from Birdofredum Sawin."

MS5   Holograph manuscript, "Another letter from B. Sawin Esqr."

NP7   "Leaving the Matter Open," *National Anti-Slavery Standard,* 27 July 1848, p. 32, cols. 5–6.

NP8   "The Pious Editor's Creed," *National Anti-Slavery Standard,* 4 May 1848, p. 194, cols. 3–4.

NP9   "Letter from Hosea Biglow. . . . A Letter from a Candidate

. . . ," *National Anti-Slavery Standard*, 1 June 1848, p. 2, col. 5.

NP10   "Letter from Birdofredum Sawin," *National Anti-Slavery Standard*, 6 July 1848, p. 20, cols. 5–6.

NP11   "Another Letter from B. Sawin, Esq.," *National Anti-Slavery Standard*, 28 September 1848, pp. 70–71, cols. 6, 1–2.

c1   *The Biglow Papers*, Cambridge: George Nichols, 1848.

c2   *The Biglow Papers*, Cambridge: George Nichols, 1848 ("Second Edition" or second printing).

BG   *The Poetical Works of James R. Lowell*, 2 vols., Boston: Ticknor and Fields, 1858 ("Blue and Gold Edition"), vol. 2.

DE   *The Poetical Works of James Russell Lowell*, Boston: Fields, Osgood, & Co., 1869 ("Diamond Edition").

HE   *The Poetical Works of James Russell Lowell*, Boston: James R. Osgood and Co., 1876 ("Household Edition").

RE   *The Writings of James Russell Lowell in Ten Volumes*, Boston and New York: Houghton, Mifflin and Co., 1890 ("Riverside Edition"), vol. 8.

EE   *The Complete Writings of James Russell Lowell . . . in Sixteen Volumes*, Boston and New York: Houghton, Mifflin and Co., 1904 ("Elmwood Edition"), vol. 10.

3.17	than to] RE; than c1
3.29	communications] BG; correspondences c1
4.13	I] HE; I also c1
10.35	it] BG; *not present* c1
11.5	work] RE; work of c1
11.23	contains] BG; contains a portion of c1
15.7	alio] BG; alii c1
*21.11	25] EDITOR; *v* c1
28.9	about] RE; around c1

273

EMENDATIONS

28.10	composition] BG; compositions c1
28.26–29	dame. Daughter of . . . Pierian store, She] BG; dame, Who c1
28.31	divine] BG; detect c1
28.32	dunce.] c2; ~ c1
29.22	bees;] BG; ~ ." c1
29.26	(to] RE; —~ BG
29.26	day)] RE; ~ , BG
29.28	that] RE; which BG
30.5	Nay] RE; And BG
30.8	some] HE; the BG
30.22	curve decorous] HE; decorous curve BG
30.22	each] HE; every BG
31.17	with] BG; to c1
31.28	inaptitude] BG; inaptitude, I know not c1
32.10	verses,] RE; verses, as c1
32.16	further] DE; farther BG
32.31	soon'z] HE; soon's BG
33.15	acrost] HE; across BG
33.21	"it] DE; ~ BG
33.22	wil'-] HE; wild- BG
34.3	hol'] DE; hole BG
34.5	Joe,] DE; ~ BG
*34.6	le's] DE; less BG
34.23	LEAVING] c1; The following tale is from the pen of the Revd Mr Wilbur of Jaalam. It is gratifying to us to meet him in the walks of elegant literature. We regret that the crowded state of our columns prevents us from inserting his letter enclosing the poem. His remarks on Parables, Apologues, & Fables are very interesting, & his observations on Prior & Gay would form a valuable contribution to a more exclusively literary journal. LEAVING MS1
34.24	TALE.] NP7; ~ MS1
34.25	WILBUR,] NP7; ~ MS1
34.27	where,)] NP7; ~) MS1
*34.29	and] NP7; & MS1

36.11	Anglo-Saxon] NP7; AngloSaxon MS1
36.35	worst.] NP7; ~ MS1
37.22	crop] HE; grain MS1
37.27	"must] NP7; ~ MS1
38.15	But] NP7; but MS1
39.1	To turn now . . . matters, there] BG; There c1
39.2	should] RE; would c1
39.27	be] RE; is c1
39.30	into] RE; in c1
39.31–32	schoolmistress] RE; schoolmaster c1
40.12	sourfaced-] BG; unwilling- c1
43.6	delighfle] DE; delightful c1
43.6	masures] DE; measures c1
44.1	Scioppius,] BG; ~ c1
45.35	Qua[kers] . . . . ."] DE; ~ c1
50.26	Southun] BG; Southern c1
53.19	lot] BG; set c1
53.20	guess they 'll] RE; they will c1
58.34	have] HE; has c1
59.8	along o'] BG; ahavin' c1
59.18	'tever] BG; ever c1
*59.29–30	in'my. / [Verse paragraph break] / Wal] EDITOR; in'my. / Wal c1
63.33	fer] BG; for c1
64.9	Gomara] BG; Diaz c1
64.28	persuasion] RE; oratory c1
*64.31	city,] BG; ~ c1
64.37–65.1	Echetlæus at Marathon and] BG; *not present* c1
65.13–15	Do we not . . . day of Rest?] RE; *not present* c1
65.34	pro] RE; *de* c1
66.9–10	in the time of] BG; to c1
*72.2	princerple] RE; principle c1
72.25	ign'ance] DE; ignorance c1
73.4	start] BG; drive c1
74.11	for] BG; for some c1
76.14	should] RE; would c1
82.6	and] BG; *not present* c1

EMENDATIONS

83.26	p'litikle] BG; p'litickle c1
83.34	Donatus] RE; Austin c1
83.34–35	St. Jerome's tutor] RE; a saint's name c1
84.18	Presidunt] RE; President c1
84.19	war is] BG; war's c1
84.33	an'] HE; and c1
85.14	An'] HE; And c1
85.18	gret] HE; great c1
86.6	Dermoc'acy's] RE; Dermocracy's c1
88.1	fore-fathers] BG; four fathers c1
88.2	slep'] BG; slept c1
88.3	swep'] BG; swept c1
88.11	Sammle's] BG; Samwell's c1
88.33	—H.W.] BG; not present c1
89.6	she'd] RE; she c1
89.34	Ἅπας] HE; Ἅπας c1
90.1	civerlized] RE; civilized c1
90.2	ruther] BG; rather c1
91.30–34	The sagacious Lacedæmonians . . . out of ear-shot.] BG; not present c1
92.7	Faneuil] DE; Fanueil c1
94.18	bound] RE; knit c1
95.5	thut] RE; that c1
97.12	permiscoous] RE; promiscoous c1
97.19	aristoxy's a] HE; aristoxy is c1
99.2	consuetude] BG; suetude c1
99.3	by] BG; in c1
*103.4	DU] c1; do MS2
103.4	cause,] c1; ~ — MS2
*103.5	Ez] c1; As MS2
103.5	Payris] BG; Paris MS2
103.7	infarnal] c1; infernal MS2
103.7	Phayrisees] BG; Pharisees MS2
103.8	wal] c1; well MS2
*103.9	an'] c1; & MS2
*103.11	Thet] c1; That MS2
*103.14	nothin'] c1; ~ MS2

*103.14	aint] c1; ain't ms2
103.14	extravygunt,—] c1; ~ — ms2
103.15	Purvidin'] c1; Pervided ms2
*103.16	Fer] c1; For ms2
*103.16	hev] c1; have ms2
103.17	eye-teeth] c1; eyeteeth ms2
103.19	Partic'larly] c1; Particklerly ms2
*103.21	O'] c1; Of ms2
103.21	taxes,] c1; ~ ms2
103.23	wut] c1; whut ms2
103.24	thru] c1; through ms2
103.26	vote,—] c1; ~ — ms2
103.27	custom-houses] c1; custom houses ms2
*103.29	sen'] c1; send ms2
103.30	sartin] c1; certain ms2
103.31	orthydox conditions] c1; orthydocks condishuns ms2
103.32	dolls.] c1; ~ ms2
103.32	ann.,] c1; ~. ms2
104.1	recommend] c1; reckomend ms2
*104.2	'ould] c1; would ms2
104.3	special] c1; speshul ms2
*104.6	tu] c1; too ms2
104.6	sartin;—] c1; ~ ; ms2
*104.8	wut] c1; what ms2
104.8	party] c1; Party ms2
104.10	privit] c1; pryvit ms2
104.12	spout] c1; shout ms2
104.15	his,] c1; ~ ms2
104.16	good-sized] c1; goodsized ms2
104.26	gov'ment] c1; guv'ment ms2
104.28	Wut's his'n unto] c1; Whatever's his to ms2
*104.30	Frum] c1; From ms2
*104.30	air] c1; are ms2
104.32	souperscription] c1; souperscripshun ms2
105.1	conscience] c1; conshunce ms2
105.2	description] c1; descripshun ms2

EMENDATIONS

*105.4	hez] c1; has MS2
105.5	every thin'] c1; everythin MS2
105.7	marcies] c1; mercies MS2
105.9	princerple] c1; principle MS2
105.10	But, O] c1; But oh MS2
*105.11–26	I du believe . . . kind o' doughface.] c1, RE; *not present* MS2
105.27	wutever] c1; whatever MS2
105.28	'll] c1; Will MS2
105.30	kindness,] c1; ~ ; MS2
105.31	Thet bombshells, grape, an'] c1; I do believe that MS2
105.31	'n'] c1; 'n MS2
106.7	heth] c1; hath MS2
106.7	ben] c1; been MS2
106.8	heth] c1; hath MS2
106.9	'll] c1; will MS2
106.10	me] c1; me./H.B. MS2
107.17	scenes.] c2; ~ c1
108.16	continue miraculous (even . . . discerned as such)] BG; (even if for a moment discerned as such) continue miraculous c1
108.19	(Acts x. 11, 12)] RE; *not present* c1
109.11	(as it may . . .) of the mind] BG; of the mind (as it may truly be called) c1
109.12	wellnigh] RE; quite c1
109.17–18	the unintelligence we have carefully picked up] BG; intelligence c1
110.25	fidgeting] DE; fidgetting c1
110.26	this] BG; the c1
110.27	in that] BG; *not present* c1
110.32–33	something to his disadvantage] BG; of him c1
111.9	D.Y.,] BG; *not present* c1
111.10	capitals),] DE; ~) c1
111.20	of our Saviour to King Abgarus, that] RE; *not present* c1
111.21–22	755, that of the Virgin to the magistrates of

	Messina] BG; 755 c1
111.22–24	that of the Sanhedrim . . . to his brother Lodovico,] RE; *not present* c1
111.24–26	that of St. Gregory . . . nun of Girgenti,] BG; *not present* c1
111.27	themselves] BG; itself c1
111.33	DEER SIR] c1; Deer sir MS3
111.33	gut] c1; got MS3
111.34	and] c1; & MS3
111.35	and] c1; & MS3
111.36	em] c1; 'em MS3
112.3	knock] c1; nock MS3
112.5	—H.B.] c1; LETTER FROM A CANDIDATE FOR THE PRESIDENCY IN ANSWER TO SUTTIN QUESTIONS PROPOSED BY HOSEA BIGLOW MS3
112.6	DEAR SIR,—You] c1; Dear Sir,/[next line] you MS3
112.8	natur] c1; nater MS3
112.10	straight-spoken] c1; straightspoken MS3
112.12	feetur,] c1; ~ MS3
112.13	wunt] c1; wun't MS3
112.24	wunt] c1; wun't MS3
112.24	so,—] c1; ~ — MS3
*112.25	An',] BG; And MS3
112.27	wich] c1; which MS3
112.28	talence] c1; talents MS3
112.31	lawth;] c1; loath, MS3
112.33	wile] c1; while MS3
113.1	Constitution,] c1; ~ MS3
113.2	preudunt] c1; prudent MS3
113.2	statesmun] c1; statesmen MS3
*113.4	*ware*] c1; *where* MS3
113.5	it,—] c1; ~ , MS3
113.6	du,—] c1; do, MS3
113.7	thet,] c1; that MS3
113.7	it,] c1; ~ MS3
*113.8	wuz] c1; was MS3

113.8	thru] c1; through MS3
113.11	civlyzation] c1; civlysation MS3
113.11	*doos*] c1; *does* MS3
*113.14	hed] c1; had MS3
113.16	So 'st] BG; So 's MS3
113.20	Yes, Sir] c1; Yes sir MS3
*113.21–114.4	Ez to the . . . to grout about?] c1; *not present* MS3
114.6	them,—] c1; ~ , MS3
114.8	ahem:] c1; ~ ; MS3
114.10	pint] c1; ~ , MS3
114.12	haint] c1; hain't MS3
114.13	princerples] BG; principles MS3
114.14	hevin'] c1; havin' MS3
114.15	Wig] c1; whig MS3
114.15	Tory] c1; tory MS3
114.16	canderdate] RE; candidate MS3
114.17	parpendicler] c1; parpendiclar MS3
114.19	an' thin'] c1; an'thing MS3
114.19	particler] c1; particlar MS3
114.28	Light-house] c1; Light house MS3
115.3–6	question / I 'm RIGHT . . . South by North] c1; question, / You've cause to know that I am right, / And say you wunt make no suggestion / As to who 'll git the biggest bite MS3
120.26	I SPOSE] c1; LETTER FROM BIRDOFREDUM SAWIN. ⟨ Another letter from Mr Sawin, in which the hero expresses a modest willingness to yield to the wishes of his countrymen & allow his name to be used in connexion with the Presidency. / [*short rule*] / ⟨ (The following was enclosed to us by Mr Biglow who states that it was apparently "wrote from Veery Cruse".) / [*short double rule*] / I spose MS4
120.27	myself,—] c1; ~ , MS4
*120.27	holl] c1; whole MS4
120.27	me.] c1; ~ ; MS4
*120.28	Wen] c1; When MS4

120.31	'twuz] c1; 'twas MS4
120.32	nuther] c1; nutther MS4
120.33	Wy] c1; Why MS4
120.33	t'other] c1; tother MS4
120.34	be;] c1; ~ , MS4
121.2	one,—] c1; ~ , MS4
121.3	liquor] c1; licker MS4
121.3	one;] c1; ~ , MS4
121.4	drink;] c1; ~ , MS4
121.5	then] c1; than MS4
121.9	gut] c1; got MS4
121.10	it,] c1; ~ MS4
121.11	git] c1; get MS4
121.13	pickins;] c1; ~ , MS4
121.14	So,] c1; ~ MS4
121.15	*myself*] c1; myself MS4
121.15	gret] c1; great MS4
121.15	it.] c1; ~ : MS4
121.16	Now, le' me] c1; Now lemmy MS4
121.17	-eends] c1; -ends MS4
121.17	'em:] c1; ~ , MS4
121.18	on 't;] c1; ~ , MS4
121.19	haint] NP10; hain't MS4
121.19	right,] c1; ~ MS4
*121.19	gut] c1; got MS4
121.20	hendy] c1; handy MS4
121.20	cal'late] c1; callylate MS4
121.20	on 't.] c1; ~ ; MS4
121.21	broke,—] c1; ~ — MS4
121.21	b'lieve),—] c1; ~) MS4
121.21	kep'] c1; ~ MS4
121.22	'em;] c1; ~ , MS4
121.23	'em.] c1; ~ , MS4
121.25	could n't] c1; couldn't MS4
121.25	break,—] c1; ~ , MS4
121.25	lef'] c1; left MS4
121.31	wenever ther' 's] c1; whenever there 's MS4

EMENDATIONS

121.32	opperlunt] c1; oppilent MS4
121.32	thunder,] c1; ~ MS4
121.34	vullinteered] c1; vullunteered MS4
122.1	reg'lar] DE; reglar MS4
122.2	time,] c1; ~ MS4
122.4	pufficly] c1; puffictly MS4
122.5	precious] c1; preshus MS4
122.6	mill-sites] c1; millsites MS4
122.9	take,] c1; ~ MS4
122.9	fer;—] c1; for; MS4
122.12	gold mines] c1; goldmines MS4
122.12	Chiny] BG; chiny MS4
122.13	acomin'] c1; a comin MS4
122.16	Although,] c1; ~ MS4
122.16	anywares] c1; anywheres MS4
122.16	locks,] c1; ~ MS4
122.18	'xpect] HE; guess MS4
122.19	all-fiered] c1; all fiered MS4
122.19	th'] c1; the MS4
122.19	awfle] c1; orfle MS4
122.20	fergut] c1; forgot MS4
122.21	drownded.] c1; ~ ; MS4
122.23	Preudence] RE; Prudence MS4
122.27	tip,] c1; ~ MS4
122.28	tea-leaves] c1; tealeaves MS4
122.29	bust] RE; broke MS4
122.29	river.] c1; ~ ; MS4
122.30	't is] c1; 'tis MS4
122.32	deepot] c1; Deepot MS4
122.34	is,] c1; ~ MS4
122.35	along,—] c1; ~ — MS4
122.35	shakin'] NP10; ~ MS4
122.36	aint] NP10; ain't MS4
123.1	't aint] c1; 'taint MS4
123.1	t' other] c1; tother MS4
123.1	on;] c1; ~ , MS4
123.2	doos n't] c1; doesn't MS4

123.3	gret] c1; great MS4
123.4	ye] c1; you MS4
123.5	reg'lar] c1; reglar MS4
123.6	smoth'rin'] c1; smothrin MS4
123.7	smashes.] c1; ~ ;— MS4
123.8	hed,—] c1; had, MS4
123.9	may n't] c1; may nt MS4
123.10	licked] c1; whipped MS4
123.12	sheer] c1; share MS4
123.12	on,—] c1; ~ , MS4
123.15	privits;] c1; ~ ? MS4
123.17	would n't] c1; wouldn't MS4
123.17	grave-stun;] c1; gravestone. MS4
123.18	licks,—] c1; ~ , MS4
123.18	hoppers;] c1; ~ , MS4
123.20–23	It may suit . . . jest the murder] c1; No, glory is a kind o' thing I shan't pursue no furder, / All *that*'s the off'cers' parquisite, & yourn is all the murder; / It may suit folks that go agin a body with a soul in't / Who aint contented with a skin without a bagnet hole in 't MS4
123.25	GLORIOUS FUN] c1; "glorious fun" MS4
123.28	wuz,] c1; was MS4
123.30	stan'in'] c1; standin MS4
123.30	*seemed*] c1; seemed MS4
123.30	cent'ry] c1; cen'try MS4
123.34	inside;] c1; ~ , MS 4
123.35	is,] c1; ~ MS4
124.1	hunderd] c1; hundred MS4
124.1	frum] c1; from MS4
124.2	roasted;] c1; ~ . MS4
*124.3	on'y] c1; only MS4
124.3	revellin'] c1; revelling MS4
124.3	me] c1; ~ , MS4
124.5	now;] c1; ~ , MS4
124.7	'T 'll] c1; 'Twill MS4
124.11	Now,] c1; ~ MS4

EMENDATIONS

124.11	man,] c1; ∼ ms4
124.13	can'idatin'] c1; candidatin ms4
124.14	't wunt] c1; 'twunt ms4
124.15	can'idate] c1; candidate ms4
124.16	soffies;] c1; ∼ , ms4
124.17	tu] DE; to ms4
124.18	did,—] c1; ∼ — ms4
124.19	run,] c1; ∼ ms4
124.20	anywares] c1; anywhere's ms4
124.21	aint] NP10; ain't ms4
124.21	can'idates] c1; candidates ms4
124.22	leg,—] c1; ∼ — ms4
124.23	wy] c1; why ms4
124.23	parfect] c1; perfect ms4
124.24	pin;)—] c1; ∼ ;) ms4
124.25	princerples] BG; principles ms4
124.26	gret] c1; great ms4
124.27	war,—] c1; ∼ , ms4
124.28	on 't] c1; on't ms4
124.29	wile] c1; while ms4
124.30	WOODEN LEG!] c1; "wooden leg!" ms4
124.31	settisfied] c1; satisfied ms4
124.32	ONE EYE PUT OUT!] c1; "one eye put out!" ms4
125.1	people likes;] c1; People likes, ms4
125.3	please,—] c1; ∼ , ms4
125.5	it 's] c1; its ms4
125.7	idee] c1; Idee ms4
125.8	thru] c1; through ms4
125.10	thet] c1; who ms4
125.12	Sech] c1; Such ms4
125.12	BLOODY BIRDOFREDUM] c1; *bloody Birdofredum* ms4
125.15	Presidunt,] c1; President ms4
125.16	ne'ssary] c1; necessary ms4
125.16	residunt] c1; resident ms4
125.18	yeller.] c1; ∼ ; ms4
125.19	haint] c1; hain't ms4

125.19	climes,] c1; ~ ms4
125.20	sometimes)],] c1; ~ ,) ms4
125.21	haint] c1; hain't ms4
125.21	ye] c1; you ms4
125.23	then,] c1; ~ ms4
125.23	No'thern] c1; Northern ms4
125.26	Institootion] c1; Institution ms4
125.27	But,] c1; My ms4
125.28	next.] c1; ~ ms4
125.29	Yourn,] c1; ~ ms4
125.30	BIRDOFREDUM SAWIN] c1; Birdofredum Sawin ms4
127.22	should] RE; would c1
128.33	and too] RE; (too) c1
129.27	to raise] RE; in raising c1
132.14	me!] BG; ~ ? c1
133.15	should] RE; would c1
134.5	the] RE; *not present* c1
134.23	I SPOSE] c1; I spose ms5
134.24	'way] c1; ~ ms5
134.25	kin'] RE; kind ms5
134.26	unannermously] HE; unanimously ms5
134.26	Preserdential] RE; Presidential ms5
134.29	sorrerd,] c1; ~ ms5
134.30	forrerd:] c1; ~ . ms5
134.35	want] c1; need ms5
134.35	thund'rin'] c1; thundrin ms5
134.35	patchin',] c1; patchin' ms5
135.3	number] c1; only ms5
135.5	masses] c1; people ms5
135.5	Country's] c1; Country ms5
135.7	Coz] c1; Cos ms5
135.10	But] c1; Wal, ms5
135.12	An'] c1; And, ms5
135.12	wile] c1; while ms5
135.14	hum] c1; home ms5
135.18	hail] c1; hale ms5

135.20	pop'lar] c1; poplar ms5
135.23	ole] c1; old ms5
135.24	name)—] c1; ~) ms5
*135.25–29	Wenever an Amerikin ... tenth is mine; / An'] bg; Now, ms5
135.29	't aint] c1; 'tain't ms5
135.29	'n'] c1; 'n ms5
135.31	thing,] c1; ~ ms5
135.32	sing;] c1; ~ , ms5
136.2	layin'] re; layin ms5
136.3	wich] c1; which ms5
136.6	bar-rooms] c1; barrooms ms5
136.7	Agethrin'] c1; A gethrin' ms5
*136.7	Demmercrats] c1; demercrats ms5
*136.7	and] np11; & ms5
136.8	An'] c1; And' ms5
136.13	him,—] c1; ~ , ms5
136.15	aturnin'] c1; a turnin' ms5
136.17	Birdofredum] c1; ~ — ms5
136.17	Cass] c1; ~ — ms5
*136.17	*twenty six*] editor; twenty six ms5
136.22	a] np11; a a ms5
136.23	deff'rence] re; diffrence ms5
136.23	cust,] c1; ~ ms5
136.26	Gin'ral] c1; Ginral ms5
136.27–28	He hez n't ... there is agoin';] c1; *not present* ms5
136.30	Coz] c1; Cos ms5
136.30	pleases:] c1; ~ ; ms5
136.31	Gin'ral] c1; Ginral ms5
136.31	neither;—] c1; ~ ; ms5
136.33	ultry] c1; ~ , ms5
136.34	warm,] c1; ~ ms5
136.34	sultry);] c1; ~ ,) ms5
137.1	't ware] c1; 'twere ms5
*137.4	deffrent] editor; diffrent ms5
137.8	Turn all] c1; And turn ms5
137.9	secon'-handed] c1; secondhanded ms5

*137.11–25	Webster sot matters . . . . 'ere Gin'ral's spurs.] c1, BG; *not present* MS5
137.26	reg'lar] c1; reglar MS5
137.29	kep'] c1; ~ MS5
137.30	ole] c1; old MS5
137.32	fur 'z] c1; fur's MS5
137.35	steddles] RE; staddles MS5
138.1	it 's] c1; its MS5
138.3	disgusted,—] c1; ~ , MS5
138.4	aint] NP11; ain't MS5
138.7	recollec'] RE; recollect MS5
138.7	'z] c1; 's MS5
138.10	dror] c1; draw MS5
138.11	No'thun] c1; Northun MS5
138.11	'll] c1; will MS5
138.14	wut.] c1; ~ ; MS5
138.16	stan'] BG; stand MS5
138.16	Buren;—] c1; ~ , MS5
138.17	thet 'ere] BG; thetere MS5
138.18	doos;] c1; ~ , MS5
138.23	aint] NP11; ain't MS5
138.24	quarrils.] c1; ~ ; MS5
138.25	ye] c1; you MS5
138.26	aspoutin'] c1; a spoutin MS5
138.29	ough' ter] BG; oughter MS5
138.30	'an] c1; than MS5
138.31	by,] c1; ~ MS5
138.31	vote,] c1; ~ MS5
138.32	*is n't*] c1; isn't MS5
138.33	South,] c1; ~ MS5
*138.33	min';] c1, HE; mind, MS5
138.34	ongrateful] BG; ungrateful MS5
138.34	set] c1; ~ , MS5
138.34	nowers] c1; nowheres MS5
*138.34	fin'.] c1, HE; find; MS5
138.35	nigger,] c1; ~ MS5

EMENDATIONS

139.1	figger;] c1; ~ , ms5
139.2	'an] c1; than ms5
139.2	gunnin',] np11; gunnin' ms5
139.4	shou'dered] c1; shouldered ms5
139.4	t'] c1; to ms5
139.6	'T worn't] c1; Tworn't ms5
139.8	more.] c1; ~ , ms5
139.9	ollers;] c1; ~ , ms5
139.13	starn,—] c1; ~ , ms5
139.14	State] c1; state ms5
139.14	consarn.] c1; ~ ; ms5
139.15	'z] c1; 's ms5
139.15	run] c1; ran ms5
139.15	ahoein'] c1; a hoein ms5
*139.18–25	heart; / He done . . . . ole fool, it] c1, he; heart. / "You darned ole fool," sez I, "it ms5
139.25	gret] c1; great ms5
139.26	master,] c1; ~ ms5
139.27	on] he; of ms5
*139.28–34	on; / Ez fer . . . . 'n a cent."] c1, he; of." ms5
139.35	an'] de; & ms5
139.36	pis'nous] c1; pisonous ms5
140.1	som'ers] c1; somwers ms5
140.4	leg,] c1; ~ ms5
140.4	coz] c1; cos ms5
140.4	begun] c1; began ms5
140.4	chafe,] c1; ~ ms5
140.5	'long side o' me] bg; just by my side ms5
140.6	ring,] c1; ~ ms5
140.8	wile] c1; while ms5
140.8	min'] he; mind ms5
140.9	then,] c1; ~ ms5
140.10	behin'] he; behind ms5
*140.11–14	creepin' grad'lly . . . to look, they] c1, re; fust I knew, the ms5
140.16	gun,] c1; ~ ms5

140.17	an'] BG; & MS5
140.18	b'lieve] c1; believe MS5
140.18	alligatur] c1; alligator MS5
140.20	However] c1; Howsever MS5
140.21	agin.] c1; ~ ; MS5
140.23	You're] c1; you're MS5
140.23	pinned;] c1; ~ , MS5
140.25	fammerly] c1; famerly MS5
140.25	me] c1; ~ , MS5
140.25	frum] HE; from MS5
140.25	hum] NP11; home MS5
140.27	trudge."] NP11; ~ ". MS5
140.30	kep'] c1; ~ MS5
140.30	sin,] c1; ~ MS5
140.31	in;] c1; ~ , MS5
140.32	He] c1; (~ MS5
140.32	(although] c1; ~ MS5
140.33	hut] c1; hurt MS5
140.34–141.1	So 'st he . . . wuz it. / Fin'lly,] c1; And then MS5
141.1	door,] c1; ~ MS5
141.2	Sez,—] c1; ~ , MS5
141.2	Ef] c1; ef MS5
141.2	quick;] c1; ~ , MS5
141.4	keep;] c1; ~ , MS5
141.5	up,] c1; ~ MS5
141.6	immertate] c1; imertate MS5
141.7	thin'] c1; ~ MS5
141.9	Buff'lo] c1; Buf'flo MS5
141.9	chaps,] c1; ~ MS5
141.10	Scriptur'l] c1; Scripturl MS5
141.11–12	Not by a . . . meet'nhus aint sotter;] c1; *not present* MS5
141.15	I guess we 're] c1; We're livin MS5
141.15	land,—] c1; ~ , MS5
141.16	Yourn,] c1; ~ MS5
141.17	SAWIN.] NP11; ~ MS5

EMENDATIONS

146.2a	Dō', don't.] RE; not present c1
*146.22–24a	Fence, on the . . . opinions; a trimmer.] BG, HE; not present c1
147.15a	Less, let's, let us.] BG; not present c1
148.22a	snaked] HE; snake c1
148.36a	Steddles] RE; Staddles c1
151.22–23b	loon, 97] RE; loon, 69. Austin, St., profane wish of, 48, note c1
153.12a	Sir] BG; ∼. c1
155.21–22a	—letters to and from, 111] BG; not present c1
155.23a	Tripoli, 93] BG; Tripoli, 63. Diaz, Bernal, has a vision, 28—his relationship to the Scarlet Woman, ib c1
155.40–41a	Donatus, profane wish of, 83, note.] RE; not present c1
155.5b	D.Y., letter of, 111.] BG; not present c1
155.12b	Echetlæus, 64.] BG; not present c1
156.37a	fidgety] BG; fidgetty c1
156.13–15b	Gomara has . . . Scarlet Woman, ib.] BG; not present c1
157.34–36a	—meeting-house ornamented with imaginary clock, 129] B7; not present c1
157.2b	Biglow, 114] BG; Biglow, 92—meeting-house ornamented with imaginary clock, 116 c1
157.34–35b	Lacedæmonians, banish a great talker, 91.] BG; not present c1
159.34–36b	(a worthy representative of Massachusetts), 82, 87, 88] RE; 46, 54, 56 (a worthy representative of Massachusetts) c1
161.3a	89, note] HE; 58 c1
162.37b	89, note] HE; 58 c1
163.4a	employment] HE; employer c1
163.14–16a	Sin, wilderness . . . what, 102. Sinai, suffers outrages, 102] HE; Sinai, suffers outrages, 74. Sin, wilderness of, modern, what, 74 c1
163.21–23b	Taylor, General . . . its origin, 136] DE; Taylor

zeal, its origin, 126—General, greased by Mr. Choate, 129, 130 c1

163.24–25b Tesephone, banished for long-windedness, 91.] BG; *not present* c1

163.27–28b Thaumaturgus, St. . . . the Devil, 111.] BG; *not present* c1

163.38b 58, *note*] HE; 15 c1

164.35–36a Virgin, the . . . of Messina, 111.] BG; not present c1

Rejected Substantives

The following list records substantive variants in texts published after copy-text and rejected as nonauthorial in the present text. The reading of the present edition appears to the left of the bracket; the authority for that reading, followed by a semicolon, the variant reading, and the source of that reading appear to the right of the bracket. *Not present* indicates that the reading of the present edition does not appear in the text or texts cited to the right of the semicolon. An asterisk preceding page and line numbers indicates that the reading is discussed in the Textual Notes. The reading of any unlisted edition may be presumed to agree with the reading to the left of the bracket (the exception is 38.14; "Leaving the Matter Open" was not printed in c1 or AE).

The following texts are referred to:

MS1   Holograph manuscript, "Leaving the Matter Open."

MS4   Holograph manuscript, "Letter from Birdofredum Sawin."

MS5   Holograph manuscript, "Another letter from B. Sawin Esqr."

NP7   "Leaving the Matter Open," *National Anti-Slavery Standard*, 27 July 1848, p. 32, cols. 5–6.

NP10   "Letter from Birdofredum Sawin," *National Anti-Slavery Standard*, 6 July 1848, p. 20, cols. 5–6.

NP11   "Another Letter from B. Sawin, Esq.," *National Anti-Slavery Standard*, 28 September 1848, pp. 70–71, cols. 6, 1–2.

c1   *The Biglow Papers*, Cambridge: George Nichols, 1848.

c2   *The Biglow Papers*, Cambridge: George Nichols, 1848 ("Second Edition" or second printing).

BG   *The Poetical Works of James R. Lowell,* 2 vols., Boston:
      Ticknor and Fields, 1858 ("Blue and Gold Edition"),
      vol. 2.

DE   *The Poetical Works of James Russell Lowell,* Boston:
      Fields, Osgood, & Co., 1869 ("Diamond Edition").

HE   *The Poetical Works of James Russell Lowell,* Boston:
      James R. Osgood and Co., 1876 ("Household Edition").

AE   *The Biglow Papers,* Boston: Houghton, Mifflin and Co.,
      1885 ("Aldine Edition").

RE   *The Writings of James Russell Lowell in Ten Volumes,*
      Boston and New York: Houghton, Mifflin and Co., 1890
      ("Riverside Edition"), vol. 8.

EE   *The Complete Writings of James Russell Lowell . . . in
      Sixteen Volumes,* Boston and New York: Houghton,
      Mifflin and Co., 1904 ("Elmwood Edition"), vol. 10.

3.13	virtues of] c1; *not present* AE
10.30	learn] c1; learned EE
15.32	et] c1; e DE
*17.30–31	seligens, et forte succidum] c1; *not present* BG
27.10	as] c1; as a AE
28.5	have] c1; *not present* AE
38.14	rights] MS1; right NP7, BG, DE
41.16	noted] c1; quoted AE
*47.1–48.17	Contents. . . . INDEX 151] c1; *not present* DE, HE, AE, RE, EE
63.10	Thet] c1; The AE
64.11	apostolical] c1; apostolic AE
78.20	Mexican] c1; Mexicans BG, DE, HE, RE, EE
*84.12	eyes o'] c1; eyes 'o AE
84.29	folks's] c1; folk's AE
99.2	consecrated] c1; concentrated EE

REJECTED SUBSTANTIVES

99.34	*divos*] c1; *not present* DE
109.15	about even] c1; even about AE
122.15	vow] MS4; von NP10
125.25	Libbaty's] MS4; Libbaty o' NP10
*127.9a	44] c1; 44 [new page] Am't bro't forward, 100 BG
128.6	examples] c1; example AE
*138.1	about] MS5; upon NP11, c1, c2, BG, DE, HE, AE, RE, EE
138.3	clean] MS5; clear NP11
140.17	cut an'] BG; cut the NP11, c1, c2
141.6	hev] MS5; her NP11
141.9	jine] MS5; give NP11
148.25b	*t*] c1; *to* EE
*151.22–23b	loon, 97] c1; loon, 118. "Atlantic," editors of. See *Neptune* EE
*152.25a	Hosea] c1; Hosea, Esquire DE, HE, RE, EE
152.22b	same] c1; some AE
154.25–26b	Convention, what, 84, 85. Convention, Springfield, 84] c1; Convention, Springfield, 102. Convention, what, 102 EE
154.37–42b	Country lawyers, sent . . . about exposed, *ib.*] c1; Country, our, its boundaries more exactly defined, 192—right or wrong, nonsense about exposed, *ib.*—lawyers, sent providentially, *ib.* DE, HE, RE, EE
156.12a	in] c1; in the HE, RE, EE
157.29b	Kinderhook, 133.] c1; *not present* EE
*158.9a	often] c1; of ten AE
158.5b	grew] c1; grow HE, RE, EE
159.36a	108—] c1; *not present* EE
*159.11b	North,] c1; North, the DE, HE, RE, EE
162.37a	in] c1; in the AE
163.2–3b	South Carolina, futile . . . to anchor, 94.] c1; *not present* AE
164.4a	adventure] c1; adventures AE

*164.28b   Wife-trees, 128] c1; Wife-trees, 214. Wilbur,
                  Mrs. Dorcas (Pilcox), an invariable rule of,
                  193—her profile, 194 DE, HE, RE, EE
165.11–12b   Wilbur, Mrs., an . . . her profile, 78] c1; *not
                  present* DE, HE, RE, EE
165.13–14b   Wildbore, a vernacular . . . to escape, 90.] c1;
                  not present AE

Textual Notes

17.30–31   In c1 the text of Wilbur's "Operis Specimen" ends
            abruptly in mid-sentence at the bottom of the last
            of the twelve pages of preliminary matter—
            "Notices of an Independent Press" and the
            advertisement for Wilbur's book. These pages are
            numbered separately from the rest of the book to
            give the appearance of being "inserted." BG and
            DE attempted to preserve the bibliographical
            autonomy of this preliminary material (though it
            is not numbered separately in these editions),
            and the four Latin words were dropped in order to
            justify the margins. In HE, RE, and EE a period
            follows "præcipue." I have rejected this curtailing
            of Lowell's Latin because the evidence suggests
            that it reflects not an authorial decision on
            Lowell's part, but rather a compositorial necessity.

21.11   Change of page numbers was required whenever
            new plates of *The Biglow Papers* were made;
            hereafter such changes will not be noted. When
            page numbers are given in this and the other two
            lists (Pre-copy-text Substantive Variants and
            Rejected Substantives), the page number to the
            left of the bracket is that of the present edition
            regardless of the authority cited immediately to
            the right of the bracket; the page number cited to
            the right of the semicolon is that of the text
            whose symbol follows first (should there be more
            than one) the emended or variant reading.

28.27   Lines 28.29–30 are written in the left-hand margin
            of this notebook page. They were not included
            in the printed poem, however, until BG.

34.6   The same change in the spelling of "less" occurs in DE at 34.7 and 34.8.

34.29   In the manuscript of "Leaving the Matter Open" Lowell commonly wrote the ampersand & for the word *and;* hereafter this is not noted in the list of Emendations.

47.1–48.14   In DE and HE the table of contents of *The Biglow Papers* was incorporated into the general table of contents of these collected editions of Lowell's poems. In both RE and EE the table of contents, with several paper titles shortened, preceded "Notices of an Independent Press." The present edition restores the "Contents" to its original position in the volume, altering only the page-number references. Substantive variants in editions after c1 are not noted (BG follows the text and format of c1).

49.32   Wilbur's footnotes to Hosea's verses appeared first in c1. Their absence in the manuscripts and newspaper printings is hereafter not noted in this list of variants.

59.16   Hosea's "Few refleckshuns" on Sawin's letter are enclosed in brackets and inserted into the verse in NP2; in c1 they are placed, as in the present edition, at the bottom of the page in footnote fashion.

59.29–30   Line 59.29 comes at the bottom of the page in c1; to have allowed space for the break in the verse which appears in NP2 (and presumably in the manuscript from which the newspaper printing was set) the printer would have had either to cut the page short by two lines of type or to have started the next page with an indented line. Neither alternative would have been typographically attractive. Besides the evidence of the newspaper printing, and the circumstantial bibliographical evidence of c1, the sense of the verse also argues for a verse paragraph break.

64.31   There is space for the comma in c1; probably the type dropped before the plates were stereotyped.

72.2   The same change in the spelling of "principle" occurs in RE at 83.3, 83.6, 83.11, and 83.14.

84.12   Similar misplacements of apostrophes which could possibly lead to substantive misreadings occur in AE at 114.29 ("'o" for "o'") and at 124.18 ("s'" for "'s").

103.4   The same change in the spelling of "do" occurs between manuscript and c1 at 103.12, 103.20, 103.28, 104.3, 104.11, 104.19, 104.27, 105.3, 105.10, 105.11, 105.19, 105.27, 106.3, 121.13, and 122.23.

103.5   The same change in the spelling of "as" occurs between manuscript and c1 a second time in this line and at 103.22 (twice), 104.18 (twice), 106.10, 112.9, 112.30, 113.2, 113.4, 113.5, 114.5, 114.13, 114.22, 114.30, 120.34, 121.3, 121.14, 121.20, 121.29, 121.32 (twice), 122.3, 122.6 (twice), 122.29, 122.31, 122.32, 122.33, 123.1, 123.5 (twice), 123.11 (twice), 123.13, 123.32, 124.11, 124.15, 124.17, 124.22, 124.26, 125.2, 125.11, 125.12, 125.13 (twice), 125.21, and 138.18.

103.9   Except at the beginning of lines, Lowell usually used the ampersand instead of writing out "and" in manuscript; these were printed out in the newspaper printings; and in c1, with only a few exceptions, the "d" was replaced by an apostrophe.

Hereafter this is not noted in the list of
Emendations.

103.11   The same change in the spelling of "that" occurs
between manuscript and c1 at 103.14, 103.30,
104.23, 104.25, 104.27, 104.31, 105.2, 105.4,
105.5, 105.12, 105.19, 105.29, 106.1, 106.5,
112.7, 112.8, 112.11, 112.13, 112.19, 112.22,
112.29, 112.31, 112.32, 113.7 (twice), 113.10,
113.13, 113.23, 114.2, 114.10, 114.17, 115.3,
120.27, 120.35, 121.9 (twice), 121.16, 121.19,
121.25, 121.30, 122.9, 122.10 (twice), 122.11,
122.12, 122.23, 122.34, 122.35, 122.36, 123.9
(twice), 123.18, 123.19, 123.20, 123.25, 123.31,
123.35, 124.3, 124.4, 124.10, 124.16, 124.18,
124.31, 124.33, 124.36, 125.1, 125.3, 125.8,
125.13, 125.17 (twice), and 135.33.

103.14   The addition of an apostrophe occurs in the
following words between manuscript and c1, the
word in manuscript having neither the final "g"
nor an apostrophe: nothin' (112.8, 114.14, 124,12,
124.23, 125.6), abeggin (122.7), abolishin'
(138.6), abrilin' (123.6), adyin' (120.30), agoin'
(112.18, 138.10), alayin' (122.31), amazin'
(122.4), anythin' (125.20), bakin' (123.5),
beginnin' (112.14), bein' (112.9, 113.7, 114.31,
122.28, 124.4, 135.20, 136.18, 136.33, 137.34,
139.28, 141.8), blazin' (122.5), blessin'
(121.5), bringin' (120.29), brustlin' (114.30),
cantin' (105.6), choosin' (112.30), combinin'
(125.2), comin' (121.32), consarnin' (114.6),
edgin' (137.29), endurin' (138.15), everlastin'
(122.33), feelin' (120.33), fightin' (124.9), fittin'
(138.4), flowin' (122.1), follerin' (121.6),
gittin' (114.28), givin' (141.1), goin' (123.14,
137.27), grantin' (105.4), growin' (141.5),
hearin' (114.24, 123.32), keepin' (121.13),

ketchin' (123.31), knowin' (139.16), leavin'
(121.16), 'lectioneerin' (124.29), levyin'
(103.21), lightnin' (137.8), losin' (112.32,
121.11), -makin' (123.4), meanin' (120.27),
missin' (124.34), mornin' (138.30), mortifyin'
(120.31), ownin' (125.20), playin' (139.7),
privateerin' (114.22), puddin' (121.31), readin'
(140.32), runnin' (124.17), seein' (134.34,
136.15), speakin' (121.24), sutthin' (114.24,
121.17, 124.32, 125.2, 125.7, 135.7), sweetnin'
(121.27), tellin' (112.19), temptin' (139.12),
-thinkin' (125.10), tusslin' (115.1), underpinnin'
(112.16), usin' (121.10), willin' (120.32), and
writin' (124.10).

103.14   The omission of the apostrophe in "ain't" also
          occurs between manuscript and c1 at 112.18,
          121.20, 135.23, 135.31, 138.23, and 139.25.

103.16   The same change in the spelling of "for" occurs
          between manuscript and c1 at 103.33, 104.6,
          104.12, 104.15, 104.29, 106.5, 113.5, 120.26,
          120.35, 121.6, 121.9, 121.11, 121.12, 124.5,
          124.15, 124.16, 124.17 (twice), 124.19, 124.24,
          124.28, 124.32, 124.35, 125.22, 125.24, and
          125.25. It should be noted that while Lowell's
          handwriting is rarely difficult to read, it is
          sometimes virtually impossible to determine
          whether he has written an "o" or an "e" for the
          middle letter of "for." In these instances I have
          read the letter as "o," and have noted the
          emendation above.

103.16   The same change in the spelling of "have" occurs
          between manuscript and c1 at 106.6, 106.10,
          114.19, 121.5, 123.3, 124.11, and 124.26.

103.21   The substitution of an apostrophe for the "f" in
          "of" also occurs between manuscript and c1 at

104.4, 104.31, 105.2, 105.5, 105.8, 112.28, 113.4, 114.23, 121.11, 122.19, 123.16, 123.33 (o' knives), 124.15, 124.30, 125.8, and 125.13 (twice).

103.29   An apostrophe replacing a final "d" of a word in manuscript occurs in c1 also in the following words: behin' (140.14), han' (137.32), hol' (124.34), kin' (114.27, 120.31, 121.24, 121.28, 122.17, 123.3, 123.11, 124.15, 124.21, 124.31, 124.33, 137.1, 137.30, 138.7, 138.24, 139.7, 140.7), stan' (113.1, 137.33), and thousan' (103.32, 103.33).

104.2   The "w" of "would" in manuscript is replaced by an apostrophe in c1 also at 122.25 (twice), 122.27, 122.29, 122.31, 122.33, 124.13, and 134.32.

104.6   The same change in the spelling of "too" occurs between manuscript and c1 at 112.26, 122.8, 123.2, 124.27, 124.34, and 125.9.

104.8   The same change in the spelling of "what" occurs between manuscript and c1 at 112.24, 113.9, 113.19, 115.1, 121.18, 121.29, 122.10 (twice), 123.4, 123.28, 124.18, 124.20, 124.24, 124.28, 124.36, 125.3, 125.4, and 125.13.

104.30   The same change in the spelling of "from" occurs between manuscript and c1 at 114.31, 134.24, and 137.30.

104.30   The same change in the spelling of "are" occurs between manuscript and c1 at 105.32, 114.7, and 125.11.

105.4   The same change in the spelling of "has" occurs between manuscript and c1 at 112.27, 114.30, and 124.24.

105.11–26   When these lines were added to the poem in c1,
             "'uthout" at 105.25 as spelled "without"; the
             dialect spelling of the word is the reading of RE.

112.25   Both the apostrophe replacing the "d" of the
             manuscript "And" and the comma appear in c1,
             but in reverse order; BG corrected this error.

113.4   The same change in the spelling of "where"
             occurs between manuscript and c1 at 120.26,
             120.27, 120.30, 121.18, 122.2, 122.4, 122.5,
             122.6, 124.1, 124.17, 139.14, and 139.27.

113.8   The same change in the spelling of "was" occurs
             between manuscript and c1 at 120.30, 120.32,
             120.34, 121.20, 121.34, 122.3, 122.5 (twice),
             122.33, 123.1, 123.30, 123.35, 124.1, 124.2,
             124.4, and 124.25.

113.14   The same change in the spelling of "had" occurs
             between manuscript and c1 at 120.28, 121.21,
             122.23, 123.14, 123.25, and 123.34.

113.21–114.4 "Permiscoous" at 113.25 is the reading of RE.

120.27   The same change in the spelling of "whole" occurs
             between manuscript and c1 at 122.15, 122.27,
             122.30, 124.28, and 135.21.

120.28   The same change in the spelling of "when" occurs
             between manuscript and c1 at 121.23, 122.34,
             123.10, 124.34, and 138.23.

121.19   The same change in the spelling of "got" occurs
             between manuscript and c1 at 122.12, 123.11,
             123.12, 123.13, 123.29, 124.11, and 124.25.

124.3   The "l" of "only" in manuscript is replaced by an
             apostrophe in c1 also at 124.10, 125.26, 136.18,
             and 136.29.

127.9a   Here and also in the right-hand column of figures
            it was necessary to carry the account over to a
            new page in BG. A similar problem and solution
            occurs in HE.

135.25–29   There is a draft of these four lines in a notebook
            which Lowell dated 22 August 1850 (bMS Am
            765:960, Houghton Library, Harvard
            University):
                Wenever an Amerikin distinguished politishin,
                Gits kind o' oneasy & begins definin his
                    posishin,
                And to the [word undeciphered] people takes
                    the tallest kind o' shine,—
                Wal, I for one, feel sure he aint gut nothin to
                    define,
            "An'" (135.29) is the reading of RE and the present
            edition; in BG the word was spelled out "And."

136.7   The same change in the spelling of "demercrats"
            (either singular or plural) occurs between
            manuscript and c1 at 137.4, 137.26, and 137.33.

136.7   In no edition of *The Biglow Papers* did Lowell
            replace the "d" with an apostrophe, his usual
            practice (see textual note 103.9); I have chosen
            to let the newspaper reading stand rather than
            regularizing the spelling on my own authority. It
            is possible, though unlikely, that Lowell preferred
            in this instance the "d" to an apostrophe.

136.17   The number appears in italics first in c1, but
            retains in that text an unauthorized hyphen added
            in NP11. I have rejected the hyphen since the
            use of that mark in compound numbers was not
            Lowell's usual practice.

137.4   NP11 standardized Lowell's dialect spelling
            "diffrent," a change which stood in subsequent

texts. In RE, however, the "i" was emended to "e", the usual spelling of the word elsewhere. The reading of this edition—"deffrent"—follows the spelling of copy-text as emended in the first syllable by RE.

137.11–25   "'Ere" (137.25) is the reading of BG and the present edition; the spelling of c1, the text in which the lines first appear, is "air."

138.1   "Upon" is the reading of the newspaper text of Sawin's "Third Letter" (NP11); Lowell's manuscript (MS5), from which the newspaper printing was set, clearly reads "about." Because I have discovered no evidence that Lowell authorized this change between the two texts, and because the newspaper compositor in three other places obviously misread Lowell's manuscript—"her" for "hev" (141.6), "give" for "jine" (141.9), and "cut the" "cut an'" (140.17)—and one of these misreadings ("cut the") was not corrected by Lowell until BG, I have decided to follow the reading of copy-text. Unlike the other newspaper misreadings, this would easily have escaped Lowell's notice.

138.33   The authority for the semicolon is c1; the "d" was not replaced by an apostrophe, however, until HE.

138.34   The authority for the period is c1; the "d" was not replaced by an apostrophe, however, until HE.

139.18–25   "Let her" (139.23) is the reading of HE and the present edition; in c1, the text in which the lines first appear, the reading is "jest let."

139.28–34   "On" (139.28) is the reading of HE and the present edition; in c1, the text in which the lines first appear, the reading is "of."

140.11–14   "An'" (140.12) is the reading of RE and the present
             edition; in c1, the text in which the lines first
             appear, the word is spelled "and."

146.22–24a   In BG, the original source of the emendation, "on
             the" is printed in italics. Inconsistent with the
             practice of c1, this was altered to roman type
             in HE.

151.22–23b   The rejected index entry belongs to *The Biglow
             Papers, Second Series*. The indices of both series
             were combined when the First and Second Series
             were printed together in DE, HE, and RE. The index
             of the First Series was again printed independently
             in EE, but the index of the Second Series in EE
             continued to appear in the combined form.

152.25a   When the index of the Second Series was
             combined with that of the First Series in DE,
             Hosea Biglow acquired the title he had been
             without in c1 and BG. Because "Esquire" is,
             however, the reading of the index of the Second
             Series, I have rejected it from the present edition.

158.9a   The great majority of errors in AE—mostly of
             punctuation and therefore not recorded—resulted
             from its plates' being set from a late printing of
             c1 (probably the 1881 printing called "Twelfth
             Edition" on the title page). The plates of this
             "first" edition, stereotyped over a quarter century
             before, were by this time extensively battered,
             and sheets printed from them were often illegible.
             In this particular instance, "often," end-lined
             hyphenated in c1, is read as two words in AE
             because the hyphen had disappeared from the
             plates of c1 some years before. Plate wear also
             accounts for the rejected substantive recorded at
             63.10.

159.11b   "The" is the reading of the index of *The Biglow
           Papers, Second Series*. When the index of the First
           Series was separated from the combined indices
           of DE, HE, and RE, the definite article found its way
           into the text of the First Series in EE.

164.28b   Mrs. Wilbur's Christian and maiden names were
           first given in *The Biglow Papers, Second Series*,
           and fully noted in that volume's index, allowing
           her, by virtue of the alphabet, to precede her
           husband. When the indices of both series were
           combined in DE, this elevation continued. I have
           regarded "Dorcas (Pilcox)" as the reading of the
           Second Series and have accordingly rejected
           these names from the present edition and have
           returned Mrs. Wilbur to her original position.

Verse Division

The following list records lines of verse which come at the bottom of a page in the present text and which, when transcribed from this text, should be separated from the line of verse at the top of the following page by a space of one line. There is no break in the verse following lines not recorded in this list.

Page

28   Who flashed the pan, and who was downright dunce.

32   Ther Sabbath-breakin' to spy out.

35   He said one day to brother North,—

36   Pick you the best, I'll take the worst."

50   O' them nigger-drivin' States.

51   This ere cuttin' folks's throats.

71   Sez he shall vote fer Gineral C.

72   Sez they did n't know everythin' down in Judee.

82   Holl Fourth o' Julys seem to bile in my veins.

86   Thet hev any consarn in 't, an' thet is the end on 't.

88   Sneaks down stairs to bolt the front door o' the Tooleries.

95   An' so git red on 'em soon," sez he.

96   They all on 'em know the old toon," sez he.

97   Then our priv'leges tryin' to proon ?" sez he.

124   An' tell 'em thet 's percisely wut I never gin nor—took !

137   Lonesome ez steddles on a mash without no hayricks on.

Word Division

List I records compounds or possible compounds hyphenated at line-ends in copy-text and resolved as either hyphenated or one word as listed below. Extant manuscripts of *The Biglow Papers,* other Lowell manuscripts of the period, and the word as printed elsewhere in copy-text have been the basis for these resolutions. *List II* records compounds or possible compounds hyphenated at line-ends in the present text which should be transcribed as given; words hyphenated at line-ends in the present text and not listed below should be transcribed as one word.

List I

4.3	pancratic	91.23	Divinely-granted
8.22	newspapers	106.14	newspaper
9.13	side-hills	106.17	puppet-show
9.26	weather-cunning	106.20–21	horseback
10.3	purblind	108.8	puppet-pranks
10.11	broad-howling	109.7	ANTI-SLAVERY
10.16	flybite	109.20–21	eavesdroppers
11.19	world-renowned	115.20	outposts
24.16	safe-keeping	117.28	ante-electionary
28.20	school-dame	127.18b	long-bow
31.35	sweet-water	127.33	ready-churned
32.1	scrub-oak	128.19	money-trees
39.30	hornbook	129.26	mirage-Pisgah
42.11	over-particular	129.28	half-believing
42.21	self-denial	131.11–12	bombshell
61.21	Salt-river	142.28	undertow
63.1	Anglosaxon	145.35b	*free-trade*
63.24	Bay-state	146.26b	*antislavery*
63.33	ahollerin'	152.10a	loadstone
66.28	Anti-Christ	152.22a	fourscore
66.33	pulpit-cushion	153.6b	cow-bell
82.3	cross-purposes	153.23b	peri-wig

154.34a	powder-cart	163.26a	cornerstone
156.22–23a	field-sports	163.27a	keystone
156.6b	season-ticket	164.32b	bombshells
160.24a	*post-mortem*		

List II

3.30–31	gaily-painted	102.35–36	ninety-nine
9.34–35	well-meaning	106.20–21	horse-back
10.13–14	wild-glaring	111.31–32	round-robins
10.21–22	snake-tressed	119.18–19	lemon-parings
11.20–21	Anglo-Saxon	127.32–33	bread-trees
23.2–3	title-page	128.8–9	back-garden
40.10–11	niggard-geniality	129.15–16	before-stated
49.19–20	fli-time	130.11–12	Astræa-forsaken
58.11–12	wider-viewed	132.12–13	gore-smeared
64.25–26	mackerel-fisher	133.9–10	goodly-sized
93.6–7	fellow-beings	156.22–23a	field-sports

Appendix

Appendix: "Letter from Rev. Mr. Wilbur"

The following letter preceded "The Pious Editor's Creed" when those verses were printed in the *National Anti-Slavery Standard,* 4 May 1848, p. 194. Lowell did not reprint the letter in *The Biglow Papers,* but used parts of it in Wilbur's afterwords to No. vii, "A Letter from a Candidate . . ." (116.20–117.2), and the "Introduction" (27.20–31). Arthur Voss reprinted, with minor inaccuracies, the letter as it appeared in the *Standard* ("An Uncollected Letter of Lowell's Parson Wilbur," *The New England Quarterly* 26, September 1953: 396–99). The text below is that of Lowell's fair-copy manuscript from which the newspaper publication was set; it differs only in accidentals from the latter. The manuscript of one folded sheet (four pages) is of gray, ruled, wove paper, 12¼ × 15¼ inches, and is written in black ink. It is addressed "For / Sydney H. Gay / N⁰ 142 Nassau St, / New York." and postmarked Cambridge, April 29.

LETTER FROM REV. MR. WILBUR.

J A A L A M , April 28ᵗʰ 1848.

E S T E E M E D   S I R : —

Your favor of the 16ᵗʰ of the current month only came to hand on the day before yesterday, being the 26ᵗʰ instant. The mails arrive at this place with considerable irregularity, though I believe we are as much favoured as other towns of the same size. Our worthy & efficient postmaster (who also conducts an extensive variety store) informs me that the difficulty is not in the circumference but at the centre, & that the system will never revolve with smoothness & regularity till the axle at Washington is either replaced with a new one or plentifully & effectually greased. If this should ever meet the eye of the Honᵇˡᵉ Postmaster General, I trust that no offence will be taken as none is meant, &, indeed, I will not take it upon me to affirm that this high public functionary was intended to be typified in the axle abovementioned. It is impossible for conjectural criticism to define the precise application of figurative & metaphorical diction,

& the meaning of the above may be as multiform as that of the Beast in Revelations, whereof in the course of my reading I have noted two hundred & three several interpretations by as many different commentators. *Non nostrum est tantas* &c. I have myself ventured upon a two hundred & fourth which I embodied in a discourse preached on occasion of the demise of the late usurper Napoleon Buonaparte, & which met with very general acceptance on the part of my people. It is true that my views on this important subject were ardently controverted by Mr Shearjashub Holden, the then preceptor of our academy (in other respects a highly amiable & sensible individual, with a somewhat inadequate knowledge of the Greek tongue), but he has been lately removed by the hand of Providence & I had the melancholy satisfaction of reaffirming my cherished sentiments in a sermon delivered on the Lord's day immediately succeeding his funeral. This might seem like taking an unfair advantage, but I had previously learned that he had left provision in his last will (being unmarried) for the publication of a posthumous tractate in support of his own erroneous interpretation. But, lest this should seem like an aberration from the subject of this communication, I forbear saying more at present. I should be pleased at a more convenient season to favour you with my speculations on this topic more at large, unless deemed of too exciting a nature for your columns. It would be necessary in that contingency that you should be supplied with type of the Grecian character.

Immediately upon the receipt of your favour of the 16th inst. I stepped over to Mr Biglow's farm, where I found him engaged in felling a fine peartree of the Harvard variety raised by his father (deceased June 8th 1843) from a scion procured by me from the parent stock on one of my annual visits to Cambridge during the season of the literary festivities of Commencement, & which had perished during the previous summer of what Mr B. denominated *fire-blight*. I myself incline strongly (from an entomological bias) to the *scolytus pyri* theory, & a debate sprung up between us which engendered no little heat on both sides & for the time rendered me oblivious of the object of my mission. The sight of your letter on my study-table as I was seating myself to write a few lines on the subject for the Cultivator, recalled your commission to my mind, & I sent my little son Seneca (now aged nine years, it being vacation-time with us) to name your request to Mr B. He returned presently with the subjoined verses which Mr B. happened to have in his pocket & as to the merits of which I refrain from expressing any opinion, though I may add that Mr B. knows more about poetry than peartrees. There is not a schoolboy at present under my tutelage who would not be ashamed to mention the *fire-blight* in this connexion, & I can assure parents who have entrusted me with their offspring that he might securely reckon on being well breeched if he did.

Mr B. sent a message with his verses to the effect that, as it was a duty to clothe the naked, he had prepared a coat which would fit a great number of persons, & that he should be pleased to furnish any applicant with a cloak of similar quality & material without extra charge. The sentiment is unobjectionable, though I do not approve of scriptural allusions in matters purely laical.

In regard to the collected edition of Mr B.'s productions, it has been delayed by the press of geoponic occupations incident to an agricultural population in the vernal season. You have been rightly informed that it would be introduced by some prefatial matter of my own. Far be it from me to claim any credit for the popularity which I am pleased to hear the bucolick strains of my talented young parishioner have acquired. If I know myself, I am tolerably free from the itch of vanity, though I may be allowed to say that I was not backward to recognize a certain wild, puckery, & subacidulous flavour in them not wholly unpleasing to a palate cloyed with the sugariness of tamed & cultivated fruit, & it may be that a few touches of my own here & there have rendered them more acceptable albeit from no other cause than my larger literary experience.

It is with regret I add that I cannot find room at present for the lad you mention. One of the adolescentules under my charge will probably not tarry later than the next Commencement, & I shall then be pleased to receive your relative, if Providence permit. The liberality of my excellent friend Mr Buckingham of the Boston Courier in giving to my prospectus the gratuitous advantage of his deservedly large circulation has filled all the vacancies of my little society.

There are several matters whereon I could wish to dilate more fully but I am loath to burthen you with the postage of a supplementary sheet. I enclose herewith a recipe which I have found invaluable in cases of obstinate ague.

Yours with respect
Homer Wilbur A.M.

Pastor of the First Church (& indeed the only church, the other being a small band of seceders worshipping in the schoolhouse) in Jaalam.